Sounding the Break

NEW WORLD STUDIES

J. Michael Dash, *Editor*

Frank Moya Pons and
Sandra Pouchet Paquet,
Associate Editors

Sounding the Break

AFRICAN AMERICAN AND CARIBBEAN ROUTES OF WORLD LITERATURE

Jason Frydman

University of Virginia Press

Charlottesville and London

University of Virginia Press
© 2014 by the Rector and Visitors of the University of Virginia
All rights reserved
Printed in the United States of America on acid-free paper
First published 2014

9 8 7 6 5 4 3 2 1

Library of Congress Cataloging-in-Publication Data

Frydman, Jason, 1976–
  Sounding the break : African American and Caribbean
routes of world literature / Jason Frydman.
      p. cm. (New World studies)
  Includes bibliographical references and index.
  ISBN 978-0-8139-3572-0 (cloth : alk. paper)
  ISBN 978-0-8139-3573-7 (pbk. : alk. paper)
  ISBN 978-0-8139-3574-4 (e-book)
  1. American literature—African American authors—History
and criticism. 2. American literature—20th century—History and
criticism. 3. Caribbean literature—20th century—History and
criticism. 4. Race in literature. 5. Identity (Psychology) in literature.
6. African diaspora in literature. 7. Literature and history. I. Title.
PS153.N5F78 2013
810.9'896073—dc23
                                                    2013030493

A book in the American Literatures Initiative (ALI), a collaborative
publishing project of NYU Press, Fordham University Press, Rutgers
University Press, Temple University Press, and the University of Virginia
Press. The Initiative is supported by The Andrew W. Mellon Foundation.
For more information, please visit www.americanliteratures.org.

Contents

Acknowledgments

THIS BOOK benefited from the generous support of family, friends, colleagues, libraries, and research foundations, all of whom deserve mention but some of whom I fear I may omit. I would like to thank the Research Foundation of the City University of New York (CUNY), the Tow Foundation, and the Whiting Foundation for enabling research that took me all around the Atlantic. Such research would have been much more difficult without the assistance of the librarians and archivists at Brooklyn College and the CUNY Graduate Center; the University of the West Indies, Mona; the Schomburg Center for Research in Black Culture; the Centre des archives nationales d'outre-mer in Aix-en-Provence; the American University in Cairo; the American University of Beirut; and Columbia University. I am very grateful to my editors at the University of Virginia Press, Cathie Brettschneider, Ellen Satrom, and J. Michael Dash, for shepherding this book through the submission and production processes, and in particular for placing my manuscript with readers who saw what this book could be when I could not. Tim Roberts and the editors at the American Literatures Initiative offered patience and meticulous care with the manuscript. I would like to thank the publishers Taylor and Francis Ltd. for allowing me to reproduce sections of "World Literature and Diaspora Studies" from *The Routledge Companion to World Literature*, edited by Theo D'haen, David Damrosch, and Djelal Kadir, as part of Chapter 5. An earlier version of Chapter 2 first appeared in *MELUS: Multi-Ethnic Literature of the United States*, issue 34.4 (2009), and is reprinted by permission of the journal.

At Columbia University, Farah Jasmine Griffin made crucial suggestions while I was conceptualizing this project, and Frances Negrón-Muntaner and Brent Hayes Edwards also offered valuable feedback during its early stages. David Damrosch and Joseph Slaughter have been tirelessly reliable sources of feedback and wisdom, and both this book project and my professional trajectory owe much to them. At Brooklyn College, I would like to thank all my colleagues in the English Department, especially our department chair Ellen Tremper for her encouragement and expert navigation of academic bureaucracy; James Davis, Joseph Entin, and Martha Nadell for their seasoned advice on research and teaching; and my Caribbeanist colleagues Rosamond King, Tamara Mose Brown, and Vanessa Pérez for their camaraderie. CUNY's Faculty Fellow Publication Program allowed me to share earlier drafts of two chapters with a congenial group of peers under the charismatic leadership of Shelly Eversley: Maria Bellamy, Amy Robbins, Jody Rosen, Charity Scribner, and Vanessa Valdés. At the American Comparative Literature Association, Theo D'haen, David Damrosch, and Djelal Kadir invited me to participate in an extremely productive set of seminars on world literature, while Michael Allan co-organized with me a similarly productive seminar that has deeply marked this book.

Numerous cities have also marked this book, and I would not have been in as good a position to write in them were it not for numerous friends and colleagues. In New York, beyond those already mentioned, I would like to thank Bina Gogineni, Kairos Llobrera, Emily Lordi, Richard So, and Elda Tsou. In Cairo, Walter Armbrust, Aaron Jakes, Mara Naaman, and Lucie Ryzova were constant companions. In Beirut, Dahlia Gubara and 'Ali Wick shared with me their expertise on archives and historiography, as well as their libraries and *sharmut*; while Christine Boustany and Kamran Rastegar offered friendship and hospitality in the Chouf. In Kingston, Carolyn Cooper, Mariano Paniello, and Clavell Lynch ensured the success of my research trips.

Finally, I would like to thank my family. I owe my abiding interest in histories and textures of the diasporic voice to my late grandparents, may they rest in peace. My parents and my sister patiently endured all those voyages, physical and intellectual, that made me difficult to reach. My daughter Hadley has kept my storytelling fresh by demanding so many stories "from my mouth." My son Sasha has arrived just in time to see this project finally fulfilled. And my wife, Elizabeth Holt, has been a bottomless source of love and ideas. This book, and my life as I know and want it, would not have been possible without you.

Introduction

EDWARD WILMOT BLYDEN, born to free Igbo parents in St. Thomas, Danish West Indies, crossed the Atlantic to Liberia in 1851 to complete the education denied to him in the United States. Ordained in 1858, he soon became Fulton Professor of Greek and Latin at Liberia College. Prolific, widely traveled, educated in not only Christian theology and the classics but Arabic traditions as well, Blyden's historical vision of Africa inspired its diaspora. "You who do not know anything of your ancestry," Marcus Garvey advised in a Jamaican pamphlet of 1914, "will do well to read Blyden, one of our historians and chroniclers, who have done so much to retrieve the lost prestige of the race, and to undo the selfishness of alien historians and their history which has said so little and painted us so unfairly."[1] As Blyden left the Americas for Africa, Europe was apprehending a world-historical shift in the literary terrain. Goethe attested in 1827: "National literature is now rather an unmeaning term; the epoch of world literature [*Weltliteratur*] is at hand, and everyone must strive to hasten its approach."[2] There was a sense of newness, of a break, that only "now" was something called "world literature" "at hand," in need of everyone's striving to "hasten" it along. "World literature" for Goethe was an international vanguard action of "a silent, almost secret congregation" reading, commenting, writing, performing, and translating across national boundaries, "less a set of works than a network," in David Damrosch's formulation.[3] In this sense, Blyden's intellectual itinerary would prove to be of an utterly world-literary sort, putting him in touch with learned Fula Muslims, European Orientalists, and Beiruti literati. At the same time, Goethe meant by world literature a transhistorical global archive available for intertextual engagement, exemplified by his *West-östlicher Diwan*, a collection of poetry inspired by the fourteenth-century Persian poet

Hafez. And in that sense too, Blyden's work in and on Africa would connect him with archives of world literature, routed through Africa—from the monuments of the Nile Valley to the orature of West Africa, from Greek and Latin texts to biblical and Islamic scriptures—in ways that, as this sprawling geography perhaps suggests, deeply trouble Goethe's sense of novelty in 1827.

Goethe grounded his historical sense of world literature's contemporary emergence economically. The resumption of "neighborly relations" in Europe after the turmoil of the French Revolution and Napoleon's conquests, in conjunction with Europe's extensive imperial relations, "newly" enabled the global circulation and translation of texts. "This movement has been in existence only a short time it is true," Goethe insists, "but long enough for one to form an opinion on it and to acquire from it, with business-like promptitude, both profit and pleasure."[4] Not only do economics materially enable, "with business-like promptitude," the print and the post, the networks and the archives of world literature, but they figure its practice, which yields "both profit and pleasure." Goethe saw world literature as both "spiritual intercourse" and "foreign trade," or, as Fritz Strich writes, "intellectual barter, a traffic in ideas between peoples, a literary market to which the nations bring their intellectual treasures for exchange."[5] This, for Goethe, is new in 1827.

Three years before Blyden boarded a ship bound from the Americas to Monrovia to continue his education, Marx and Engels published *The Communist Manifesto*, meeting Goethe's sense of the new with what has come "in place of the old local and national seclusion and self-sufficiency": "We have intercourse in every direction, universal inter-dependence of nations. And as in material, so also in intellectual production. The intellectual creations of individual nations become common property. National one-sidedness and narrow-mindedness become more and more impossible, and from the numerous national and local literatures, there arises a world literature."[6] For Marx and Engels, as for Goethe, writing in the first half of the nineteenth century, the recent past was a time neither of "universal inter-dependence" nor of "intercourse in every direction" in material or intellectual terms, but of "narrow-mindedness." Only now, these proclamations from Germany insist, does "there arise a world literature" that is "common property."

A little-studied piece of Blyden scholarship appears in the pages of *The People of Africa*, a slim 1871 volume compiled and published with the support of the New York–based American Colonization Society. It is his translation of an Arabic letter received in the mid-1860s by Liberia

College along with a shipment of Arabic books from the printing press
of the recently founded, fellow missionary institution of the Syrian Protestant College in Beirut. "From the city of Beirut, in the country of
Syria, to the noble lords living in Central Africa. Peace to all," it opens,
continuing:

> O ye Noble Lords !
>
> We have learned of the existence of tribes south of the great desert, whose
> dialect is the noble Arabic language, and that they extend from there to the
> central countries of Africa. As we desire information respecting them, we
> have taken this method for that purpose, hoping that whoever may chance
> to receive this paper will favor us with answers to the subjoined questions,
> by the hand of the head of the College of Liberia, which country is west from
> your country, as we have understood. By this means you will establish a con-
> nection between yourselves and the learned men of the College of Beirut, and
> the chief of its printing department; and this may be an advantage to you.[7]

The "learned men of the College of Beirut" wrote to "whoever may
chance to receive this paper," hoping to hasten the interconnectedness
of the College of Beirut with the "tribes south of the great desert, whose
dialect is the noble Arabic language." They inquired about the geography, the religion, and above all the reading and writing habits of Arabo-
phone "Central" Africa: "Are there among you many books—what are
the names of the principal and most valuable ones? Are there among you
any authors—on what subjects have they written?" At Blyden's request,
Ibrahima Kabawee, "a Mandingo priest" passing through Monrovia,
composed a response to the letter from Beirut in the Maghrebi script,
reproduced by photo-facsimile in *The People of Africa*. A gesture of
what Katie Trumpener identifies as transperipheral cosmopolitanism
enabled by but also skirting the edges of an Anglo-American missionary
infrastructure, Blyden and Kabawee would take up the invitation to link
Beirut to Monrovia in a world-literary conversation in Arabic between
"whoever chanced to" get caught up in it.[8]

Kabawee declares that "the Koran is the chief of all books; men know
it and do not know it; they see it and do not see it; they hear it and do
not hear it."[9] His list of "books in our country" begins with the *Maqamat* of al-Hariri (1054–1122). Common property for some time north,
south, east, and even west of the Sahara if we consider their appearance
in Muslim narratives of the New World, it is the most important non-
sacred work in the portrait of West African letters offered by Blyden and
his scribe Kabawee.[10] The *Maqamat* of al-Hariri, along with those of

al-Hamadhani, are the foundational texts of the *maqama* tradition in Arabic, and subsequently also in Hebrew, Persian, and Syriac. Written in rhymed, rhythmic prose (*saj'*), *maqamat* (often translated as "assemblies" or "settings," "*séances*" in French) episodically recount the travels of rhetorically gifted, roguish trickster figures through the social geography of the Islamic world. In keeping with Arabic practices of *adab*, the scribe of the king of Musadu cites the *Maqamat* of al-Hariri as a source of political wisdom in his epistle to the government of Liberia, the second Arabic manuscript facsimile included in the volume. This diplomatic use of the genre points to the incomplete ability of the emergent nineteenth-century European category "literature" to translate the *maqama* and its relationship to *adab*, a performative field of wisdom and morals, aesthetics and manners.[11]

In his efforts to comprehend and portray West African literary practices, Blyden could not have found better interlocutors for this terminological difficulty than the intellectuals of post-1860 Beirut he would soon meet, eager to engage in literary correspondence with "whoever may chance to receive" their invitation. During his time studying Arabic at the Syrian Protestant College in 1866, he would cross paths with figures such as Butrus and Salim al-Bustani, who at precisely this moment were negotiating Arabic's place within European categories of knowledge, literature among them.[12] Kabawee's response to "the learned men of the College of Beirut," and Blyden's translation of it, showcase both the troubles and opportunities these kinds of negotiations have presented to the worlding of literature. According to Blyden's translation, Kabawee describes his king as "skilled in literature and in war." Consulting the facsimile reproduction of the letter, we see that Blyden has rendered as "literature" the Arabic word *'ilm*, which generally means knowledge, even scientific and religious knowledge.[13] As though marking a break with what literature was coming to mean, Blyden's rendering of *'ilm* as "literature" testifies to the tensions and fault lines produced by that imperially mediated process Aamir Mufti describes as the "integration of widely dispersed and heterogeneous sociocultural formations into a global ensemble" called literature.[14]

Working at the fault lines of Liberia College's conflicted mission, Blyden incorporated al-Hariri into the Anglophone curriculum of Liberia College, bringing it in line with the Arabic curriculum of the Sahel. During senior exams in 1870, Blyden invited "a learned Muslim from Kankan" to sit in as the students read from the English translation of the French Orientalist Silvestre de Sacy's edition of the *Maqamat* of al-Hariri:

Our Mohammedan visitor happened to have with him the whole of the fifty Makamat in elegant manuscript. He followed the students as they read, repeating after them in an undertone. Of course he could not judge of the translation, as he understood not a word of English. I communicated with him in Arabic. After the students had read I requested him to read the same portion, that they might hear his pronunciation. He read in the musical cantilating manner of the East, and the listener who had travelled in these countries might have fancied himself on the banks of the Nile, or on Mount Lebanon.[15]

Embodied in the voice of the learned Muslim from Kankan, the *Maqamat* of al-Hariri mediate the literary and linguistic convergence of multiple intellectual networks: that traced in the travels of al-Hariri's hero Abu Zayd throughout the Islamic world; that traced in the travels of "African Moslems" who, Blyden observes, "are continually crossing the continent to Egypt, Arabia, and Syria";[16] Blyden's repetition of those itineraries, alluded to here but documented more fully in *From West Africa to Palestine* (1873); and the itinerary of the *Maqamat* themselves, relayed initially via manuscript from al-Hariri's native Iraq to the libraries and madrassas of the Islamic world and subsequently via printed Orientalist editions and translations to the libraries of Europe and beyond (some of which might own a copy of *The People of Africa* as well). Blyden's participation in and documentation of Arabic textuality from Monrovia to Beirut extends its worldly itinerary to the New World, not only via printed texts such as *The People of Africa*, but through the extensive lectures he gave as a leading intellectual of the African diaspora promoting Liberia's "promise" for the global redemption of the black race. Blyden put into practice and called into being a nineteenth-century transoceanic and trans-Saharan textual community translating between Arabic and English, *'ilm* and literature, as they negotiated the legacy of old world literary routes still visible beneath the imperial institutions and discourses through which a new world literary order was announcing itself.

Blyden's transatlantic, circum-Mediterranean labors exemplified the "transnational circuits of intellectual advance" that Goethe, Marx, and Engels theorized, according to Stefan Hoesel-Uhlig, yet they also drew attention to anterior literary networks long inclusive of and scattered across Africa, from the Nile to the Atlantic, the Mediterranean to south of the Sahara.[17] In a speech written in the years immediately following the *Manifesto*'s 1848 publication and titled "The Claims of the Negro Ethnologically Considered," Frederick Douglass had also unsettled the promises of a vanguard cosmopolitanism emanating out of European centers of knowledge production. Responding to the world-literary networks and archives of comparative philology and Orientalism and of Egyptology and the classics at a time when "all that is solid melts into air" and "all that is holy is profaned," Douglass declaimed:

> It is somewhat remarkable, that, at a time when knowledge is so generally diffused, when the geography of the world is so well understood—when time and space, in the intercourse of nations, are almost annihilated—when oceans have become bridges—the earth a magnificent hall—the hollow sky a dome—under which a common humanity can meet in friendly conclave—when nationalities are being swallowed up and the ends of the earth brought together—I say it is remarkable—nay, it is strange that there should arise a phalanx of learned men—speaking in the name of science—to forbid the magnificent reunion of mankind in one brotherhood.[18]

As insuperable natural divisions give way to engineered spaces of "friendly conclave," Douglass makes "strange" the proclamation of a "silent, almost secret congregation" practicing a vanguard cosmopolitanism. This "phalanx of learned men—speaking in the name of science" is rather shown to sabotage the idyll of world literature as a "magnificent reunion of mankind in one brotherhood."

Uttering scientific speech "to forbid" such a reunion despite its manifest possibility—at a time "when oceans have become bridges—the earth a magnificent hall—the hollow sky a dome—under which a common humanity can meet in friendly conclave"—Douglass's "phalanx of learned men" inherit and embody a material and discursive supremacy that not only produced the transatlantic African diaspora but continually misrecognized and worked to erase the role of Africa and its diaspora in world history. Joseph Roach observes, "Although Africa in fact plays a hinge role in turning the Mediterranean-centered consciousness of European memory into an Atlantic-centered one, the scope of that role largely disappears." But it is not gone completely: "it leaves its historic traces amid the incomplete erasures, beneath the superscriptions, and within the layered palimpsests of more or less systematic cultural misrecognition."[19]

The novels, stories, poetry, and theater discussed in this book—from W. E. B. Du Bois and Zora Neale Hurston to Alejo Carpentier and Derek Walcott to Maryse Condé and Toni Morrison—are an archive of these palimpsests, excavations of "historic traces" attesting to the *longue durée* of a world literature extending from before Goethe's now to a twentieth-century Atlantic and Caribbean.[20] Inheritors of Blyden's nineteenth-century encounter with al-Hariri, these authors stage African diasporic literary genealogies to excavate the *longue durée* of a world literature "sedimented," as Fredric Jameson has it, in the mutually constituting genres of oral and textual, elite and vernacular cultural production.[21] The twentieth-century New World ironies of Socratic dialogue in the signifying dialogism of Du Bois's *The Quest of the Silver Fleece*, the spectral Afro-Asiatic trails of Hurston's Moses stories, the Andalusian echoes in the verbal duels and African epics of Carpentier's Caribbean, the circuits of animal tales linking krik-krak to Aristophanes to the *Panchatantra* in Walcott's *Ti-Jean and His Brothers*, the structures of *A Thousand and One Nights* decentering the Francophone West African novel in Condé's *Ségou*, and the Afro-Greek conjuring of Islamic origins in Morrison's *Song of Solomon*—these rhizomatic palimpsests evoke a deep history of worldly narrative and generic traffic from the Indian Ocean up the Red Sea, around the Mediterranean and across the Atlantic.

Read by Du Bois, Garvey, and others as a chronicle of West Africa's historic cosmopolitanism, Blyden's crossings with Arabic manuscripts and recitations, with transcontinental trade and scholarship, "host prior such moments," as Ian Baucom argues, "not autonomous but invested by a range of pasts which are not, in fact, past."[22] This legible "sedimentation" of worldly lines of circulation, translation, and exchange offers a historiography of world literature inhospitable toward declarations heralding it as newly emergent.[23] The twentieth-century diasporic inscription of Africa into anterior world-systemic networks and archives—stretching from the Nile Valley and classical antiquity to the Malian empire and medieval al-Andalus—asserts a different *durée* for world literature, one that shares a historiographical logic with Black Atlantic periodization, and so with Paul Gilroy's observations regarding "the catastrophic rupture of the middle passage" and "the concept of Jubilee . . . a special break or rupture in the conception of time defined and enforced by the regimes that sanctioned bondage."[24] Rather than imagining world literature through a narrative of steady progress through "empty, homogeneous time," this historiography lays out, in Saidiya Hartman's words, "a story written against the narrative of progress," an ongoing story of unfreedom that persists across "one definitive moment . . . that has yet to cease happening."[25] Conjuring another, prior moment, before the break, world literature offers itself as an archive where spectral and obscure traces of anteriority evoke those faded or foreclosed cosmopolitan circuits running through a diasporic idea of

Africa before European hegemony, extending to our own contemporary moment through the works of Du Bois, Hurston, Carpentier, Walcott, Condé, and Morrison.

The "narrative of progress," against which the Black Atlantic's story accumulates, is the stuff of Goethe's "profit and pleasure," the "business-like promptitude" of his world-literary "now." Yet synchronic and diachronic affiliations with transcontinental and transoceanic networks of reading, writing, and recitation open up what David Scott calls "an archaeology of black memory . . . an exercise, literally and metaphorically, of re-membering, of putting back together aspects of our common life so as to make visible what has been obscured, what has been excluded, what has been forgotten."[26] Writing after the break, Blyden's histories and chronicles, his itineraries and crossings, make visible the subterranean streams of what Mufti calls "heterogeneous and ancient cultures of reading and writing," of performance and recitation, at work in the New World, which twentieth-century writers of the African diaspora bring to the surface like Edouard Glissant's "fugitive memories" from the "chasms" of the ocean, like Derek Walcott's "archaeology of fragments lying around, from the broken African kingdoms, from the crevasses of Canton, from Syria and Lebanon, vibrating not under the earth but in our raucous, demotic streets."[27]

Inheriting Goethe, Marx, and Engels, though, preeminent European theorists continue to imagine world literature as consonant and coterminous with European economic and discursive ascendance. Franco Moretti and Pascale Casanova together conjure a literary world system emerging around the turn of the nineteenth century whose "centers" lie in Western Europe and whose "peripheries" lie everywhere else. Moretti's *Atlas of the European Novel* asks readers to "recognize in the geographical variation and dispersal of forms the power of the center over the enormous periphery."[28] In the case of the novel form, he argues: "In cultures that belong to the periphery of the literary system (which means: almost all cultures, inside and outside Europe), the modern novel first arises . . . as a compromise between a western formal influence (usually French or English) and local materials."[29] Casanova's "world republic of letters" complements Moretti's model by attending to the adjudication of "literary value" by "cosmopolitan intermediaries—publishers, editors, critics, and especially translators" who largely operate out of Paris and set the "Greenwich meridian" of literary time.[30] Moretti's "atlas" and Casanova's "meridian" render world literature through a Eurocentric grid of space and time that both predetermines their conclusions and occludes networks and archives that sound time across the depth of the Atlantic. Rather than a positivist sociology, apprehending world literature's *longue durée* through the African diaspora turns on intertextual traces and echoes, spectral genealogies and fragile networks; as Hartman writes, "the identification with Africa is always already after the break."[31]

While numerous critical discourses—postcolonial, transnational, relational, planetary—have addressed the cosmopolitan engagements of African diasporic literary production, the specific nexus of world literature and the literature of the African diaspora has gone largely unremarked. Studies of world literature have neglected the engagement, critique, and revision of the idea by writers of the African diaspora, while studies of African diaspora literature have passed over its formative engagement with the world literature idea. This reciprocal oversight has neglected the opportunity to link up the foundational work on African diasporic cultural and intellectual formations pioneered by George Shepperson and Earl Lewis with methodologically resonant approaches informing comparative literature's transnational, disciplinary circuitry from Goethe to Claudio Guillén and David Damrosch.[32] Thirteen years after Goethe heralded the epoch of world literature and five years before Douglass published his *Narrative*, Henry B. Stanton, president of the American Anti-Slavery Society would recognize abolitionist literature as a "literature of the world" at the 1840 World Anti-Slavery Convention.[33] The Goethean discourse of *Weltliteratur* also sits at the heart of a foundational scene of twentieth-century diasporic, modernist literary production. When René Maran became the first black writer to win the Prix Goncourt in 1921 for his novel *Batouala*, it catalyzed an international and interracial literary traffic that not only resembled but invoked Goethe's coinage. The US mainstream and African American press both responded enthusiastically to the success of Maran, the Martinique-born son of Guyanese parents, who up to that point was working as a colonial administrator in the French Central African colony of Ubangi-Shari, which provided the characters and setting for the novel. As Michel Fabre has noted, Americans frequently took the award to indicate "the absence of racial prejudice in France" and also "Africa's artistic potential."[34] Reporting from Paris, Ernest Hemingway wrote an account of "la querelle de *Batouala*" in the *Toronto Star Weekly*, both reviewing the political uproar caused by the preface's denunciation of French imperialism and praising the artistry of the narrative itself.[35] Putting aside Hemingway's opinion that "to be translated properly, however, there should be another Negro who has lived a life in the country two days' march from Lake Tchad and who knows English as René Maran knows French," the publishing houses of Thomas Seltzer in New York and Jonathan Cape in London quickly put out Adele Szold Seltzer's translation in 1922.[36] In 1923 Countee Cullen's poem "The Dance of Love (After Reading René Maran's *Batouala*)" appeared in *Opportunity*, the publication of the United States–based National Urban League. *Les Continents*, a Paris-based periodical founded by Kojo Tovalou Houénou where Maran himself played an active editorial role, would reprint this poem in 1924 as part of a short feature titled "La jeune poésie afro-américaine." Alain Locke, who would soon go on to edit *The New Negro* anthology, prefaced Cullen's poem with a brief introduction to "the youngest generation of Africo-American culture[, . . .] brilliantly represented by a whole host [*toute une pléiade*] of young poets: Claude McKay, Jean Toomer, Langston Hughes, and Countee Cullen."[37] Locke links "their importance from a racial point of view" precisely to the literary traffic initiated by the prize-winning *Batouala*: "Doesn't the poem about René Maran's 'Batouala' itself imply the future enrichment of art by this new movement of the African genius, by this new intellectual commerce between the continents?"[38]

Locke taps Goethe's economic metaphor of world literature to proleptically herald "this new movement of the African genius" exemplified by Cullen's poetic rewriting of Maran's novelistic description of a ceremonial, orgiastic frenzy in Ubangi-Shari. Even before his years of study at the University of Berlin, Locke admired Goethe's call for worldliness in the arts. His first major statement on the subject, "Cosmopolitanism and Culture," composed at Oxford University while he was a Rhodes scholar, even opens with a reference to Goethe.[39] Locke's invocation of the discourse of world literature in the context of *Batouala*'s Parisian triumph echoes how Paris's role in "consecrating" international literary value catalyzed Goethe's own thinking. It was in response to French adaptations of his play *Torquato Tasso* that Goethe made his inaugural proclamation to his secretary Johann Peter Eckermann on January 22, 1827, that "national literature is now rather an unmeaning term; the epoch of world literature is at hand." Locke's preface to *Les Continent*'s paradigmatic short feature "La jeune poésie africo-américaine," then, makes manifest the author's ongoing conversation with Goethe. The familiar metaphor of "intellectual commerce" frames his emergent vision of what poet and critic Melvin

Dixon—while looking at precisely this scene of circulation, translation, and exchange but not specifying the connection between Locke and Goethe—calls "world black literature."[40]

Locke's mapping of the intellectual commerce between a poem by an African American riffing on a novel by an Antillean colonial administrator who claims merely to be a "recording instrument" for a village in Ubangi-Shari charts an influential modernist economy of forms consonant with European models of world-literary formation.[41] Brent Hayes Edwards notes how the technological metaphor of the recording instrument "marks the interface between the oral and the written" in *Batouala*, which has offered a foundational model for subsequent African and diasporic entries into metropolitan circuits of literary production and consumption.[42] Casanova defines the primitive accumulation providing such access to world-literary markets as "the transposition of oral practices to written form . . . to create literature and thus convert folk tradition into literary wealth."[43] While in *The New Negro* Locke would fully embrace this "alchemical" teleology of "transmuting popular cultural and linguistic forms . . . into cultural and literary gold," he also witnessed the precarious material status of Afro/diasporan literary capital.[44] Much of the correspondence between Locke and Maran concerned their mutual efforts to secure translation deals for *The New Negro* and various novels of Maran. This became especially urgent during World War II, with Maran a poor, hungry refugee in Bordeaux: "Book reviews and articles [in the African American press] contained appeals for the publication of his works in the United States; after the Liberation, [Locke and Mercer Cook] bought several manuscripts from him and sent him provisions as delicately as possible."[45]

Locke's role in *Batouala*'s post-publication history, then, registers an ambivalent engagement of African diaspora writing with the category of world literature. The discourse of world literature helps Locke mediate contemporaneous practices of transnational modernism, of "cosmopolitan styles" and "synthetic vernaculars,"[46] yet it also endorses a top-down vanguardism in which elite transformations of vernacular forms underwrite the *entrée* to the world-literary market. During the century after this emergent global modernist moment, market forces will continue to inherit and impose upon African diaspora literature this developmental discourse. In the chapters that follow, we will attend to the ways a series of twentieth-century writers of the African diaspora negotiate this imposition as they fashion the vernacular itself as a repository of cosmopolitan traces, New World palimpsests of ancient discursive technologies conjoining oral and scribal modes of dissemination, from recitation to transcription to lining-out. Reclaiming the terrain of world literature from vanguardist triumphalism and nationalist teleologies, the authors analyzed in this study instead attend to the ways orality and literacy, as Roach observes, "have produced one another interactively over time."[47] Linking up New World vernacular forms with bards, griots, storytellers, scribes, orators, and scholars, their works inscribe themselves and the cultures of the African diaspora in a *longue durée* of worldly circulation and generic sedimentation shuttling between breath and text. In the face of elusive verbal itineraries and conservative historiographical protocols, they reckon with but also flaunt Glissant's reliquary of "uncertain evidence," "extremely fragile monuments," "frequently incomplete, obliterated, or ambiguous archives."[48]

Drawing upon this catalogue, W. E. B. Du Bois makes the literary a site of historiographical contest and redress, articulating radical temporal and spatial coordinates of world literature for a subsequent tradition of twentieth-century African diaspora writing committed to conjuring a cosmopolitan past. Chapter 1, "World Literature and Antiquity: Classical Surrogates in W. E. B. Du Bois's Black Belt," looks at Du Bois as a transitional figure between nineteenth- and twentieth-century writers in the "vindicationist" tradition of black historiography of the ancient world, defined by Wilson Jeremiah Moses as "the project of defending black people from the charge that they have made little or no contribution to the history of human progress."[49] Whereas figures such as Martin Delany and George Washington Williams had tended to read the archive of antiquity through reified national and racial lenses tracking a monolithic succession of civilizations, Du Bois, on the other hand, evokes the ancient world as a cosmopolitan scene of circulation, translation, and exchange. Egypt, Ethiopia, Greece, and Rome emerge as hybrid entities in a fluid, transculturating, world-historical milieu, a milieu to be revisited in the Conclusion's reading of Heliodorus's fourth-century AD *Aithiopika*, a Hellenistic romance about the fate of a white child born to a royal Ethiopian couple in Meroë.

Du Bois's doubly revisionist historiography alloys a treatment of Greece and Rome as a site from which to read African origins and stolen legacies with a more speculative hermeneutics for reading the present. For in *The Souls of Black Folk* and *The Quest of the Silver Fleece*, the verbal arts of Greece and Rome are blasted "out of the homogeneous course of history" to form a "constellation" with African American culture.[50] The schoolhouses of Tennessee and the country roads of

Alabama are palimpsests from which Du Bois excavates traces of classical regimes of orality and literacy. These traces stage the mysterious temporal conundrums, affinities and aporias, and genealogical pathways down which black culture comes to carry forth a cosmopolitan antiquity. Such mysteries encode a diasporic poetics of world literature that upsets the hierarchies and teleologies leading from European centers to global peripheries, from raw orality to refined literacy, and from folk to elite culture, then current among Du Bois's modernist contemporaries. This diasporic poetics offers new ways of drawing together diverse strains of global modernism, contributing to the efforts of scholars such as Rebecca Walkowitz and Matthew Hart, who have employed notions of "cosmopolitan styles" and "synthetic vernaculars," respectively, to cut across stubborn linguistic, racialized, and geopolitical categorical divisions.[51]

Du Bois's intertextual alignment of country schoolhouse teachers, activists, and preachers with Mediterranean figures such as Homer and Cicero sets the black vernacular tradition within a cosmopolitan archive of world literature, one in which orality and literacy, folk and elite culture "have produced one another interactively over time." While readers of Du Bois have long debated his valuation and valencing of vernacular culture, Zora Neale Hurston represents a world-literary figure intimately and thoroughly aligned with it. Chapter 2, though, "World Literature in Hiding: Zora Neale Hurston, Biographical Criticism, and African Diasporic Vernacular Culture," presents a portrait of Hurston and her work that runs counter to their critical and popular canonization as familiar, intimate, and vernacular. An analysis of the numerous institutional entanglements of Hurston's life and career reveals the degree to which the familiar, intimate, vernacular Hurston paradoxically emerges from the conditions of textual production she often struggled against as a student, theatrical producer, performer, anthropologist, essayist, letter-writer, and novelist. Her posthumous reception and canonization continue to evade the range of discursive stances she aimed to achieve with regard to the worldliness of African diasporic vernacular culture, enmeshed as it is in linguistically and geographically overdetermined oral and textual genealogies.

It has long been noted how in Hurston's work on stage and in print, story, song, gesture, and dance ground moments of what VèVè Clark calls "diaspora literacy," cueing mutual recognition across multiple sites of the African diaspora.[52] Less attention has been paid to Hurston's presentation of hybrid technologies such as recitation, lining-out, and transcription as long-lived vernacular practices with deep historical roots. They not only mediate between performance and writing; they serve as mechanisms through which Hurston inscribes African diaspora verbal arts in worldly networks and archives that reach back to stories of Moses scattered along narrative pathways reaching from the Middle East to West Africa and that conjoin "characteristics of Negro expression" with, for example, Elizabethan rhetorical conventions.[53] The deep history she presents of a vernacular always already crucially involved with cosmopolitan textuality mitigates critiques leveraged against her work, most notably by Richard Wright, for being anachronistically invested in folk orality, while also making visible aspects of her work and persona occluded by overinvestment in her folkishness. As with "la querelle de *Batouala*," this revisionist account of Hurston's canonization draws attention to the material production of world literature, a contradictory, racialized business of art, marketing, and celebrity formation particularly pressing for writers of the African diaspora.

Immanent processes of commodification, no less than the networks and archives of world literature's *longue durée*, shape Hurston and Du Bois's engagement with "modernist notions of culture" that, according to Michael Denning, "named those social sites where the commodity form and its law of value did not yet rule—the high arts, on the one hand, and the lifeways of 'primitive' peoples, on the other."[54] Crossing and confounding these twin poles, the work of Du Bois and Hurston summons the verbal technologies and world-systemic traffic of the cosmopolitan past to reimagine the New World moment. Their contemporary, the Cuban writer Alejo Carpentier, likewise draws on performative and textual traces of this cosmopolitan past in order to undermine the racialized, literary-anthropological primitivism that admittedly dogs his avant-garde quest for a New World poetics. Thus Chapter 3, "Whiteness and World Literature: Alejo Carpentier, Racial Difference, and Narrative Creolization," analyzes the trajectory of the Cuban writer's engagement with African diasporic culture from *negrismo* to surrealism to marvelous realism. Carpentier's appropriations of blackness share many of the motives and details of global modernisms' various, overlapping strains of avant-garde primitivism; this chapter reads how early works from *¡Écue-Yamba-Ó!* (1933) to *El reino de este mundo* (1949) problematically gift to the Americas as a whole the particular racialized experiences and practices of African diasporic subjects. Nonetheless, in articulating a scribal—as opposed to what Jerome Branche calls a "neobozalic"— register of blackness, partly through West African Muslim figures such as the Haitian revolutionary Mackandal, these texts revise Eurocentric paradigms of orality and literacy securing the globe-spanning, literary-ethnographic surreal.[55]

Los pasos perdidos (1953) further revises modernist literary-ethnographic protocols. Through the figure of a Latin American New Yorker, Carpentier self-reflexively exposes the discursive tropes that textually mediate subject positions frequently associated with whiteness, such as the ethnographic voyeur, the scribe amongst the unlettered, and the fair intellectual rejuvenated by consorting with darker-skinned folk. "El camino de Santiago," published in *La guerra del tiempo* (1958), continues to excavate racialized textual devices by conjoining marvelous or magical realism with a revisionist historiography of world literature. Set in the world of sixteenth- and seventeenth-century Spain and Cuba, the story unveils the baroque, creolized origins of oral and written narrative traditions—in particular the *libro de caballería*, or book of knightly adventure—that remain foundational for New World writing. Resuscitating the narrative and generic circulation, translation, and exchange of al-Andalus through tropes such as *'aja'ib*—Arabic for "marvels"—Carpentier philologically connects a narrative tradition anterior to colonial Europe to the contemporary magical realist moment through a spectral genealogy before European hegemony to a time of Arab and Islamic empire. The hegemony of a US book market that racializes Latin American literary production, though, obstructs the generic struggles with whiteness immanent in Carpentier's exemplary texts, displacing and reasserting world literature's racial blind spot at a formal juncture meant to deal explicitly with it.

Chapter 4, "Dialectics of World Literature: Derek Walcott between Intimacy and Iconicity," tracks how the St. Lucian lays bare, as well as fashions his participation in, a commodified field of "hypercanonical" world literature. Walcott poetically tropes exhaustion as a response to the critical and political frameworks that have produced him as an "exemplary" postcolonial, West Indian, and Afrodiasporan poet/playwright. A circulating icon of diasporic contradictions, Walcott stages, but ultimately disavows, the world-literary dialectic of postcolonial irony, repetition, and reversal that might seem to underwrite his access to and success on the world-literary stage. This disavowal turns on recontextualizing New World creolization, linking its vernacular creations to the *longue durée* of world literature's recursively creolizing networks and archives. So, for example, when an opening chorus of frogs chants "Greek-croak, Greek-croak" in the "folk" drama *Ti-Jean and*

His Brothers, the African-derived Caribbean krik-krak storytelling tradition and the ancient Greek comedies of Aristophanes mutually articulate one another.[56] And they do so not as a far-fetched juxtaposition between folk and classical art but as a cipher of the cosmopolitan circuit of animal stories traveling from West Africa to India.

These stories have simultaneously functioned along a continuum encompassing courtly mirrors for princes and rustic fireside anecdotes as they have shuttled between oral performance and textualization in compendia such as the *Panchatantra*, *Kalila wa Dimna*, and *Aesop's Fables*. Walcott's own poetic work uncannily inhabits this shuttling continuum, moving toward a poetics of intimate recitation. He recuperates practices of intimate recitation from the *longue durée* of world literature oscillating "from hand to mouth" between elite and vernacular idioms and contexts. This "hand to mouth" intimacy inscribes his oeuvre into a transhistorical, transcontinental chain of individually enacted poetic transmissions operating outside hypercanonical dialectics that have figured Walcott as a diasporic icon, or resolution, of critical and political contradictions.

The historical novels of Guadeloupean author Maryse Condé similarly recuperate material circuits of global narrative traffic obscured by racialized processes of canonization. They uncover ghostly literary genealogies in the ways a West African saga explicitly indebted to the nineteenth-century French adventure novel reveals the specter of *A Thousand and One Nights* in the European novel and in the ways a rewriting of *Wuthering Heights* in Guadeloupe helps uncover the specter of New World racial taxonomies in Emily Brontë's text. These gestures, as explored in Chapter 5, "Material Histories of World Literature: Intertextuality and Maryse Condé's Historical Novels," overdetermine world literature's narrative genealogies and disrupt nationalist genealogical narratives. By placing the Bambara kingdom in a dynamic material context, Condé's African saga *Ségou* deromanticizes both the griot and the heroic historiography of Africa. This move to materially historicize Ségou enacts Condé's efforts—through attention to the far-reaching mercantile systems of Africa and the Mediterranean basin—to include West Africa in world literature's history of circulation and translation, specifically through intertextuality with *A Thousand and One Nights*, which disorients and reorients the relations between French literature and its colonized Francophone affiliates. Furthermore, *Ségou* dramatizes how West African genealogical practices of reincarnation, both narrative and familial, disrupt the assimilation of local storytelling into a deterritorialized, universal narratology.

Its title evoking the transmigration of souls folded into the narrative structure of *Ségou*, Condé's *La migration des coeurs* reincarnates Brontë's *Wuthering Heights*. Like *Ségou*, *La migration des coeurs* allows Condé to comment on genealogical processes, both through the concerns of its characters and through the formal construction of the novel. Also like *Ségou*, *La migration des coeurs* conjoins material history and intertextuality to disrupt genealogical expectations and desires. The economic history of Caribbean plantation economies inverts the timeline of origin and revision in the relationships between *Wuthering Heights* and *La migration des coeurs* and also between the Caribbean and English gothic traditions. Painting the gothic as a world-literary genre fed by narrative, architectural, and conceptual elements generated and disseminated by racial and colonial contests in the Caribbean, Condé's text reroutes, pluralizes, and decenters lines of narrative exchange. The multidirectional and overdetermined genealogical explorations of *La migration des coeurs*, and *Ségou*, serve Condé's larger skepticism toward investing the past with identitarian dreams of singular origins. As in Carpentier's and Walcott's writing, creolization appears as a recursive process extending backward through time, while also projecting itself forward into what Glissant calls "its unforeseeable whirl."[57]

Condé's impious embrace of overdetermined origins and contingent futures informs her impatience with cultural nationalist pieties, as hallmark essays such as "Order, Disorder, Freedom, and the West Indian Writer" make clear. Her intertextual literary practices conform with her critical impatience; by contrast, her contemporary Toni Morrison's intertextual literary practices often work counter to her own cultural nationalist critical commitments, a contradiction explored in Chapter 6, "'Healing' World Literature: Toni Morrison's Conflicts of Interest." While Morrison's texts and dreadlocked image circulate globally as a symbol of the African American ancestor figure she theorizes, her novels expansively imagine their kin and kind. Her thematic treatment of ancestry and genealogy often turns on formal engagements that work counter to the notion of linear, singular descent implicit in metaphors of rootedness privileged for their "didactic" and "healing" capacities. Approached through a rubric of world literature that the texts themselves invite through geography and intertextuality, Morrison's work consistently poses alternatives to these healing, nationalist genealogies, tracing highly trafficked lines of descent across multiple eras of world history.

Two novels in particular, *Song of Solomon* and *Paradise*, stage the tension between restorative local commitments and worldly filiations and affiliations. *Song of Solomon* has typically been read as the genealogical quest of its protagonist through an African American, cultural nationalist, symbolic geography aligning the North with literacy, disenchantment, and alienation and the South with orality, magic, and authenticity. This chapter will identify those threads of the novel that not only confound this symbolic geography but radically globalize it. Following textual clues to Africa, Europe, and the Middle East, an alternative to the cultural nationalist vernacular paradigm emerges that firmly plants the novel, and African American cultural genealogies, in world literature's swirling history of circulation and translation, orality and textuality, rootedness and cosmopolitanism. Written twenty years after *Song of Solomon* yet revisiting that novel's historical moment and conversations, *Paradise* engages cultural nationalist politics at formal and thematic, as well as local and global, levels. A generational divide amongst the inhabitants of an all-black town in Oklahoma poses one model of black solidarity against another, pitting nation-based political allegiances against Pan-African spiritual ones. When the town consolidates and regenerates itself through a stunning act of collective violence against women that effectively dismisses diasporic spiritual commitments, the novel limns the tragic incommensurability of identity-based ethics, politics, and aesthetics. Morrison's work tensely charts these overlapping and embattled terrains of filiation and affiliation that both serve and haunt African diaspora writing. Entanglements and genealogies from the cosmopolitan past offer the call of recognition but also prefigure future misrecognitions, silences, and betrayals.

1 World Literature and Antiquity

Classical Surrogates in W. E. B. Du Bois's Black Belt

LIKE EDWARD WILMOT BLYDEN at Liberia College, W. E. B. Du Bois briefly held a professorship of Greek and Latin at Wilberforce University. Alongside their humanist enthusiasm for Greco-Roman culture, both men inherited and promoted a counter-discourse of antiquity increasingly marginalized over the course of the nineteenth century and well into the twentieth, an intellectual shift whose story Martin Bernal has popularly documented in his *Black Athena* volumes. This counter-discourse emphasized the variously shaded African roots of classical antiquity, reminding an amnesiac Europe of Greece and Rome's debts to Egypt and Ethiopia, as recorded by ancient and modern sources alike. Du Bois, furthermore, proceeded to significantly refashion this counter-discourse, with significant consequences for how we read the literature of the African diaspora within the field of world literature. The vindicationist historiography of his predecessors, as Wilson Jeremiah Moses writes, "sought to defend Africans by proving the African origin of ancient civilizations and demonstrating the indebtedness of modern humanity to those civilizations."[1] Exploding the linear calculus by which "the riddle of Egypt . . . led to Greece," in the words of Jeremy W. Pope, Du Bois taps a hermetic strain of classical historiography to subtly thread an esoteric, palimpsestic hermeneutics of antiquity.[2] Supplementing a teleological history of successive monolithic civilizations, Du Bois in the historical treatise *The Negro* attends to the rhizomatic, cosmopolitan networks of the ancient scene, crisscrossed by obscure histories and mysterious affinities.

These obscure histories and mysterious affinities provide the hermetic key to deciphering the allusive textures of *The Souls of Black Folk* and *The Quest of the Silver Fleece*. Both texts make plain that Du Bois shares with Goethe "a sense of classical antiquity as the ultimate treasury to plunder for themes, formal models, and even language," as David Damrosch writes.[3] Yet for Du Bois, this foundational archive of world literature is not merely an impressive collection of artifacts, destined to inspire intertextual engagement by *littérateurs* or to elevate the minds of the oppressed and disenfranchised. Radically calling into question racialized hierarchies of elite and folk culture, this archive persists embodied in the vernacular practices of the Black Belt, where preachers, teachers, activists, and ordinary folk are what Joseph Roach calls "surrogates" who carry it forth as if in unbroken communion with an antiquity whose loci always bear hermetic traces of Afro-Oriental relations and inversions.[4] Du Bois's hermeneutics of world literature thereby brushes the surfaces of text and performance against the grain in order to excavate living traces not only of "African survivals" but of a cosmopolitan circum-Mediterranean antiquity. By modeling twentieth-century African diaspora literature's spectral continuity with this revised classical scene, Du Bois galvanizes a counter-discourse of world literature that charts an alternative to ideologies of literary-anthropological cultural nationalism and global modernism that did and continue to spatially and temporally subordinate the cultural products of Africa and its diaspora within world literature. It also offers a reading protocol attentive to oscillatory and fragmentary processes of memory and transmission, an anti-positivist protocol that sutures the poetics of diaspora to the foundational, nineteenth-century German discourses of world literature.

From the late eighteenth century onward, the semiotics of classical antiquity became a prime vehicle for touting Europe's world-historical ascendance. From the Greek Revival in architecture to the pedagogy of the French *lycée*, Prussian *gymnasium*, and English public school, imperial self-regard aped the spatial and linguistic forms of Greece and Rome, their vaunted origins. Surveying the globe-spanning archive of world literature available for plunder, Goethe warned: "We should not think that the truth is in Chinese or Serbian literature, in Calderón or the Niebelungen. In our pursuit of models, we ought always to return to the Greeks of antiquity in whose works beautiful man is represented."[5] The elite emplotment of an expansionist European culture as the revival of classical virtue, reason, beauty, and might invited many skeptical second looks at antiquity as a site of origins. Edward Gibbon, author of *The History of the Decline and Fall of the Roman Empire*, wrote: "Unfortunate inhabitants of the forests, these proud Greeks took everything from strangers. The Phoenicians taught them the use of letters; the arts, the laws, all that elevates man above the animals, they owed to the Egyptians. These last brought them their religion, and the Greeks in adopting it paid the tribute that ignorance owes to wisdom."[6] Annotating eighteenth-century philhellenism, Gibbon sardonically reminds readers of Greece's Afro-Semitic tutelage. Around the same time, Constantin-François de Chaseboeuf, comte de Volney, extended this theme. Standing before the ruins of Thebes, "the pride of the ancient kingdom of Ethiopia" (here signifying Meroë, Nubia, Sudan, and parts of Abyssinia), he writes: "There a people, now forgotten, discovered, while others were yet barbarians, the elements of the arts and sciences. A race of men now rejected from society for their *sable skin and frizzled hair*, founded on the study of the laws of nature, those civil and religious systems which still govern the universe."[7] Countering Europe's possessive investment in Greco-Roman transcendence, Gibbon and Volney exemplify a counter-discourse attentive to the inescapable legacy of Greece and Rome's neighbors, even and especially those with "sable skin and frizzled hair."

African American writers participated in this counter-discourse from the early days of the republic. David Walker's *Appeal*, a millenarian condemnation of New World slavery first published in 1829, took a "retrospective view of the arts and sciences," stating that "learning originated [with] the sons of Africa," for "the Egyptians, were Africans or coloured people, such as we are—some of them yellow and others dark—a mixture of Ethiopians and the natives of Egypt—about the same as you see the coloured people of the United States at the present day."[8] This foundational learning "was carried thence into Greece, where it was improved upon and refined. Thence among the Romans . . . and it has been enlightening the dark and benighted minds of men from then, down to this day."[9] Frederick Douglass would echo Walker's civilizational timeline in "The Claims of the Negro Ethnologically Considered" (1854), reiterating that "Greece and Rome—and through them Europe and America have received their civilization from the ancient Egyptians. This fact is not denied by anybody. But Egypt is in Africa. Pity that it had not been in Europe, or in Asia, or better still in America!"[10] Dickson D. Bruce Jr. reads such "pictures of the African past" as "strongly influenced by the need to come to terms with black double-consciousness . . . looking for aspects of the African background that were closely tied to western civilization but were distinctively black."[11]

This historiography of antiquity emphasizes the linear continuity leading from Egypt to Greece and Rome, and subsequently to contemporary Euro-American culture. Further setting the stage for Du Bois's revision of classical historiography, African diaspora writers such as Blyden and Martin Delany would revisit the ancient sources in order to explore the more radical possibilities latent in the "close ties" between "distinctively black" origins and "western civilization." There has been a tendency to group these figures with the earlier vindicationists, overlooking the esoteric streak running through works such as Blyden's "The Negro in Ancient History" (1869) and Delany's *Principia of Ethnology* (1879). Maghan Keita, for example, argues: "Blyden sets the tone for those who will follow in the way he uses classical material to make the point of an African presence in and contribution to the Classical Age documented in the classical sources themselves."[12] Africa, in this construction, derives its value from its "presence in and contribution to the Classical Age." As such, it remains consistent with the long vindicationist tradition discussed above and reaching back to Phillis Wheatley's invocation of Terence in her late eighteenth-century poem "To Maecenas": "one alone of Afric's sable race" to receive the Muses' "partial grace."[13] Pope argues that for such literary and historical gestures, "the analytical center of gravity, the philosophical point of reference . . . the *telos*," remains Greek and Roman.[14]

Blyden admittedly had a "reverence for Greco-Roman culture," as Valentin Mudimbe records.[15] "No modern writers," Blyden declared, "will ever influence the destiny of the race to the same extent that the Greeks and Romans have done."[16] Nonetheless, the classical sources accumulated by Blyden, and later by Delany, render the ancient Ethiopians, as the former writes, "above mortals, associates of the gods."[17] From among many similar passages in Homer, he representatively cites out of the *Iliad*: "Yesterday Jupiter went to Oceanus, to the handsome Ethiopians, to a banquet, and with him went all the gods."[18] Diodorus Siculus accounts for the Ethiopians' privileged status on Mt. Olympus: "They were the first to be taught to honour the gods and to hold sacrifices and processions and festivals and the other rites by which men honour the deity; and that in consequence their piety has been published abroad among all men, and it is generally held that the sacrifices practised among the Ethiopians are those which are the most pleasing to heaven."[19]

Whereas in Walker's *Appeal*, Egyptian arts and sciences were "improved upon and refined" in Greece, the classical sources track a degradation of divine knowledge as colonizing Ethiopians disseminated their rites and practices up the Nile, whence the Egyptians triumphantly disseminated them in turn throughout the circum-Mediterranean, founding, for example, the royal house of Danae in Sparta and Colchis on the Black Sea, "descended from the army of Sesostris," as Herodotus records and Blyden cites.[20]

Writing from Philadelphia, Delany also follows Diodorus and notes how the sacred system of writing that transmitted the divine wisdom of worship and architecture, astronomy and medicine, "is understood only by the priests of the Egyptians, who learn it from their fathers as one of the things which are not divulged, but among the Ethiopians everyone uses these forms of letters."[21] These Egyptian Mysteries, the basis of Greek and thence Roman hermetic knowledge, were the common possession of Ethiopia that through successive iterated colonial mimicries lost their originary plenitude. For Delany, the Greeks and Romans mourned the deterioration of the "combined wisdom of Ethiopia and Egypt, comprising their ethics, religion, philosophy, literature, arts, science and wealth," through "the mysterious allegory of the Garden of the Hesperides."[22] Delany interprets this lapsarian myth of the inaccessible tree of immortal knowledge to refer to the increasingly distant hermetic encoding of Ethiopia and Egypt's "Lost Arts": "Such were their discretion, caution, prudence, judgement, care and jealousy of others, that whatever they desired to conceal, was exhibited in such a manner, that while it was perfectly plain and comprehensible to themselves, the design was obscure and unintelligible to others."[23] Thus, rather than allowing Ethiopia and Egypt to derive their value from their "presence in and contribution to the Classical Age," Delany presents that age as increasingly cut off from the fullness of Africa's foundational knowledge. A self-reflexive hermeneutic game authorizes this reading, for the hidden mourning allegorized in the Garden of the Hesperides remains legible only through the form of Ethiopian and Egyptian knowledge: "perfectly plain and comprehensible to themselves . . . obscure and unintelligible to others."[24]

Du Bois will appropriate this hermetic deployment of the classical archive to similarly insinuate the palimpsestic layers beneath the classical allusions that articulate the material and spiritual aspirations of *The Souls of Black Folk* and *The Quest of the Silver Fleece*. The veiled, esoteric legacy of the African mysteries conjures an African antiquity incompletely assimilated by "western civilization" and disrupts the linear timeline favored by vindicationists. Blyden, for example, suggests that history unfolds according to multiple rhythmic lines, advising against the "mistake" of assuming that "the Negro is . . . in the same groove, with the European."[25] Du Bois figures this polyrhythmic sensibility in

The Souls of Black Folk as a "veiled unanswered sphinx" gazing upon the "wofully unorganized . . . sociological knowledge [of] the meaning of progress, the meaning of 'swift' and 'slow' in human doing."[26] These variable rhythmic lines structure "the double life every American Negro must live, as a Negro and as an American, as swept on by the current of the nineteenth while yet struggling in the eddies of the fifteenth century" (122).

Such temporal conjunctions and disjunctions animate the increasingly audible "conceptual echo chambers" Alexander Weheliye traces between Du Bois, Walter Benjamin, and Jacques Derrida.[27] Out of this intellectual tradition, for example, Ian Baucom theorizes "a nonsynchronous contemporaneity in which an older deep-structural form," Du Bois's fifteenth century, for example, "inscribes, reasserts, and finds itself realized" in the nineteenth.[28] Charles Lemert poses the anti-positivist, anti-historicist argument that we should read Du Bois as a "Derridean before the fact." His "hauntological" historiography undermines "the intoxicating sign of History's Progress" implicit in the disciplinary history and social sciences that remain unable to answer Du Bois's sphinx: "Why should Aeschylus have sung two thousand years before Shakespeare was born?"[29] Rather, polyrhythmic temporalities "delineate the grounds of empirical knowability," in Weheliye's formulation.[30] As signaled by Du Bois's constant allusions, latent in this empiricism are the ways his moment plays host to antiquity, "an apparitional moment," as Baucom describes, "in which the 'wreckage' of the past accumulated in the present becomes manifest."[31]

The antiquity Du Bois alludes to, however, neither integrates fully into the upward swing of "western civilization" nor hews to what Wilson Jeremiah Moses dubs the "ethnic chauvinism" of Blyden's and Delany's exceptionalist narratives of African antiquity.[32] Du Bois reconstructs an ancient scene that is as plural and polyrhythmic, as cosmopolitan and mysterious, as the present. He was not the first, however, to identify the cosmopolitanism of the African diaspora as an extended, if tragic, replay of ancient routes out of Africa. Often cited as the first African American disciplinary historian, George Washington Williams argues that this cosmopolitanism "antedates all profane history," writing: "And while the great body of the Negro races have been located geographically in Africa, they have been, in no small sense, a cosmopolitan people. Their wanderings may be traced from the rising to the setting sun."[33] Du Bois's 1915 volume *The Negro* systematically develops this claim, one regularly set down in smaller instantiations on the pages of the *Crisis*, with its enthusiasm for Egyptology, as well as in his lectures and essays.[34] "Of the ancient world gathered about the Mediterranean," he wrote of Africans, "they formed a part and were viewed with no surprise or dislike, because this world saw them come and go and play their part with other men."[35]

Du Bois emphasizes the quotidian ordinariness of the African presence in antiquity, replacing the shroud of romance with material details of the ancient world-system. Tracking the trade that brought sub-Saharan Africa into relation with the circum-Mediterranean, he states: "Gold, skins, ivory, kola nuts, gums, honey, wheat, and cotton were exported, and the whole Mediterranean coast traded in the Sudan."[36] Documentation of this trade reaches back to "a thousand years to 700 B.C., or about the time that Pharaoh Necho of Egypt sent out the Phoenician expedition which circumnavigated Africa," and Du Bois notes not only that the Phoenicians and Carthaginians later recorded many such voyages but that these may have been "an attempted revival of still more ancient intercourse."[37] The rounding of the African cape, of course, stood as one of the purported triumphs of a resurgent Europe's "Age of Discovery." That Afro-Semitic coalitions routinely conducted such navigations undercuts Vasco da Gama's achievement and reiterates for Du Bois the elusive "meaning of progress, the meaning of 'swift' and 'slow' in human doing."

This subtle revisionist critique sediments layers of historical repetition beneath the annals of European culture. A palimpsestic rhetoric emerges to insist upon the cosmopolitan histories woven into narrative and plastic artifacts. Byzantine crafts, for example, hold within their forms the history of the Nupe, in modern Nigeria, who trace their origins to Egypt and "who recognized the suzerainty of the Byzantine emperor."[38] Lest historians of the ancient world think of sub-Saharan Africa as "the inert recipient of foreign influence," Du Bois uncovers the mercantile-artisanal trail by which "the Byzantine people learned certain kinds of work in bronze and glass" from the Nupe.[39] Such shuttling, palimpsestic histories constitute the norm in Du Bois's account of the ancient world, where "merchants have passed to and fro for thirty centuries" and "Arabian, Jewish, Egyptian, Greek, and Roman influences spread slowly upon the Negro foundation."[40] There is a fantastic ambiguity in this last claim, allowing readers to just as easily imagine a Negro foundation spreading slowly along the routes of trade outside Africa as to imagine this plurality of influences spreading within Africa itself. This strategic undecidability provides a rhetorical key for Du Bois's cultural analyses. Typically, then, when confronting the popular prejudices against African fetishism, Du Bois cites Goethe's *Prometheus* as the best text for understanding this "severely logical way of accounting for the world."[41]

That a Greek revival in Europe's late second millennium would surrogate an African religious system nicely captures Du Bois's hermeneutics of world literature and cultural history. Marked by recursive, nomadic cosmopolitan networks, his vision of antiquity underwrites a palimpsestic reading practice in which singular icons give way to plural origins that only contemporary history has come to produce as paradoxical. This revisionist historiography and its attendant hermeneutics model new uses of the classical archive delimited neither by an integrationist Eurocentrism nor by a romantic Afrocentrism. For just as Delany decodes Greek and Roman mourning for African plenitude in the Garden of the Hesperides, Du Bois invites a hermetic decoding of classical literature in *The Souls of Black Folk* and *The Quest of the Silver Fleece*. Rather than the "Lost Arts" of Ethiopia and Egypt, however, Du Bois asserts the plural origins of the ancient verbal arts, produced through a cosmopolitan traffic between orality and literacy increasingly illegible to contemporaneous teleological theorizations of popular and elite aesthetic forms, from those of cultural nationalism to those of global modernism. The interactions of text and performance Du Bois embeds in the Black Belt makes of the late nineteenth century that sort of "apparitional moment" discussed by Baucom, "in which the 'wreckage' of the [classical] past accumulated in the present becomes manifest."[42] In African American rural culture's time- and space-defying vernacular surrogations of Greco-Roman verbal arts, Du Bois articulates a palimpsestic diasporic practice that reimagines the networks and archives of world literature for a tradition of writers to come.

Combining autobiography, political advocacy, sociology, fiction, history, and musical notations, *The Souls of Black Folk* weaves numerous allusions to classical antiquity into its multidisciplinary, multimedia format. These allusions do significantly more work than decorate Du Bois's advocacy for a liberal arts, humanist education in the face of Booker T. Washington's program gearing African Americans toward manual and industrial labor. They form part of an esoteric discourse delineating the far-reaching terrain of epistemological redress knitted into *Souls*. Through this "mystical register," Cynthia Schrager argues, "*Souls* offers a powerful and problematic critique of the nexus of the terms determinism, materialism, realism, and positivism."[43] For Schrager, this critique constructs an alternative to both Washington's materialism and the positivist intellectual discourses that rationalize the persistent second-class status of African Americans. However, while *Souls* articulates a timely call for revising postbellum US history, sociology, politics, pedagogy and aesthetics, it does so partly by inserting the contemporary moment into a deep transatlantic, circum-Mediterranean cultural history through palimpsestic allusions to antiquity.

The ways African American figures inherit and inhabit classical forms and practices manage the peril of a privileged elitism that stalks *The Souls of Black Folk* and its potentially voyeuristic promise to "leav[e], then, the white world, and . . . [step] within the Veil, raising it that you may view faintly its deeper recesses" (v). Early in the text Du Bois invokes antiquity to address precisely this raced and classed peril. Explaining the predicament of the middle-class black intellectual, he writes: "The would-be black *savant* was confronted by the paradox that the knowledge his people needed was a twice-told tale to his white neighbors, while the knowledge which would teach the white world was Greek to his own flesh and blood" (3). At first glance, it appears that Du Bois simply uses "Greek" in that casual way we signify that something is foreign to us, or difficult to understand. However, "Greek" mediates a language game of reversals and substitutions traversing *The Souls of Black Folk*. Du Bois here uses Greek as a semantic stand-in for African American folk culture. Black America, at the time of Du Bois's writing predominantly Southern and agricultural, is in possession of a transformative knowledge, born of the Southern experience, for its white co-citizens. But to the black savant, often separated from this population by class, geography, and a relatively elite education, this knowledge is "Greek to his own flesh and blood." The culture that emerged from slavery, as opposed to the education which is "a twice-told tale" to white America, is equated with Greek culture in this instance.

The short story "Of the Coming of John," the penultimate section of *The Souls of Black Folk*, dramatizes the trajectory of a "would-be black *savant*" and reiterates what we may have thought was merely an offhand colloquial equation of Greek and African American folk culture. A student at the Wells Institute, a fictionalized Atlanta University, John Jones embodies the strivings of the black community of Altamaha, Georgia. "When John comes" is their refrain, for then there will be "parties," "speakings in the church," and "a new schoolhouse, with John as teacher" (142). Shedding his carefree, careless attitude to his studies after returning to the institute from a disciplinary leave of absence, John devotes himself to, among other subjects, his Greek: "He pondered long over every new Greek word, and wondered why this meant that and why it couldn't mean something else, and how it must have felt to think all things in Greek" (144). John is caught up in a dynamic of translation, of the stakes and implications of being inside or outside a language. The short story's suspense turns structurally on this dynamic: whether John will be able to translate between the social language of higher education, on the one hand, and Altamaha, on the other.

In a zero-sum formation, though, it appears that John's acquisition of the ancient Greek language coincides with his loss of that other expression of Greek, the vernacular culture of Altamaha. He gives a disastrous homecoming speech at the Baptist church, marginalizing the religious sensibilities of his community by calling for African American unity and progress under a secular aegis: "A painful hush seized that crowded mass. Little had they understood of what [John] said, for he spoke an unknown tongue" (148). With John's oratorical failure, Du Bois stages the gap between an elite discourse of secular activism led by the "Talented Tenth" and mainstream perspectives rooted in religious social organization. John spoke Greek to his hometown, and it falls on the shoulders of an "old bent" preacher to reeducate John, the would-be black savant, as to "the knowledge which would teach the white world," knowledge that has become "Greek to [John's] own flesh and blood." If John had spoken Greek to Altamaha, Altamaha spoke back in Greek, for "John never knew clearly what the old man said." Yet during the preacher's spirited sermon, he "felt himself held up to scorn and scathing denunciation for trampling on the true Religion, and he realized with amazement that all unknowingly he had put rough, rude hands on something this little world held sacred" (148–49). Du Bois conveys John's alienation from his hometown as linguistic incomprehension, a failure of translation between social languages. Arnold Rampersad identifies such moments in Du Bois's writing as the recognition of the "savage irony that, for the black man in a racist world, the acquisition of culture is a dangerous and often destructive process."[44]

However, as Eric Sundquist argues, "Du Bois refused to accept as necessary the contradiction between elite and folk culture."[45] The double referentiality of Greek bears this out: on the one hand, Du Bois uses Greek to stand in for the elite education African Americans are in need of and entitled to; on the other hand, Greek stands in for the African American folk culture that the would-be black savant risks unlearning through his or her elite education. The preacher kinesthetically reenacts this troubled relation between book learning and popular culture when he takes the podium: "He seized the Bible with his rough, huge hands; twice he raised it inarticulate, and then fairly burst into words, with rude and awful eloquence" (148–49). The book seems to stifle speech, to shut down communication; this reflects precisely what happened to John: he got book learning and subsequently "spoke an unknown tongue." As the preacher's words burst forth, he models for a bewildered John the obligation to mediate between book learning and folk culture just as the preacher mediates between scripture and orature.

John recognizes this obligation on the other side of the transformative frenzy induced by the preacher, who "quivered, swayed, and bent; then rose aloft in perfect majesty, till the people moaned and wept, wailed and shouted, and a wild shrieking arose from the corners where all the pent-up feeling of the hour gathered itself and rushed into the air" (148). Coming so late in the volume, Du Bois has prepared his readers to apprehend in this sermon, in its religious and rhetorical technologies, complex traces of antiquity. Three chapters back, in "Of the Faith of the Fathers," Du Bois introduces the "Priest or Medicine-man" as the "chief remaining institution" of African society whose "traces" remained in the New World:

> He early appeared on the plantation and found his function as healer of the sick, the interpreter of the Unknown, the comforter of the sorrowing, the supernatural avenger of wrong, and the one who rudely but picturesquely expressed the longing, disappointment, and resentment of a stolen and oppressed people. Thus, as bard, physician, judge, and priest, within the narrow limits allowed by the slave system, rose the Negro preacher. (119)

The preacher's deft mediation between sacred text and public performance culminates in the "frenzy" described multiple times throughout *Souls*. Not only harkening back to "the heathenism of the Gold Coast" (117), these scenes of "pythian madness . . . as [old as] Delphi" (115, 116) also sustain the hermetic practice of the famous oracle, the Pythia, of Greek antiquity, locating yet another source for the diasporic subject's "second-sight in this American world" (2).

As the pairing of the Gold Coast and Delphi attest, Du Bois's cultural genealogies of New World social practice systematically affiliate diverse sites of the Old World. Such revisionist affiliations appear again at Du Bois's base for teaching and research: "The college curriculum that was laid before the Pharaohs, that was taught in the groves by Plato, that formed the *trivium* and *quadrivium*, . . . is today laid before the freedmen's sons by Atlanta University" (51). This sequence, of course, replays the vindicationist origin story of Western civilization from Egypt to Greece, from orality to literacy. However, as Du Bois delves deeper into the scene of Southern education in the chapter "Of the Meaning of Progress," a palimpsestic exegesis of his key intertext, Cicero's *Pro Archia Poeta*, will reveal how what has typically been read as a human-ist endorsement of literacy actually privileges oral forms closely associ-ated with the black vernacular.

Du Bois writes how, after Emancipation, the freedmen and -women caught hold of "the ideal of 'book-learning'; the curiosity, born of compulsory ignorance, to know and test the power of the cabalistic letters of the white man" (35). In the service of this curiosity, Du Bois "taught school in the hills of Tennessee" (37). Sallying forth from Fisk University in Nashville to teach the illiterate rural peasantry, Du Bois finds a little school in a small community—between Alexandria and Lebanon!—where "but once since the war had a teacher been" (38). While they were excited to learn, students often failed to show up: "I knew that the doubts of the old folks about book-learning had conquered again, and so, toiling up the hill, and getting as far into the cabin as possible, I put Cicero 'pro Archia Poeta' into the sim-plest English with local applications, and usually convinced them— for a week or so" (40). Mediating between literacy and orality, Du Bois turns to Cicero's 62 BC *Pro Archia Poeta Oratio*, an oration on behalf of the Greek poet and scholar Archias. Archias faces exile from Rome based on a new statute expelling noncitizens from the imperial capital. Cicero defends his childhood tutor not only on legal grounds but also through a vindication of literature, which "links together all the arts which have any bearing upon the common life of mankind."[46] Carrie Cowherd argues that Du Bois here straightfor-wardly "concurs with Cicero that literature produces men, the most fully realized human beings."[47]

Yet while Du Bois has cast himself as an agent and vehicle of literacy, his oratorical channeling of Cicero's transcribed oratory hints at the lat-ter's less remarked championing of improvised oral poetry. Cicero com-ments: "How often, I say, have I seen [Archias], without writing a single letter, extemporizing quantities of excellent verse dealing with current topics!"[48] Cicero presses upon his audience the power of poetry: "The very rocks of the wilderness give back a sympathetic echo to the voice; savage beasts have sometimes been charmed into stillness by song; and shall we, who are nurtured upon all that is highest, be deaf to the appeal of poetry?"[49] Cicero then reminds his audience that Homer was claimed by the cities of Colophon, Salamis, and Smyrna: "These people then, are ambitious to claim, even after his death, one who was an alien, merely because he was a poet."[50]

In Cicero's oration on behalf of the Greek poet Archias, Du Bois may have found an echo of his own defense of African American folk culture. Stolen from Africa, the slaves and their descendants find themselves in a polity that denies them civic status, threatens them with expulsion, and considers them, like the Greeks Archias and Homer, "alien." Yet like Archias and Homer, African Americans bring the gift of improvised oral poetry. Du Bois writes:

> The Negro folk-song—the rhythmic cry of the slave—stands today not simply as the sole American music, but as the most beautiful expression of human experience born this side the seas. It has been neglected, it has been, and is, half despised, and above all it has been persistently mistaken and misunderstood; but notwithstanding, it still remains as the singular spiritual heritage of the nation and the greatest gift of the Negro people. (156)

Read through the palimpsestic, genealogical network of allusions running through *Souls*, we can recognize how the Sorrow Songs operate at the same shuttling intersection of the oral and scribal as the verbal arts of antiquity. From Homer's "tale of Troy divine" to Virgil's "love-song of Dido," Du Bois's classical intertexts map a cosmopolitan circum-Mediterranean geography traversed and tied together by the interactive mutual constitution of performance and textuality (51). The African American spirituals surrogate this cosmopolitan antiquity, bearing traces of the Gold Coast and Greece, interweaving orature and scripture as they creatively renovate the Protestant hymnal.

The allusive texture of *The Souls of Black Folk* thereby offers a model of African American poetics that sidesteps one of that tradition's most persistent structuring tensions, that between oral and literary, folk and elite idioms. We see this structuring tension at play in an argument between Arnold Rampersad and Eric Sundquist over Du Bois's respective allegiances to folk and elite cultures. Rampersad writes:

> By emphasizing the sublimity and originality of their music above all other accomplishments of black Americans, Du Bois accepted Herder's basic terms for evaluation of culture. But beyond his deep admiration for the religious songs, Du Bois was no champion of folk expression.[51]

Nearly inverting Rampersad's emphasis, Sundquist writes:

Du Bois's celebration of the folk world represented by the spirituals tempered his own commitment to a progressivist ideal that was too easily identified with elite European American culture and with his own proclaimed belief in the elevating leadership of a black talented tenth whose achievements, he argued throughout his early career, would raise up the masses below.[52]

For both critics, the orality of the "folk world represented by the spirituals" stands opposed to the literate discourses of "elite European American culture." Yet neither the circum-Mediterranean epics of antiquity nor the oratory of Cicero conform to a model that exclusively aligns orality with folk expression and literacy with elite forms.[53] Through the surrogations of the classical past articulated in the interwoven oral-scribal practices of the Sorrow Songs, the preacher's sermon, and the country schoolhouse teacher's vocation, *The Souls of Black Folk* inscribes African diasporic folk expression into a creative network spanning ancient and modern world systems whose aesthetic values elude the antinomies of orality and literacy, vernacular and elite.

The radical political and aesthetic potential of exploding these antinomies constitutes one of the structuring principles of Du Bois's 1911 novel *The Quest of the Silver Fleece*. Written out of his deep engagement with the archive of antiquity during the period between the writing of *The Souls of Black Folk* and *The Negro*, it shares the revisionist strategies of both those texts. The plot of the novel "puts into English with local applications" the story of Jason and the Argonauts, an epic parallel treated briefly in *Souls*. The circulation of this story within the novel becomes a disruptive pedagogical and political force, subverting the gendered and racialized hierarchies of the post-Reconstruction era. The mode of circulation of the Jason saga reiterates how African American rural culture surrogates, with a difference, the verbal arts and the narrative genres of antiquity, exploring the revolutionary potential of this revised surrogation. In *Quest*'s nonlinear, palimpsestic historical practice, and in its inextricable interweaving of vernacular and elite idioms, the novel lays out a foundational poetics of African diaspora and world literature that stands as an alternative to contemporaneous cosmopolitan paradigms of cultural nationalism and global modernism that continue to inflect the reception of Du Bois and the African diasporic literary tradition.

Critics long disdained *The Quest of the Silver Fleece*, as Lawrence J. Oliver recounts, for its "failed" or "flawed" deployment of realism and romance or its "randomly and unevenly developed" socialism.[54]

Recent assessments of the novel have been more favorable, parsing how it "rejects the constraints of realism and romance" and "repossesses a powerful tradition of dissent by advocating a new national errand," as well as how it helps significantly move forward the timeline of Du Bois's egalitarian radicalism, "offering both a specifically socialist critique of US economics and an alternative economic model originating in cooperative, southern black folkways."[55] These reassessments emphasize the national context of the novel, its influences, and its projected dissemination; however, *The Quest of the Silver Fleece* also demands to be read as what Franco Moretti calls a "world text," with a "geographical frame of reference [that] is no longer the nation-state, but a broader entity—a continent, or the world-system as a whole."[56] The novel maps the material and symbolic geography of the rural South's insertion into the modern financial world-system; this mapping contains a palimpsestic allegorical structure, by which the apparitions of an ancient world system come to inhabit and inspire the transformation of the present.

The Quest of the Silver Fleece features two protagonists who traverse these symbolic and material geographies, Bles and Zora. Bles, a good-natured black farm boy, arrives in Tooms County, Alabama, to attend the school of Sarah Smith, who embodies the moral uprightness of the New England abolitionists and educators. Along the way to the school, Bles meets Zora:

> Zora, child of the swamp, was a heathen hoyden of twelve wayward, untrained years. Slight, straight, strong, full-blooded, she had dreamed her life away in wilful wandering through her dark and sombre kingdom until she was one with it in all its moods; mischievous, secretive, brooding; full of great and awful visions, steeped body and soul in wood-lore. Her home was out of doors, the cabin of Elspeth her port of call for talking and eating.[57]

Rampersad insists: "The swamp stands for ignorance, sloth, superstition, paganism, and moral delinquency. It keeps the blacks wrapped in the old, miasmal mist of their pre-American past."[58] Bles, with his upwardly mobile aspirations, agrees. Urging a disdainful, reluctant Zora to learn to read, he tells her: "You see, when you're educated you won't want to live in the swamp" (50). Arlene Elder, however, counters: "The Swamp represents all that is free, wild, joyful, and loving."[59] Part of what makes the novel so gripping is the suspense surrounding Zora's ongoing relation to the swamp. "Steeped body and soul in wood-lore," will any trace of the vibrant "heathen hoyden" remain after Bles and the New England schoolmistresses get through with her?

The swamp, then, "resists easy reduction to univocal symbolic structures."⁶⁰ Its topography bears traces of other texts and histories. Walking readers through a swamp in *The Souls of Black Folk*, Du Bois writes:
"Once we crossed a black silent stream, where the sad trees and writh-
ing creepers, all glinting fiery yellow and green, seemed like some vast
cathedral, —some green Milan builded of wildwood. And as I crossed, I
seemed to see again that fierce tragedy of seventy years ago. Osceola, the
Indian-Negro chieftain, had risen in the swamps of Florida, vowing vengeance" (76). Channeling the legacy spanning from Osceola to the Dismal Swamp of Nat Turner's marronage and rebellion, as well as Martin
Delany's 1861–62 serialized novel about overthrowing New World slavery, *Blake, or The Huts of America*, Du Bois stamps what Delany calls
the "mystical, antiquated, and almost fabulous" swamp as a topographi-
cal marker of autochthonous and African rebellion against slavery and
oppression.⁶¹

On the edges of the swamp in *The Quest of the Silver Fleece*, bor-
dered on its other side by the Cresswell plantation, stands Sarah Smith's
school. Mary Taylor, a young New Englander, has just arrived to take
a teaching position. Her brother John, a Northern financier, urged her
to accept the position so she could learn as much as possible about the
Cresswells and the source of their wealth and power, cotton: "The lust
of financial dominion had gripped [John's] soul, and he had a vision of
a vast trust of cotton manufacturing covering the land" (62). The Cresswell family uses the post-Emancipation tactic of debt-peonage to keep
the sharecropping blacks poor and dependent on their paternalistic dis-
pensation: "No Negro starved on the Cresswell place, neither did any
accumulate property. Colonel Cresswell saw to both matters" (364).

It is through cotton that blacks try to acquire land and relative independence, that the old Southern aristocracy attempts to maintain their
status and their control over poor whites and blacks alike, and that
the Northern financiers attempt to dominate the global textile market.
Symbolic and material investments in the land are negotiated through
the narrative of Jason and the Argonauts. As Mary Taylor stands with
Bles looking out over the fields of cotton, she dimly perceives this
crop's kinship with the Golden Fleece. Though Miss Smith's school
puts "plough-hands all to studying Greek," the first lesson she gives to
Bles does not take place in a classroom, nor does it involve books (160).
Instead, it takes the form of the oral transmission of the legend of the
quest for the Golden Fleece, in which Jason, dispossessed prince of Iolcus, sets off to Colchis on the Black Sea to retrieve the famous Golden

Fleece. With the aid of Medea, a powerful sorceress who betrays her father the king, he succeeds. Jason later betrays Medea upon reclaiming his throne in Iolcus.

A clue to the powerfully disruptive force of this story lies within the annals of antiquity mentioned above: Egyptian settlers established Colchis, according to Herodotus, and the Greek adventurer Jason usurped the African polity. This buried tale of European colonization will be spontaneously resuscitated by the unschooled Bles, setting off a chain of unsettling inversions that set the classical archive to radical work. Here Du Bois presents the scene of oral transmission, reproduced at length:

[Mary Taylor] settled herself almost luxuriously, and began the story of Jason and the Argonauts.

The boy [Bles] remained silent. And when she had finished, he still sat silent, elbow on knee, absently flicking the jogging horse and staring ahead at the horizon. She looked at him doubtfully with some disappointment that his hearing had apparently shared so little of the joy of her telling; and, too, there was mingled a vague sense of having lowered herself to too familiar fellowship with this—this boy. She straightened herself instinctively and thought of some remark that would restore proper relations. She had not found it before he said, slowly:

"All yon is Jason's."

"What?" she asked, puzzled.

He pointed with one sweep of his long arm to the quivering mass of green-gold foliage that swept from swamp to horizon.

"All yon golden fleece is Jason's now," he repeated.

"I thought it was—Cresswell's," she said.

"That's what I mean."

She suddenly understood that the story had sunk deeply.

"I am glad to hear you say that," she said methodically, "for Jason was a brave adventurer—"

"I thought he was a thief."

"Oh, well—those were other times."

"The Cresswells are thieves now." . . .

But Bles continued.

"This is the Black Sea," he said, pointing to the dull cabins that crouched here and there upon the earth, with the dark twinkling of their black folk darting out to see the strangers ride by.

Despite herself Miss Taylor caught the allegory. (35–36)

The oral transmission of this tale first unsettles Miss Taylor because in "settling herself" to tell it "there was mingled a vague sense of having lowered herself to too familiar fellowship with this—this boy." We noted earlier that Du Bois's use of classical culture could not be assimilated into the hierarchical model that aligns orality with folk culture and literacy with elite culture. Here too the oral encounter eludes the hierarchy of "proper relations" that should obtain between white Northern teacher and black Southern "boy." Both the pleasure of recitation ("the joy of her telling") and the reciprocal structure of orality work against this hierarchy. When Bles intuits the historically prescient Herodotean version, and applies the tale to his local surroundings, not only does the reader discover that "the story had sunk deeply," but that suddenly—echoing those moments of *peripeteia* in Platonic dialogue when the position of ignorance shifts to that of wisdom—he has become the teacher and she the young naive: "Despite herself Miss Taylor caught the allegory."

The chain of oral transmission continues as Bles recites the legend of Jason and the Argonauts to Zora. Once again, the oral tale prompts an inversion of the interlocutors' hierarchical roles. Bles, in order to realize his *mission civilisatrice*, proposes an idea to Zora:

> "Zora," he whispered, "I've got a plan."
>
> "What is it?" she asked, still with bowed head.
>
> "Listen, till I tell you of the Golden Fleece."
>
> Then she too heard the story of Jason. Breathless she listened, dropping her sewing and leaning forward, eager-eyed. Then her face clouded.
>
> "Do you s'pose mammy's the witch?" she asked dubiously.
>
> "No; she would n't give her own flesh and blood to help the thieving Jason."
>
> She looked at him searchingly.
>
> "Yes, she would, too," affirmed the girl. . . .
>
> "Then we must escape her," he said gayly. "See! yonder lies the Silver Fleece spread across the brown back of the world; let's get a bit of it, and hide it here in the swamp, and comb it, and tend it, and make it the beautifullest bit of all. Then we can sell it, and send you to school." (52)

Bles single-mindedly pursues his goal of getting Zora educated. However, Zora's reception of the tale ultimately inspires a much grander vision. Rather than secretly tending a small patch of cotton to pay for her studies alone, she envisions a self-sufficient black communal cotton farm in the reclaimed swamp, "a free community" (362). Zora's interpretation of the Greek legend not only maps the allegory onto local circumstances but also seeks to change them, wresting the Silver Fleece (back) from the Cresswells with the local black peasantry. These scenes of narrative transmission and interpretation formally invoke the Athenian model of political education, an invocation reiterated later when we see Plato's *Republic* on Zora's bookshelf (399). Yet whereas aristocratic Athenian boys would receive oral instruction in epic narrative from their male elders, guaranteeing the reproduction of the ruling class and the extension of the oral epic tradition, in *The Quest of the Silver Fleece*, Du Bois maps onto the Athenian model an insurgent appropriation of oral instruction rooted in vernacular sensibilities. Over the course of the novel, literacy and literature come to bear the stamps of these insurgent sensibilities, articulating a vernacular "signifying" poetics channeling not just a rural peasantry but one that embodies ancient verbal arts which defy categorization as elite or popular.

Zora's literary education, then, while it transforms her from a youth "steeped body and soul in wood-lore" into an eloquent bibliophile, does not sever her connection with vernacular culture. Working alongside Miss Smith at the school, she remains involved in the popular life of the county:

> There were thoughts and vague stirrings of unrest in this mass of black folk. They talked long about their firesides, and here Zora began to sit and listen, often speaking a word herself. All through the country-side she flitted, till gradually the black folk came to know her and, in silent deference to some subtle difference, they gave her the title of white folk, calling her "Miss" Zora. (356)

In scenes like these and others, the reader comes to recognize how Zora closely resembles Martin Delany's Henry Blake, the protagonist in the aforementioned novel *Blake*. He too circulates among the huts and firesides to learn the conditions of the African American peasantry and their thoughts about their own conditions. Both Blake and Zora, furthermore, are presented as inheritors of the tradition of swamp resistance. The comrades of Nat Turner who Blake meets with in the Dismal Swamp "anointed him a priest of the order of High Conjurors," a scene that reiterates Delany's enthusiasm for hermetic African knowledge.[62] Yet whereas through the masculinism of *Blake* "Delany fights for black men's access to the range of models of public manhood available to white men," as Ifeoma C. K. Nwankwo writes, Zora's leadership extends the inversions that accumulate with the circulation of the Jason myth.[63]

Thus she teaches Bles to quit "looking down upon her with thoughts of uplift and development" and "to be [a] co-worker—nay, in a sense to be a follower" (400). Precisely the question of "uplift and development" is at stake here, both at the level of political strategy and poetics. The viability of Zora's plan to convert the swamp into a self-sufficient commune with a model farm and school depends on her ability to mediate between Tooms County vernacular and the Alabama legal code. Precisely the vernacular tradition of "wearing the mask" enables her to dupe Colonel Cresswell into inadvertently signing "a contract of sale . . . [that] will stand in law." His lawyer warns him: "'There's but one way to break it, and that's to allege misunderstanding on your part.' Cresswell winced. It was not pleasant to go into open court and acknowledge himself over-reached by a Negro" (411). Set in motion by her reception of the "Quest of the Golden Fleece," Zora's *Bildung*, while in some ways tracing the familiar path of the *mission civilisatrice* such as acquiring literacy and abandoning "heathenism," also sustains a savvy and subversive orality.

The classical allusions that signpost Zora's educational path anchor this orality in dialogic Socratic irony as much as in the dialogism of the black vernacular. This nonlinear suturing of antiquity to the Black Belt in a narrative about the integration of that region into early twentieth-century global finance capital offers a counterpoint to teleological, financialized discourses of black and global literary modernism. Introducing *The New Negro*, Alain Locke celebrates the *entrée* of Harlem into a cosmopolitan literary geography of urban "race capitals" including Dublin and Prague.[64] For Pascale Casanova, such entries into literary modernity are "alchemically" underwritten by "the transposition of oral practices to written form . . . to create literature and thus convert folk tradition into literary wealth."[65] Locke's own formulation lends itself ideally to this economic coding: "Not merely for modernity of style, but for vital originality of substance, the young Negro writers dig deep into the racy peasant undersoil of the race life."[66] In this passage "from countryside to city . . . from medieval America to modern," writers refine raw folk "substance" into "literary gold."[67]

The rural institutions of *The Souls of Black Folk* and *The Quest of the Silver Fleece*, however, channel a cosmopolitan antiquity whose verbal arts resist this sort of developmental theorization. Figured partly from textual strategies Du Bois self-consciously stages to ward off his own elitist tendencies, the preacher, the country schoolhouse teacher, and the grassroots activist incarnate effigies of ancient bards, orators, and philosophers who do not redemptively sublimate demotic orality through elite literacy. Instead, their mediations between the oral and the textual scramble the aesthetic values presently ascribed to those categories in order to conjure an alternate vision of world literature, not as an elite modernist space structured through transcending nationalist teleologies, but as a living archive throwing up hermetic apparitions of ancient cosmopolitan networks in "unlikely" demotic spaces.

Like global modernists such as H.D., Ezra Pound, St.-John Perse, T. S. Eliot, and James Joyce, Du Bois perceives the early twentieth-century strewn with the traces of antiquity. Eliot, in his review of Joyce's *Ulysses* (1922), has canonically assessed the relationship between avant-garde modernism and classical antiquity:

> In using the myth [of the *Odyssey*], in manipulating a continuous parallel between contemporaneity and antiquity, Mr. Joyce is pursuing a method which others must pursue after him. . . . It is simply a way of controlling, of ordering, of giving a shape and a significance to the immense panorama of futility and anarchy which is contemporary history. It is a method already adumbrated by Mr. Yeats, and of the need for which I believe Mr. Yeats to have been the first contemporary to be conscious. . . . No one else has built a novel upon such a foundation before.[68]

In Eliot's own poetry and that of Pound, ruins and fragments of the classical past indeed testify to the "futility and anarchy which is contemporary history." In order to bring *Ulysses* into line with the narrative of cultural decline running through *The Waste Land* and *The Cantos*, Eliot occludes and refashions Joyce's playful palimpsests. Likewise, Du Bois, whose *Quest* antedates *Ulysses* by eleven years, employs "the mythical method" not to disparage his present but to animate how, in Benjamin's phrasing, "what has been comes together in a flash with the now to form a constellation."[69] For both Du Bois and Joyce, vernacular figures mysteriously surrogate antiquity—and contemporaneity does not necessarily pale by comparison. Instead, this monadic constellating of the present and the past sets Du Bois and Joyce as equally apart from what Claudia Tate calls the "laments" of Anglo-American modernism as from the literary-anthropological cultural nationalisms of Harlem and Dublin.[70] So while critics such as Houston A. Baker Jr. warn that "Africans and Afro-Americans—through conscious and unconscious designs of various Western 'modernisms'—have little in common with Joycean or Eliotic projects," it may be worthwhile to draw more variegated lines through global modernism.[71] For as both antiquity and vernacular culture increasingly featured in the alchemy of modernist world literature, authors turned this conjunction to other ends than lamenting decline or aestheticizing the folk into the redeemable coin of authenticity. As the next chapter will show, attention to vernacular culture's traces of worldly verbal itineraries, moving back and forth between orality and literacy across the continents, can salvage from critical neglect the discursive aspirations of figures as canonical within African diaspora and world literature as Zora Neale Hurston.

2 World Literature in Hiding

Zora Neale Hurston, Biographical Criticism, and African Diasporic Vernacular Culture

ZORA NEALE HURSTON has emerged as a figure of world literature strongly associated with her accessible mappings of African diasporic vernacular culture. Tracking the transnational continuities of black social practices and performances, her literary-anthropological cosmopolitanism has prompted Françoise Lionnet to compare her to the Egyptian goddess Isis, "the wanderer who conducts her research, establishes spatio-temporal connections among the children of the diaspora, and re-members the scattered body of folk material so that siblings can again 'touch each other.'"[1] With her reliance on family metaphors, Lionnet suggests that Hurston's writings keep it all in the family, so to speak, an authentic African diasporic family circumscribed by "folk material." In light of the revisions of antiquity considered in the previous chapter, however, the allusion to Isis invites an expanded field of relations: as an ancient Egyptian figure, Isis belongs to a tradition claimed by European, Afrocentric, and Semitic origin stories.[2] This historiographic overlap, which Hurston strategically invokes throughout her career in representations of Moses, to be discussed below, reflects a revisionist project of global cultural geography that works counter to narrowly construing Hurston's affiliation with black folk material. Whereas recent critical works on seminal early twentieth-century diasporic figures such as Du Bois, Langston Hughes, and Claude McKay have emphasized the diverse global connections of their texts and biographies, intersecting with China, India, and Russia, Hurston remains predominantly circumscribed within an Afrodiasporan context. However, renewed attention to the biographical, ethnographic, and literary terrain upon which such a critical position relies offers a more diversified portrait of Hurston's intersectional mapping of African and diasporic culture, a mapping that relies on prolific transculturations as well as a vernacular aesthetic crucially involved with textuality. Her work, like that of Du Bois, inserts black vernacular culture into the *longue durée* of world literature, attuned to the traces of discursive fields and hybrid oral-literate verbal technologies inhabiting, extending, and redoubling the transcontinental networks and archives of the cosmopolitan past accumulating in the New World.

This worlding of Hurston's oeuvre runs against the dominant trends shaping and delimiting her own career and posthumous canonization. Valerie Boyd, for example, in her 2003 biography of Hurston, *Wrapped in Rainbows*, refers to her as "Zora" throughout the book. This gesture of familiarity, even intimacy, extends similar gestures reaching back to Alice Walker's acts of literary-filial devotion, chronicled in her 1975 *Ms.* magazine piece, "In Search of Zora Neale Hurston," that helped resuscitate popular and critical interest in Hurston's life and writings. Hurston's writings set the stage for this intimate treatment, as she commonly employs a rhetoric of familiarity with her readers, from the authorial "I" of her ethnographic *Mules and Men* (1935) to that of her best-selling autobiography *Dust Tracks on a Road* (1942).[3] Furthermore, her expert and pioneering use of the African American vernacular, what she termed "the idiom—not the dialect—of the Negro," obscures the artifice of that endeavor, making it easy for readers to feel an unmediated access to the author "behind" the words of novels such as *Their Eyes Were Watching God* (1937).[4] The dazzling vernacular of her personal correspondence, which Carla Kaplan has made widely available with the recent publication of *Zora Neale Hurston: A Life in Letters* (2002), has intensified this feeling of unmediated access. In sum, a combination of narrative, ethnographic, epistolary, critical, and biographical discourses has produced Hurston as a world-literary figure with whom her audience feels an intimacy as familiar as the vernacular she has been so strongly identified with. However, an analysis of the numerous institutional entanglements of Hurston's life and career reveals the degree to which the familiar, intimate, vernacular Hurston paradoxically emerges from the exemplary, racialized conditions of textual production she often struggled against as a student, theatrical producer, performer, anthropologist, essayist, letter writer, and novelist. Her posthumous reception and canonization continue to evade the range of discursive stances she aimed to achieve with regard to the worldliness of African diasporic vernacular culture, enmeshed as it is in linguistically and geographically overdetermined oral and textual genealogies.

Hurston's first novel, *Jonah's Gourd Vine* (1934), tells the life story of an African American preacher, John Pearson, from his youth in Notasulga, Alabama, to his professional rise and fall in Eatonville, Florida. While the novel contains many signature elements of literary-anthropological global modernism, it does not merely represent an instantiation of what Pascale Casanova formulates as "the transposition of oral practices to written form . . . to create literature and thus convert folk tradition into literary wealth."[5] *Jonah's Gourd Vine* exemplifies the ways Hurston's vernacular poetics aspire to exceed a mythic folk orality and is structured around narrative moments where orality and textuality intersect in vernacular culture, culminating in the protagonist being called to the pulpit to orally mediate the written Word. Harryette Mullen's discussion of the vernacular mediation of "the Bible as sacred text and sublime speech" helps orient Hurston's effort temporally and geographically. "As the written record of a divine voice inspiring its authors to write and its readers to speak holy words," she argues, "[the Bible] mediates the historical and mythic dislocation from primarily oral cultures to one in which literacy has the power of a fetish."[6] Mullen continues, "African-Americans, in the process of acquiring literacy . . . fuse the inspiriting techniques of Christian prayer and biblical textuality with African traditions of oral and visual expressiveness."[7] Drawing on the work of scholars such as Robert Farris Thompson, she links African American practices of mediating between visual signs and spoken words to precolonial African practices.

Beginning with *Jonah's Gourd Vine*, Hurston's work is similarly attuned to the recursive mediations back and forth between text and speech in African and diasporic cultures. Early in the novel, John leaves his poor hill-folk "over the creek" and migrates to Alf Pearson's plantation, where before Emancipation his mother was a slave and gave birth to John, allegedly fathered by Mr. Pearson. His high yellow complexion and strapping physique gain him a job—and the Pearson last name—straightaway. True to the European *Bildungsroman* genre that *Jonah's Gourd Vine* transplants to the American South, Mr. Pearson also sends John to get lettered: "Well, you get over there in de A B C class and don't let me ketch you talkin' in school."[8] John develops a crush on fellow student Lucy Potts and aspires to memorize and declaim texts as well as she does. With this art of "speaking pieces," Hurston interlaces orality and literacy, a hybrid performance that anticipates John's calling as a preacher.

Throughout the entire courtship of John and Lucy, we encounter this interplay of writing and the oral tradition. When John goes to help his mother and stepfather "over the creek," Lucy writes flirtatious rhymes in her letters to him:

> Sweet Notasulga, Chocklit Alabama Date of kisses, month of love, Dere John, you is my honey. I won't never love nobody else but you. I love choir practise now. Sugar is sweet, and lard is greasy, you love me, don't be uneasy.
> Your darling,
> Lucy Ann Potts (45)

Robert Hemenway in his literary biography of Hurston explains how rhyming like this belongs to "a traditional mode of verbal lovemaking among southern rural black folk, very possibly African in origin. . . . Certain formulas and rhymes were set, others improvised at the moment."[9] While Hurston dramatizes scenes of John and Lucy's "verbal lovemaking," she also shows how members of a folk community textualize their own oral traditions—displacing the agency of textualization from an urban, lettered elite back to the rural community itself. This displacement refracts Hurston's complicated efforts to locate her own writing career within an increasingly privileged literary and academic milieu whose expectations and protocols will ignore or misread such vernacular patterns of self-textualization and operating back and forth between oral and written traditions, rather than dwelling in a romanticized mode of pure orality.

Nonetheless, in the world of *Jonah's Gourd Vine*, literacy pays: "There was no doubt about it now. John was foreman at Pearson's. His reading and writing had improved to the degree where Alf could trust him with all the handling of supplies" (85). Hurston's novel demonstrates a continuity here with the African American literary tradition in which mastering letters represents a survival strategy, offering the literate African American opportunities not made available to his or her unlettered peers. John's improved literacy gives him access to more money, power, and responsibility in white-dominated socioeconomic institutions. However, as Hurston dramatizes the changes to the socioeconomic structures of the South at the end of World War I, textuality will also serve another goal celebrated in the African American oral tradition—outwitting white power: "Do what they would, the State, County and City all over the South could do little to halt the stampede. The cry of 'Goin' Nawth' hung over the land like the wail over Egypt at the death of the first-born. The railroad stations might be watched, but there could be

no effective censorship over the mails" (151). As the white power structure of the South tries legal and illegal means to stop the Great Migration for better jobs, more money, and maybe some relief from Jim Crow,
writing helps the African American population put one over on them. In
this, it echoes the numerous interminglings of orality and textuality in
Jonah's Gourd Vine, the first book published by an author who would
become famous for being "true somehow to the unwritten text of a common blackness."[10] What Hurston suggests, though, is that even before
she wrote, black folks had been writing that text.

Jonah's Gourd Vine relies heavily on the actual lives of Hurston's
parents. John and Lucy Pearson are models of John and Lucy Hurston;
in fascinating ways, though, they are also models of Hurston herself.
Hurston and others represent Zora Neale Hurston as a figure of orality mediating between the vernacular and textuality, creating for herself
personal, artistic, and professional opportunities that, in turn, motor further mediations between orality and textuality. Hurston's career negoti-
ates expectations and limitations that reflect institutionalized discourses
about race, the vernacular, and writing that she variously depends on,
plays with, and resists. In *Dust Tracks on a Road*, for example, she presents her first experience of literary patronage. One afternoon, two young
white ladies visit Hurston's Negro school:

> So we took our readers and went up front. We stood up in the usual line,
> and opened to the lesson. It was the story of Pluto and Persephone. It was
> new and hard to the class in general. . . .
>
> Then it came to me. I was fifth or sixth down the line. The story was not
> new to me, because I had read my reader through from lid to lid, the first
> week that Papa had bought it for me.
>
> . . . Some of the stories, I had reread several times, and this Greco-Roman
> myth was one of my favorites. I was exalted by it, and that is the way I read
> my paragraph.[11]

The young Zora's oral rendering of the written text of a translated Greco-
Roman oral-derived myth earns her the praise of the white visitors, who
invite her to lunch with them the next day at their hotel. They ask her
to do some more readings, after which they present her with a cylinder
full of pennies. Over the next weeks and months, Mrs. Johnstone and
Miss Hurd would send Zora, among other things: "Gulliver's Travels,
Grimm's Fairy Tales, Dick Whittington, Greek and Roman Myths, and
best of all, Norse Tales" (594). While ancient myth and folktales had
been part of the children's literature canon since the nineteenth century,

one must pause at the preponderance of such literature in the patronage packages. Perhaps, Hurston might be subtly suggesting, Mrs. Johnstone and Miss Hurd see in young Zora, like a later patron would, "a wonderful child of nature who was so unspoiled."[12] A blend of condescension and Herderian romanticism, nineteenth- and twentieth-century attitudes commonly figured the collective Greek and Norse creators of the mythology and folklore passed on to Hurston, and also African Americans, as children of nature, as Hurston well knew. At the same time, Hurston's enthusiasm for written versions of oral-derived mythology and folklore falls in line with her work as anthropologist, folklorist, and writer. She emphasizes this lifelong continuity in her autobiography while dodging the condescending implications possibly at work in her patrons' gifts. Hurston nonetheless figures herself, even at such an early stage in her life, at the intersection of oral and written traditions, institutionalized expectations, and her own affinities and abilities.

Following classical tropes of the African American literary tradition, *Dust Tracks on a Road* links the quest for literacy, and institutions of literary production, to Northern migration. She eventually secures a place for herself at Howard University in Washington, DC, where her textualization of rural black oral traditions will promote her even farther northward. She publishes her first story, "John Redding Goes to Sea," in *Stylus*, Howard's major literary journal. Set in Eatonville and full of its proverbs, idioms, and conjure, the story caught the attention of Charles S. Johnson, founder of the magazine *Opportunity*: "He wrote me a kind letter and said something about New York. So, beginning to feel the urge to write, I wanted to be in New York" (682). Illustrative of the often ironic interwovenness of oral and written cultural production, even though "the urge to write" propelled her to New York, before long she is known as a "raconteur" and "storyteller" of "bodacious charm."[13] At rent parties and swank affairs at A'Lelia Walker's "Dark Tower," *Opportunity* award dinners and literary salons, Hurston would regale listeners with her Eatonville inheritance and personal verve. Hemenway offers a potent suggestion about this aspect of Hurston's life: "Hurston was engaged in a more-or-less conscious process of bringing Eatonville folklore to a wider audience during the Renaissance years. Arna Bontemps indicated that those who knew her during the twenties were not at all surprised by some of the tales in *Mules and Men*. They had heard them before during Zora's tale-telling feats at parties."[14] In a sense, then, Hurston prepares her audience orally to receive her forthcoming literary work. During the Harlem Renaissance, members of this audience would often be the very cultural gatekeepers who would evaluate her literary production: Jessie Fauset, literary editor of the *Crisis*; Charles S. Johnson, founder and editor of *Opportunity*; and enthusiasts, patrons, and promoters such as Carl Van Vechten, Fannie Hurst, Annie Nathan Meyer, and Alain Locke. By performing her Eatonville-inspired folkloric material, setting it in the full complement of voice and gesture, improvisation and spontaneity, Hurston enhances its future appreciation. Perhaps, then, when editors and people with access to publishing institutions read her material, it would resonate with their memories of its richly dramatic presentation: Johnson would go on to publish her stories "Drenched in Light" and "Spunk"; Locke would include "Spunk" in *The New Negro*; and Hurst and Meyer would enable Hurston's studies with Franz Boas at Barnard College. Hurston's savvy self-presentation as a figure of orality (in person and in print) preemptively addresses the institutions of literary reception she is subject to.

Written subsequent to her studies with Boas, Hurston's work in anthropology echoes and extends this dynamic interplay between the oral and the written over an increasingly hemispheric and transatlantic field of cultural production. She uses oral traditions to textually frame the continuities of African diasporic culture. She writes in *Tell My Horse* about "Brother Anansi, the Spider, that great culture hero of West Africa who is personated in Haiti by Ti Malice and in the United States by Brer Rabbit."[15] *Their Eyes Were Watching God* reiterates Hurston's approach to articulating an African diasporic cultural geography through oral and performative traditions. In the Muck, the Everglades work camp where Janie and Tea Cake spend the bean-harvesting season, a group of Bahamians perform the African-derived "jumpin' dance." When the whole work camp performs it one night, Hurston textually links this Afro-Caribbean dance to African American culture through a folktale about Big John de Conquer: "How he had done everything big on earth, then went up tuh heben without dying atall. Went up there picking a guitar and got all de angels doing the ring-shout round and round de throne."[16] "The culture hero of the American Negro folk tales," Big John de Conquer prompts a ring-shout, a performative tradition that for Hurston, and Paule Marshall after her, is a cipher of African diasporic culture.[17] Migratory labor, dance, and storytelling combine to delimit the diasporic cultural geography future authors and readers would overwhelmingly associate with Hurston's work, inserting her into a canon of hemispheric American culture-workers including the Cuban Jose Martí and the Haitian Jean Price-Mars.[18]

And yet while using oral and performative traditions to articulate an African diasporic cultural geography, Hurston does not circumscribe this geography as exclusively African, oral, or performative. In *Dust Tracks on a Road*, for example, she explains the delight she brings to the musical theater troupe she traveled with as lady-in-waiting:

> In the first place, I was a Southerner, and had the map of Dixie on my tongue. They were all northerners except the orchestra leader, who came from Pensacola. It was not that my grammar was bad, it was the idioms. They did not know of the way an average southern child, white and black, is raised on simile and invective. They know how to call names. (651)

The editorial politics of writing race during wartime, as Hemenway notes, would constrain Hurston's autobiographical freedom of expression, encouraging her to embrace integrationist positions and paper over national political problems.[19] So, the "map of Dixie" Hurston draws in this passage, which uses the vernacular to delineate an interracial Southern cultural geography, should be suspect. However, in the 1940s Hurston would read extensively in folklore and linguistics, concluding that many of the linguistic "characteristics of Negro expression," such as "the will to adorn," form part of an interracial Southern heritage.[20] In a private letter of 1947, she writes of the South:

> You find the retention of old English beliefs and customs, songs and ballads and Elizabethan figures of speech. They go for the simile and especially the metaphor. As in the bloom of Elizabethan literature, they love speech for the sake of speech. This is common to white and black. . . . The agrarian system stabilized in the South by slavery slowed down change and lack of communication aided this retardation, and so the tendency towards colorful language that characterized Shakespeare and his contemporaries and made possible the beautiful and poetic language of the King James Bible got left over to an extent in the rural South. The double descriptive and all of that.[21]

Hurston perceives that this reading of Southern orality "naturally lessens the stature of the Negro as a contributor to American expression." Ironically, though, Hurston exposes a certain way of celebrating the African American idiom as a product of the minstrel tradition: "From the influence of the black-face minstrels, anything quaint and humorous has been attributed to the darkies."[22] These ideas about the linguistic history of the South do not exactly mark a rupture with earlier writings such as the celebrated aesthetic treatise "Characteristics of Negro Expression," first published in Nancy Cunard's *Negro: An Anthology*

(1934). Hurston consistently resists positing notions of a vernacular culture exclusive of racial diversity or textual interactions. As discussed above, *Jonah's Gourd Vine* represents an African American folk community deftly engaged in writing rhymes and "speaking pieces." The back-and-forth play of orality and textuality in Eatonville recurs in Hurston's thoughts about Elizabethan language: "[The] songs and ballads and Elizabethan figures of speech . . . simile and especially the metaphor . . . the tendency towards colorful language that characterized Shakespeare and his contemporaries . . . made possible the beautiful and poetic language of the King James Bible." In other words, Hurston argues that the oral culture of Elizabethan England shapes the literature of that period, which through drama and religion recirculates back into English and (through colonization) American oral culture. In the rural South, furthermore, this process of recirculation is extended through figures such as the preacher who, like John Pearson, mediate back and forth between the King James Bible and the vernacular culture of black and white communities. Hurston thereby provides a model geography of European, African, and American language attentive to the recursive transculturations that propel the interweaving of oral, performative, and textual traditions in the African diaspora.

Through efforts such as these, Hurston promotes what VèVè Clark has labeled "diaspora literacy."[23] Big John de Conquer's appearance at the jumpin' dance shows how oral traditions serve Hurston's project of diasporic recognition, that is, of recognizing shared cultural features across the African diaspora while simultaneously attuned to the distinct transculturations constitutive of diasporic difference. And yet we should hesitate for a moment at the term diaspora *literacy*. Because, as mentioned above, audiences were watching and listening to Hurston early in her career as much as they were reading her:

> Her folktales and personal anecdotes seldom had been dramatized for the black artists of Hurston's acquaintance. In fact, few of the literary participants in the Renaissance knew intimately her rural South. Langston Hughes had arrived in New York for the first time after a midwestern childhood and a summer in Mexico. . . . His friend Arna Bontemps was from California. Wallace Thurman had arrived from Utah via the University of Southern California. [Countee] Cullen was from New York; Jean Toomer was from Washington, as was [Bruce] Nugent.[24]

Hurston's role as a figure of orality in the Harlem Renaissance, a role enabled by the literary accomplishments that drew her to New York, rekindles enthusiasm for and recognition of African American folk traditions. This anticipates the diasporic recognition she will promote in her books. However, that books would come to mediate vernacular culture to her audiences comments ambivalently about Hurston's relationship to the interplay of textuality and the vernacular in this modernist moment. On the one hand, her oral performances advance her written literary and academic pursuits. On the other hand, they imbricate her in institutional relationships that interfere with her own mediation between oral and written cultural production.

Hurston's oral and performative talents won her the admiration and support of her faculty advisor Franz Boas and of her literary patron "Godmother" Charlotte Osgood Mason. Both encouraged Hurston's work in the rural South collecting folklore. Her affiliation with each, though, marked Hurston in ways that would constrain and shape her recording and recirculation of folk material. She stages multiple scenarios in which her access to institutions of literacy—the university and literary patronage—enables her fieldwork and yet threatens to cut off her access to vernacular culture:

> My first six months [of collecting] were disappointing. I found out later that it was not because I had no talents for research, but because I did not have the right approach. The glamor of Barnard College was still upon me. I dwelt in marble halls. I knew where the material was all right. But, I went about asking, in carefully accented Barnardese, "Pardon me, but do you know any folk tales or folk songs?" The men and women who had whole treasuries of material just seeping through their pores, looked at me and shook their heads. No, they had never heard of anything like that around there. (*Dust Tracks on a Road*, 687)

Likewise, in her essay "High John de Conquer" she introduces us to Aunt Shady Anne Sutton:

> "Of course, High John de Conquer got plenty power!" [she] bristled at me when I asked her about him. She took her pipe out of her mouth and stared at me out of her deeply wrinkled face. "I hope you ain't one of these here smart colored folks that done got so they don't believe nothing, and come here questionizing me so you can have something to poke fun at. Done got shamed of the things that brought us through. Make out 'tain't no such thing no more."[25]

Hurston illustrates the generational tensions surrounding her own marked access to metropolitan institutions of literacy. Similarly, Hurston's access to the financial resources of those institutions marks her as an outsider, threatening once again her ability to collect folk material. In *Mules and Men* (1935), she arrives at a work camp in Polk County:

> They all thought I must be a revenue officer or a detective of some kind. They were accustomed to strange women dropping into the quarters, but not in shiny gray Chevrolets. They usually came plodding down the big road or counting railroad ties. The car made me look too prosperous. So they set me aside as different. And since most of them were fugitives from justice or had done plenty time, a detective was just the last thing they felt they needed on that "job."
>
> I took occasion that night to impress the job with the fact that I was also a fugitive from justice, "bootlegging." They were hot behind me in Jacksonville and they wanted me in Miami. So I was hiding out. That sounded reasonable. Bootleggers always have cars. I was taken in.[26]

The marks of class difference acquired in the North, such as her Chevrolet and Macy's dress, cast suspicion on Hurston, but she wins folks over with her quick wit and charisma. She sponsors "lying" contests "announced by a notice at the post office promising four prizes for the four best lies."[27] (The fact of a written notice at the post office that "brought a wide response" comments neatly on the mixed population of lettered and unlettered individuals in the community, as do many of the folktales themselves, for example, "How to Write a Letter" [43–44].) Other ways of acquiring folk material often require her to spend a lot of time with men, who, as critics Cheryl A. Wall and Mary Helen Washington note, participate to a greater extent than women in performing African American oral traditions documented by ethnographers and other collectors.[28] This gendered imbalance puts Hurston in conflict with a woman named Lucy, the ex of guitar player Slim, a major source of Hurston's material. Big Sweet, Hurston's friend and protector on the job, explains the situation to her: "She mad 'cause Ah dared her to jump *you*. She don't lak Slim always playing JOHN HENRY for you. She would have done cut you to death if Ah hadn't of took and told her" (145). In numerous ways, then, Hurston's affiliations with metropolitan institutions of literacy—which enjoin and enable her to collect oral traditions—expose her to generational, class, and gender conflicts that threaten to disable her access to those traditions.

Hurston's literary and academic pursuits put a question mark over her own authenticity as a member of the folk community. By driving her Chevrolet and collecting folklore throughout the rural South, she exhibits suspicious signs of difference and consequently risks offending elders she respects, alienating herself from a community she feels she belongs to, even jeopardizing her life. Ironically, precisely the question of authenticity motivates her quest to document African American vernacular culture. Complaining about the condescending folklore collections of certain of her white peers, she writes to Langston Hughes: "It makes me sick to see how these cheap white folks are grabbing our stuff and ruining it. I am almost sick—my one consolation being that they never do it right and so there is still a chance for us."[29] After returning from her collecting expeditions in the South and the Bahamas, Hurston chooses two media in which to redress degrading renditions of black folk traditions: anthropology and the theater. Her simultaneous efforts to establish careers in theater and anthropology run Hurston up against institutional contradictions surrounding questions of race, orality, and textuality that by her own terms result in the failure of both careers. By the terms of posterity, however, this scene of failure has been revaluated as a success, testifying to Hurston's role in anticipating and influencing new institutional orientations and desires.

When Hurston returned to New York, she successfully published "Dance Songs and Tales from the Bahamas" and "Hoodoo in America" in the academically prestigious *Journal of American Folklore*. These scholarly essays exhibit the participant-observer methods of anthropology innovated by Boas and others at Columbia University in the early twentieth century. However, Hurston struggles with the bulk of the material she had collected in Florida. Technically, like all her material collected during 1928–29, it belongs to her patron, Charlotte Osgood Mason, who financed Hurston's expedition under the terms of a contract giving her discretion over the use of the material. While preparing the manuscript, which would go through several revisions, for what would eventually become *Mules and Men*, she receives a letter from Alain Locke writing on Mason's behalf: "She thinks it would be a mistake even to have a scientific tone to the book, so soft pedal all notion of too specific documentation and let loose on the things that you are really best equipped to give—a vivid dramatizing of your material and the personalities back of it."[30] Aside from wrestling with scholarly protocols, Mason's wishes, and her own voice, Hurston contemplates using this material to pursue theatrical ideas that had been percolating for a while: "Did I tell you before I left about the new, the *real* Negro art theatre I plan?" she writes to Langston Hughes. "Well, I shall, or rather *we* shall act out the folk tales, however short, with the abrupt angularity and naivete of the primitive 'bama nigger. Just that with naive settings."[31]

Hurston conceives a folk theater that will "show what beauty and appeal there was in genuine Negro material, as against the Broadway concept" (*Dust Tracks on a Road*, 701). Through her own frustrating experiences writing skits for the Broadway revues *Fast and Furious* and *Jungle Scandals*, Hurston knew firsthand the obstacles at the production end of presenting "real," "genuine Negro material."

With the financial support of "Godmother" Mason, Hurston presents *The Great Day*—a folk production that reenacts a whole day in a Florida work camp, culminating in a Bahamian Fire Dance—at the John Golden Theatre in New York on January 10, 1932. "Despite the critics' unstinting praise," Boyd writes, "*The Great Day* was not picked up by a deep-pocketed producer and Godmother was sorely disappointed by the box office receipts. Hurston, too, was displeased by the financial figures."[32] Hurston had been trying to put herself on independent financial footing for a couple of years at this point. As the curtain falls on *The Great Day*, she finds herself over $600 in debt to Mason. Hurston had believed that "real, genuine Negro material" could establish her economically. It seems clear, though, that Hurston misapprehended her theatrical market. Dance historian Anthea Kraut suggests: "Given how easily her representation of diaspora could be subsumed by entrenched notions of black bodies as wild, uncivilized Others, the complex relationship between African, Caribbean, Southern rural, and Northern urban black vernacular idioms that Hurston set out to portray may well have remained largely invisible to spectators in the early 1930s."[33] The primitivist discourse confronts Hurston in two ways here: as a waning and unreliable popular trend for potential white audiences and as a source of anxiety for potential black audiences. Carla Kaplan comments: "It was one thing to perform black folklore to white audiences who found it new and exciting. It was altogether another thing to stage black folklore in a black context with audiences experiencing various scenarios as overly familiar, embarrassing, or belittling."[34] It seems Hurston could not or would not adapt her material in ways that would attract large audiences or "deep-pocketed producers."[35] Hurston's failure to sustain a "*real* Negro art theatre" forces her into a precarious artistic and economic position. Both for self-promotion and to promote her artistic ideas, she would produce variations on *The Great Day* (also titled *From Sun to Sun* and *Singing Steel*) numerous times in the near future, throughout Florida, in Chicago, and in St. Louis. However, the economic unviability of Hurston's theater of diasporic recognition, and her attendant debt to Mason and Mason's own ideas about how the black vernacular should be circulated, effectively directs Hurston away from scholarly, oral, and performative recirculations of the black folk tradition in ways that shape the Hurston who has become so crucial to the world-literary canon today.

While Hurston had labored to laterally transfer the oral and performative material of African diasporic culture to the oral and performative context of the stage (mediated, clearly, through writing and choreography), Mason would insist on the textualization of this material, relying on the archival endurance of the printed word. In her contract arranging for Hurston's repayment of the $600 debt, Mason writes: "In all that you do, Zora, remember that it is vital to your people that you should not rob your books, which must stand as a lasting monument, in order to further a commercial venture."[36] The institution of patronage is not the only institution that would have its say in directing Hurston's textualization of black oral traditions in *Mules and Men*. Hurston explains her publisher's marketing directives to Franz Boas:

> [Mr. Lippincott] wants a very readable book that the average reader can understand, at the same time one that will have value as a reference book. I have inserted the between-story conversation and business because when I offered it without it, every publisher said it was too monotonous. Now three houses want to publish it. So I hope the unscientific matter that must be there for the sake of the average reader will not keep you from writing the introduction.[37]

The editorial directives imposed upon Hurston in her own day become the very things her future readers celebrate. In a typical critical gesture, one critic lauds Hurston for avoiding the trappings of scholarly anthropology: "Rather than presenting classifications and analysis, she describes how various factors shape the way the collection is formed, including her patronage, her education, her position in relation to intersections of race, gender, and class, and her allegiance to African-American culture as well as to her training in anthropology."[38] Balancing Mason's desires for anti-scholastic primitive authenticity and J. B. Lippincott's market-oriented editorial strategies, Hurston manages to "hit a straight lick with a crooked stick."[39] However, the prehistory of the final manuscript reveals to what extent institutional constraints and expectations impose the innovations that will later be praised by reformers of the disciplines of ethnography and folklore.[40]

In light of these institutional constraints and expectations, Richard Wright's feeling that "Hurston *voluntarily* continues . . . the tradition which was *forced* upon the Negro in the theater, that is, the minstrel technique that makes the 'white folks' laugh" appears both right and wrong.[41] Hurston did not quite "voluntarily" compose *Mules and Men* the way she did; however, the pressure brought to bear by Mason and Lippincott do echo the limitations imposed by white producers and audiences on African American art that Wright collectively aligns with minstrelsy. Hazel Carby, in an essay that seeks to recuperate somewhat Wright's critique of Hurston, comments:

> In returning to and recreating the [Eatonville] of her childhood, Hurston privileges the nostalgic and freezes it in time. Richard Wright, in his review of *Their Eyes Were Watching God*, accused Hurston of recreating minstrelsy. Though this remark is dismissed out of hand by contemporary critics, what it does register is Wright's reaction to what appears to him to be an outmoded form of historical consciousness.[42]

Carby considers Hurston's "representation of African-American culture as primarily rural and oral . . . [to be a] discursive displacement of contemporary social crises," namely, "the migration of black people to cities."[43] However, Hurston's rendering of the Great Migration in *Jonah's Gourd Vine* stages a rural, Southern African American population dynamically intermingling orality and literacy. As the white power structure attempts to restrict their freedom of movement, blacks employ institutions of literacy, such as the US mail, to dodge those restrictions, incorporating textuality into the vernacular tradition of putting one over on the white folks. Throughout her work, the rural culture Hurston represents is rich with practices that intermesh orality and textuality: preaching texts, writing rhymes, speaking pieces.

Critics, though, commonly interpret Hurston to posit oral language as the mark of African diasporic cultural authenticity, missing the expansive worldliness she inscribes into diasporic verbal hybridity. Discussing Hurston's rendering of Moses, for example, John Carlos Rowe writes: "My own view is that Hurston reinterprets Moses in an origin story about the magic of language that will link together the traditions of writing and orality that respectively organize Euroamerican and African-American cultures."[44] In Rowe's exegesis of Hurston's Moses, he identifies Euro-American culture with writing, African and African diasporic culture with orality. Yet Hurston's own words belie this simple mapping. We have already read her comments about Elizabethan oral culture and its determinative effect on English and Southern language and literature. Here is what she writes about Moses in *Tell My Horse*:

All over the Southern United States, the British West Indies and Haiti there are reverent tales of Moses and his magic. It is hardly possible that all of them sprang up . . . coming in contact with Christianity after coming to the Americas. It is more probable that there is a tradition of Moses as the great father of magic scattered over Africa and Asia. Perhaps some of his feats recorded in the Pentateuch are the folk beliefs of such a character grouped about a man for it is well established that if a memory is great enough, other memories will cluster about it, and those in turn will bring their suites of memories to gather about this focal point, because perhaps, they are all scattered parts of the one thing. (378)

As Hurston suggests, the Pentateuch represents merely one textualization of oral traditions relating to Moses. Emerging in Palestine between the tenth and sixth centuries BC, the Pentateuch selectively compiled orally and textually transmitted stories current in the region.[45] It was assembled by Hebrew scribes in royal courts with cultural, commercial, and political ties to Egypt, Nubia, and Saba, an Amharic-language kingdom stretching across the Horn of Africa and Arabia.[46] Hurston's geographic orientation, then, not only presumes African writing by way of the ancient Egyptian, Nubian, and Amharic scripts but also suggests lines of narrative transmission along which Moses stories may have circulated both orally and textually in and out of Africa. Furthermore, "a tradition of Moses as the great father of magic scattered over Africa and Asia" should immediately call to mind the crucial role of Musa (the Arabic name of Moses) in the Islamic tradition. He appears in both the Qur'an and the Hadith. The history of Islam in Africa had already been a major part of African American historical discourse at the time Hurston was writing about Moses, being a topic of conversation from Edward Wilmot Blyden, George Washington Williams, and Anna Julia Cooper in the late nineteenth century to the 1925 republication of Omar ibn Sa'id's autobiography.[47] By the eleventh century, Islam and its texts had reached the Niger and Senegal Rivers and syncretically interacted with a variety of West African cultures and communities.[48] While the Islamic injunction to acquire literacy may not have been practiced universally, numerous forms of mediation between the written and spoken word evolved surrounding the Qur'an (which means both a reading and a recitation), the Hadith, and other religious practices.[49] Attuned to such mediations, Williams wrote about the diffusion of Islamic learning throughout Africa in his *History of the Negro*: "In the song and narrative, in the prayer and precept, of the heathen, the Arabic comes careering across each sentence, giving cadence and beauty to all."[50]

Hurston's attention to Moses conjures processes of circulation, translation, and revision central to the idea of world literature. Treating contemporary, New World African diasporic folklore as a palimpsest of ancient world-systems, she makes legible within it that "tradition of Moses as the great father of magic scattered over Africa and Asia." Animating the spectral traces of Afro-Semitic genealogies, a category of what Timothy Marr calls "American Islamicism," "all over the Southern United States, the British West Indies and Haiti," Hurston sutures the diasporic chronotope to a deep history of world literature.[51] This suturing turns on her recognition and mobilization of hybrid oral-literate techniques such as recitation and recirculation in vernacular culture. Hurston's inscription of diaspora into Old World genealogies redresses the implicit exclusion of African narrative from world literature consequent upon constructing Africa as exclusively oral.[52] Even in precolonial times, African orality was irretrievably intermeshed with textuality, as Thomas A. Hale's *Scribe, Griot, and Novelist* argues.[53] With recitations from classical mythology and the King James Bible to Brer Rabbit and Moses tales, Hurston's writing emerges from, showcases, and attunes readers to cultural practices discursively linked to Old World histories of mediating back and forth between orature and scripture, performance and textuality.

Not limited to visionaries and preachers, Hurston shows every level of the African American community participating in the back-and-forth play of oral and written cultural production. In "Spirituals and Neospirituals" she writes:

> Contrary to popular belief [the spirituals'] creation is not confined to the slavery period. Like the folk-tales the spirituals are being made and forgotten every day. There is this difference: the makers of the song of the present go about from town to town and church to church singing their songs. Some are printed and called ballads, and offered for sale after the services at ten and fifteen cents each. Others just go about singing them in competition with other religious minstrels. The lifting of the collection is the time for the song battles. Quite a bit of rivalry develops.
>
> These songs, even the printed ones, do not remain long in their original form. Every congregation that takes it up alters it considerably.[54]

African American religious minstrels print, recirculate, and innovate the spirituals, extending a recursive cycle of oral material entering the textual domain and textual material entering the oral domain. Since the eighteenth and nineteenth centuries, African American spirituals had appropriated and revised written Protestant hymns, which themselves had emerged out of an English culture whose oral and textual lineages, as we have seen, were inextricably interwoven. The religious minstrels, or balladeers, Hurston describes extend an already extant African American tradition of interweaving orality and textuality.

In a series of enthusiastic letters to Langston Hughes, Hurston conveys their own roles in a process that illustrates how popular and how developed is the practice of mediating back and forth between oral and textual cultural production in Southern African American communities of the 1920s and 1930s. I quote at length:

> In every town I hold 1 or 2 story-telling contests, and at each I begin by telling them who you are and all, then I read poems from "Fine Clothes." Boy! they eat it up. Two or three of them are too subtle and they don't get it. "Mulatto" for instance and "Sport" but the others they *just eat up*. You are being quoted in R.R. camps, phosphate mines, Turpentine stills etc. I went into a house Saturday night (last) and the men were skinning—you remember my telling you about that game—and when the dealer saw his opponent was on the turn (and losing consequently) He chanted
>
>> "When hard luck overtakes you
>> Nothing for you to do
>> Grab up yo' fine clothes
>> An' sell em to-ooo-de Jew Hah!!"
>
> (slaps the card down on the table)
> The other fellow was visibly cast down when the dealer picked up his money. Dealer gloating continued: "If you wuz a mule
>
>> I'd git you a waggin to haul—
>> But youse *so* low down-hown [?]
>> you aint even got uh stall."
>
> So you see they are making it so much a part of themselves they go to improvising on it.
>
> For some reason they call it "De Party Book." They come specially to be read to & I know you could sell them if you only had a supply. I think I'd like a dozen as an experiment. They adore "Saturday Night" and "Evil Woman," "Bad Man" "Gypsy Man"
>
> They sing the poems right off, and July 1, two men came over with guitars and sang the whole book. Everybody joined in. It was the strangest & most

thrilling thing. They played it well too. You'd be surprised. One man was giving the words out-lining them out as the preacher does a hymn and the others would take it up and sing. It was glorious!"[55]

Hurston had often found herself as a mediator between oral and textual cultural production among the literati in New York. Usually, though, she would bear the oral traditions of Eatonville and the African diaspora for literate audiences. The scene she communicates here, however, places her in a different role. She brings *Fine Clothes to the Jew* to the "job" and finds herself amazed: "It was the strangest & most *thrilling* thing." The fluency, the ease, the naturalness with which the community appropriates and improvises on Hughes's poetry suggests, in fact, that mediating back and forth between the written and the spoken word is an institution itself. Hurston recognizes in their practice of mediation the same techniques used by a preacher: "One man was giving the words out-lining them out as the preacher does a hymn and the others would take it up and sing." This scene witnesses two reversals: on the one hand, Hurston has come *to* "the folk" bearing products of the literary avant-garde (products based, of course, on the popular art of the blues); on the other hand, this band of migrant laborers has expertly appropriated the preacher's techniques of mediating textuality to "the folk."

These reversals reiterate the interwoven dynamics of textuality and orality that mark Hurston's participation in and depiction of African diasporic culture. Just as they cut across social worlds of the African diaspora, they also move beyond the boundaries of that diaspora. The preacher's masterful mediations between orality and textuality, which since Du Bois have been associated with practices emanating out of West Africa, have also been thought to derive from the "out-lining" (or lining-out) techniques of Puritan clerics. Not one to shy away from overdetermined transculturations, Hurston revisits these rhetorical practices in her historical novel *Moses, Man of the Mountain* (1939). Her Afro-Semitic Moses must fulfill an abundance of verbal tasks. Jethro instructs him that "it's always a great advantage when you're managing people to be able to speak their kind of language."[56] Not only does Moses range across registers, from the "dialect" of Midian to "high Egyptian," from the oracular timbre of Mt. Sinai and the weary pleading of a tired Emancipator, but he must also work across oral and textual media and parley his mastery of the book of Thoth and the Midianite book of magic into the "stiff" language of the Pharaonic court and the vernacular language of the Israelite folk.

Refashioning Moses as "neither reverent nor epic," as Alain Locke wrote disapprovingly, Hurston refracts the epic of Exodus through another diasporic rendering, a new iteration of the text's—and the epic genre's—worldliness carried out by means of such linguistic and tonal diversity.[57] Working through a worlded generic map of epic languages, Hurston's suggestive mapping of African and African diasporic culture repeatedly highlights such pluralistic interweavings of orality and textuality, authenticity and adaptation, formal and vernacular.[58] Forays into her manuscript histories, private letters, and unpopular novels expand the familiar portrait of Hurston as the authenticity-driven Isis "re-membering" the fragments of African diasporic vernacular culture. This metaphorization of Hurston as a healing goddess, furthermore, projects a radically cohesive authorial agency at odds with a historical figure subject to myriad institutional expectations and social contradictions. Yet the cozy intimacy her major works project obscures the evident traces of such conflicted processes of literary production, as well as Hurston's own attempts at discursive diversity. The overpowering effectiveness of her textualization of the vernacular, in conjunction with exigencies and pieties fueling the institution of literary historiography, has engendered a readerly desire for and sense of familiarity with Hurston. These have been constitutive of the revived popular and critical interest in her life and work. While wrapping Hurston in an aura of familiarity and intimacy, they have also produced a portrait of the artist that keeps her—and her worldliness—hidden in plain sight.

3 Whiteness and World Literature

Alejo Carpentier, Racial Difference, and Narrative Creolization

THE COMPLEX INTERSECTION of early twentieth-century avant-garde literature with ethnography and racial "science," exoticism and primitivism, negrophilia and indigenism, represents a well-documented aspect of global modernism. The Cuban writer Alejo Carpentier joined many white intellectuals in perceiving racial difference as an opportunity for artistic innovation: Luis Palés Matos of Puerto Rico, Miguel Ángel Asturias of Guatemala, Gertrude Stein and Carl Van Vechten of the United States, Federico García Lorca of Spain, and André Breton and Michel Leiris of France. Carpentier's artistic investment in racial difference overlaps signficantly with these writers, many of whom he crossed paths with in Paris and New York, Havana and Port-au-Prince. In the marginalized cultural expressions of colonial subjects and internal others, they found unfamiliar and exciting linguistic and performance traditions that could serve a range of projects, from articulating new nationalist ideologies to experimenting with form and genre in poetry and prose. While racial difference helped these white writers develop novel ideas and forms, many of them recognized that their modes of appropriating nonwhite cultural expressions were exploitative and sensationalistic, betraying more about the observer than the observed. Carpentier in particular struggled with the gap between his desire to "make it new" by bringing attention to African diasporic cultural expressions and the way he mediated his attention through narrative tropes—the ethnographic voyeur, the scribe amongst the unlettered, and the fair intellectual rejuvenated by consorting with darker-skinned folk—that reproduced textually racial hierarchies he sought to distance himself from.

Such struggles mark the way Carpentier's work seeks to frame, from the explicit position of the white intellectual, an antiracist New World aesthetics attentive to the historical fissures erected upon and constitutive of racial difference. His literary project continually revises the poetics of racial representation to work through discursive obstacles confronted by white Latin American as well as US modernists. At the theoretical level, Carpentier fashions the mid-century world-literary mode of magical realism as a constellation of strategies that could unhierarchically mediate the racialized terrain of American literature on both sides of the Río Grande/Río Bravo, despite the vexing discontinuities produced by the ongoing production of that border. Carpentier sharpens hemispheric continuities when, in a revisionist detour that affiliates him with Du Bois and Hurston, he grounds the emergence of marvelous and magical realism in the *longue durée* of world literature, evoking spectral, genealogical sites of circulation, translation, and revision before European hegemony—from medieval West Africa to al-Andalus—that inscribe African and diasporic performance and textuality into a deep history of cosmopolitan exchange. However, as witnessed in the case of Hurston, material processes of literary production and reception interfere with his efforts to inscribe African diaspora cultures into such worldly networks and archives. Namely, the racialization of Latin American difference in the United States' book marketplace undermines Carpentier's experimentation with marvelous realism as a mode of world literature capable of staging and deconstructing a racialized horizon of expectations that frames, and deforms, the historical specificities of African and diasporic verbal arts. The monolithic racialization of Latin American literary production as "Latin" overwrites even as it confirms the misrecognitions Carpentier lays bare as the enduring historical unconscious of New World literature.

Carpentier's literary and political commitments to African diasporic cultural expressions emerged during his early involvement with a contrarian strain of anticolonial Cuban nationalism, *minorismo*. At twenty-three years old, he served seven months in prison for signing the 1927 manifesto of the Grupo Minorista, which protested the political and cultural corruption rampant under the Gerardo Machado dictatorship in Cuba (1925–33). In the aftermath of the Cuban War of Independence (1895–98) and the Spanish American War (1898), the United States had established direct rule over Puerto Rico and indirect rule over Cuba. The influx of North American capital and culture prompted intellectuals of both islands to defensively articulate national cultures as redoubts of independence, placing Havana and San Juan in a circuit of modernist cultural nationalism including locales such as Harlem, Port-au-Prince,

São Paulo, Dublin, and Prague. The classic Puerto Rican text of Antonio Pedreira, *Insularismo* (1934), affirmed the essentially Spanish basis of Spanish Caribbean culture, and the idealized peasant figures of the Puerto Rican *jíbaro* and Cuban *guajiro*, both racialized as white, would support this affiliation. However, in both Puerto Rico and Cuba a small but influential number of artists and intellectuals would insist upon the centrality of the traditions of the islands' black populations. Infusing literary works with sensationally rendered Afro-Caribbean vernacular practices, Cuban *minorismo* or *negrismo* had its counterpart in the poetry of the white Puerto Rican Luis Palés Matos. While its practitioners were largely white and mulatto, *minorismo/negrismo* shared affinities with the Harlem Renaissance and *L'indigenisme* in Haiti, and networks of translation and collaboration emerged connecting Carpentier and Palés Matos to figures including Nicolás Guillén of Cuba, Langston Hughes of the United States, and Jacques Roumain of Haiti.

As with early twentieth-century cultural nationalist movements from Haiti to Dublin, ethnography played a crucial, if problematic, part in mediating racial difference for modernist literary treatments. The Cuban *minoristas* took inspiration from Don Fernando Ortiz, a white Cuban statesman and anthropologist. While his intellectual development would ultimately lead to his canonization as a model of progressive ethnography, his early works—some of the first "scientific" investigations of Afro-Cuban culture—framed that culture through the deprecating lenses of criminology and witchcraft. Jerome Branche, author of *Colonialism and Race in Luso-Hispanic Literature*, notes that Ortiz "made a lasting contribution to vernacular and juridical stereotyping of blacks in Cuba," helping to "establish the negative ideological and semantic parameters of the textual *negro* for the discourse of racial domination."[1] Situating the *minoristas* in this Ortizian ethnographic discourse on blackness, Carpentier's recollections candidly lay bare some of the more dubious moods and motives animating them: "Don Fernando Ortiz used to meet with us. To him we owe much of our interest in the black folklore of Cuba. There was in it an effort to recuperate traditions disdained by a whole bourgeoisie. To interest oneself in the black, in those days, was equivalent to adopting a nonconformist attitude, even a revolutionary one."[2] The laudable goal of recuperating disdained traditions went hand in hand with a problematic presentation of the white self. The embrace of Afro-Cuban "folk" culture provoked and shocked the respectable Cuban bourgeoisie, carrying nonconformist, even revolutionary cachet. This radical posture evinces what Saidiya Hartman refers to as "the facility of blackness in the other's self-fashioning": "The black body or blackface mask serve[s] as the vehicle of white self-exploration, renunciation, and enjoyment."[3] The *minoristas* deployed Afro-Cuban culture symbolically, as a response to "the false and exhausted values" denounced in the 1927 manifesto against Cuban political, economic, and cultural dependency.[4]

The novel Carpentier wrote to protest this dependency, *¡Écue-Yamba-Ó!* (1933), similarly conjoins attention to Afro-Cuban cultural expressions with their sensationalistic appropriation for aesthetic and ideological purposes. This symbolic appropriation of blackness displaces novelistic attention away from the subjective experience of his Afro-Cuban characters. For this reason, Carpentier would only consent to the republication of *¡Écue-Yamba-Ó!* in 1968 after a pirate edition began circulating, and in the prologue to the authorized edition he wrote: "I thought I knew my characters, but with time I saw that, observing them superficially, from the outside, the profound soul, the muzzled pain, the hidden pulsations of rebellion had slipped away from me."[5] *¡Écue-Yamba-Ó!*, which remains untranslated into English, takes the form of a *Bildungsroman* about the Afro-Cuban youth Menegildo Cué, set against the penetration of US economic and cultural imperialism into the Cuban interior. In a contrarian reversal of contemporaneous nationalist ideologies, which lionized peasant figures of Spanish descent, the novel offers the members of the Afro-Cuban Cué family as icons of national culture:

> The creole countryside was already yielding foreign fruits, ripening in soft-drink ads! Orange-Crush became a tool of imperialism, like the memory of Roosevelt or Lindbergh's airplane . . . ! Only the blacks, Menegildo, Longina, Salomé and their stock jealously guarded an Antillean character and tradition. The bongo, antidote to Wall Street! The Holy Spirit, venerated by the Cué family, did not admit Yankee sausages into their votive rolls! The saints of Mayeya would eat no hot-dogs! (118)

As the mass-produced commodities of the United States intrude upon the "creole" landscape, Carpentier casts an ethnographic gaze upon the Afro-Caribbean in order to represent an uncommodified Caribbean authenticity. Black Cubans, with their music and Yoruba-Catholic pantheon, "jealously guard an Antillean character and tradition" and thereby resist the corrupting, deauthenticating onslaught of Yankee commercialism. Carpentier's ethnographic interest in the formation of African diasporic culture out of African survivals and New World syncretisms honors its creative spirit of survival, yet he presents Afro-Cuban cultural resilience as if it explicitly repudiated North American imperialism rather than refracted the racialized domination and marginalization produced by Cuban, and New World, history. In this localization of national culture in Afro-Cuban cultural practices, he leaves out the ensemble of social relations that subordinate these practices in Cuban society, colonial and *comprador* social relations that equally bear witness to an "Antillean character and tradition." Rather than exploring opaque and "hidden pulsations of rebellion" (thereby "skirting," as Branche notes, "important questions related to black alterity"),[6] the novel sensationalistically makes transparently available for an island-wide Cuban identity the artifacts, linguistic elements, and religious practices of a black culture formed by subordination and exclusion. Formally, this historical marginalization of Afro-Cubans serves the *minorista* novel's modernist cultural nationalism, motivating what Roberto González Echevarría identifies as surrealist-inspired juxtapositions such as "The bongo, antidote to Wall Street!" and "The saints of Mayeya would eat no hot-dogs!"[7]

The juxtapositions of ethnographic surrealism overload the novel's traditional picaresque and *Bildungsroman* structures of subject-formation, culminating in Menegildo Cué's sensational gang-related death during a riotous performance of popular black dance music. Though mediated through a mode of modernist primitivism, the linguistic and narrative deformations of these canonical European narrative forms (already marked by and suited to deformation) embody the *minorista/ negrista* argument that Afro-Cuban practices offer autonomous, local grounds for cultural critique and aesthetic renewal. This appropriation of blackness forms a crucial aspect of the hemisphere's early twentieth-century modernist moment. As Michael North argues in *The Dialect of Modernism*, black vernacular practices mediate the literary efforts of artists such as Gertrude Stein, Ezra Pound, and T. S. Eliot to break down what Langston Hughes dubbed linguistic "standardization" in his 1926 essay "The Negro Artist and the Racial Mountain."[8] In Carpentier's creative output following the publication of *¡Écue-Yamba-Ó!*, he would continue to prominently stage Afro-Caribbean culture in his efforts to set forth distinctive New World cultural identities and formal innovations. While bearing the exploitative marks of this modernist racial economy, they nonetheless emerge from a desire to displace Europe as the privileged center of perceptual and artistic authority.

Carpentier would sharpen his articulation of this purpose during his time in the heart of that center. Shortly after his release from prison in 1928, the French surrealist Robert Desnos aided his flight to Europe, the beginning of his eleven-year expatriation in Paris. Carpentier formed part of a surrealist movement disillusioned with the European rationalism and industrial militarism that led to World War I. At the same time, he immersed himself archivally in an America constantly looking to Europe for its intellectual and artistic ideas. From this split position, he dispatched from Paris to the Havana journal *Carteles* the 1930 essay "América ante la joven literatura europea." In it Carpentier diagnoses "the spirit of imitation" marring New World letters, where, he writes, "we passed through, fifteen years late, all the fevers born in the old continent: romanticism, Parnassianism, symbolism." Meanwhile, "the Indians told their marvelous legends in our landscapes, which we did not want to see."[9] In a classic Latin American rhetorical formation, Carpentier seeks to break this Latin American dependency on European literary trends; as Carlos Alonso has written: "The demand for an autochthonous cultural expression has been the dominant concern in Latin American intellectual history. . . . This rhetorical dialectics of crisis has both characterized and structured Latin American discursive space from the outset."[10] In response to this social and cultural crisis of dependency, the same crisis that motivated his participation in the Grupo Minorista, Carpentier offers indigenous American oral traditions, "marvelous legends," as a neglected source of "autochthonous cultural expression."

A fraught counterpoint structures and destabilizes Carpentier's aesthetic project: combating European dependency by means of a racially precarious dependency on the neglected cultural expressions of the New World's nonwhite populations. Mediated through the strategies of "marvelous realism," the oral and performative traditions of the nonwhite/non-European provide an avenue for the development of hemispheric American cultural expressions untethered from Eurocentrism. Negotiating ethnographic surrealism's inspiring yet self-implicating mediations of the myths and rituals of indigenous Americans and Afro-Caribbeans, *lo real maravilloso americano*, or the marvelous American real, as has been well documented, predates, deeply influences, and significantly overlaps with Latin American magical realism. This concept conveys a New World mode of experiencing and artistically rendering a reality marked by multiple temporalities, proliferating belief systems, fantastic dreamscapes, outlandish historical events, and outsize landscapes. Leonardo Padura Fuentes, in his essay "The Marvelous Real: Praxis and Perception," comments: "It seems certain that Carpentier's initial propositions are to create a surrealism proper to America, where life is more immediate and history full of more astonishing relations than European prefabrications."[11] In the prologue to *El reino de este mundo* (1949; English translation, *The Kingdom of This World*, 1957), Carpentier elaborates an American mode of surrealist experience, but he tries to distance it from the secular, subjective enchantments of European avant-garde art, which he calls "cheap magic."[12] Carpentier privileges indigenous American and Afro-Caribbean cultural practices that offer authentic enchantment:

> Whereas in Western Europe folk dance, for instance, has lost all magical or invocatory character, rare is the collective dance in America that does not incorporate a deep ritualistic meaning, becoming almost a ceremony of initiation: such as the dances of the Cuban *santería*, or the extraordinary negro version of the festival of Corpus Christi, which can still be seen in the town of San Francisco de Yare, in Venezuela.[13]

In this instance, African diasporic culture sustains a sort of faith, a "magical or invocatory character," that European culture has lost. Carpentier incorporates these practices into the repertoire of the marvelous American real, crediting to America as a whole the specific cultural practices of the blacks of San Francisco de Yare in Venezuela. This logically suspect rhetorical maneuver produces a sort of borrowed faith: he takes the specific practices of a racialized part of the Americas and uses them to argue that the whole of the Americas offers a marvelous reality. This echoes the dubious metonymy through which ¡*Écue-Yamba-Ó!* makes the particularities of Afro-Cuban culture available to stand in for Cuban and Caribbean authenticity as a whole. The concluding sentence of *El reino de este mundo*'s prologue indicates again the problem with these metonymic substitutions. They appear as gestures of inclusivity, but they decisively answer Branche's question: "For whom is the *negrista* text written?"[14] When at the very end of his prologue Carpentier invokes "the Faustian presence of the Indian and the Black" as a point of departure for the marvelous American real, he implicitly addresses a white reader.[15] Through the metaphor of the European Faust myth, nonwhite cultural expressions acquire a diabolical alterity, however productive they may be for white literary appropriation.

In ¡*Écue-Yamba-Ó!* and the prologue to *El reino de este mundo*, then, Carpentier attempts to articulate cohesive national, regional, and hemispheric cultural identities through attention to African diasporic culture; however, the kind of attention paid reproduces textually the very hierarchies and divisions he criticizes. Carpentier's subsequent novel, *Los pasos perdidos* (1953; English translation, *The Lost Steps*, 1956), on the other hand, explicitly engages the cultural politics of cross-racial appropriations, scrutinizing the discursive tropes through which the white intellectual frames and deploys nonwhite cultural practices. Both in its politics of racial appropriation and by its fashioning a white Latin American adoptive New Yorker as the narrator-protagonist, *Los pasos perdidos* reiterates the desire for what Kirsten Silva Gruesz calls "transamerican" relevance behind Carpentier's literary project.[16] The narrator-protagonist works in the economic capital of the Americas as a commercial composer and socializes with bohemian intellectuals, artists, and performers, until his old musicology professor commissions him to travel to Latin America to find certain primitive instruments among the Indians.

During his journey into the remote reaches of the Amazon jungle, he begins a passionate, and pragmatic, love affair with Rosario, a dark-skinned woman of the region who serves as both native informant and dutiful wife. His physical description of her, an overabundance of exploitative tropes, establishes the narrator's perceptual unreliability and foreshadows the critical reversal the novel will perform:

> With the passing of morning into afternoon and afternoon into evening, Rosario grew more authentic, more real, more clearly outlined against a background that affirmed its constants as we approached the river. Relationships became established between her flesh and the ground we were treading, relationships proclaimed by sun-darkened skins, by the similarity of the visible hair, by a unity of forms giving the common stamp of works from the same potter's wheel. . . . And yet, as I looked at her as a woman, I felt myself clumsy, awkward, conscious of my own exoticism [*exotismo*].[17]

This description of Rosario's physical form, its inscription in and issuance from a gendered American landscape ripe for possession by the white man, figures her literally as the autochthonous: "sprung from the earth itself."[18] Through the doubly signifying word "exotismo," the narrator-protagonist recognizes both his own exoticizing gaze and his outsider status, staging an anxiety about his appropriation of her racialized difference that is absent from *¡Écue-Yamba-Ó!* and the prologue to *El reino de este mundo*. The narrator-protagonist continues to catalogue the differences that impose limits on his union with Rosario: "It was the thousand books I had read and of which she knew nothing; it was her beliefs, habits, superstitions, ideas of which I knew nothing and which, nevertheless, formed the basis for vital beliefs as valid as my own. My education, her prejudices, all that she had been taught, all that she valued, at that moment seemed to me irreconcilable" (107). This personal crisis refracts the larger cultural questions the novel—and Carpentier's entire oeuvre—asks about race, class, and the quest for some sort of cohesive New World identity. Yet while their backgrounds seem to unsuit them for one another, economics and desire bring them together with a novelistic force of inevitability.

A scene that closely follows the narrator's crisis suggestively transfers the question from the level of interpersonal intimacy to that of cultural creolization. The novel's protagonist encounters in the fictional Santiago de los Aguinaldos a loosely veiled performance of "the extraordinary negro version of the festival of Corpus Christi, which can still be seen in the town of San Francisco de Yare, in Venezuela" that Carpentier mentions in the prologue to *El reino de este mundo*. Departing from his earlier instrumentalized enthusiasm for that festival in the service of an artistic manifesto, in this rendering a circular procession of the icon of Santiago around the church soberly combines medieval European religious pageantry with an African-derived ring-shout. In presenting this syncretistic ritual as an *un*-sensationalized juxtaposition, *Los pasos perdidos* departs from the prologue's programmatic advocacy and *¡Écue-Yamba-Ó!*'s modernist display. Here we see instead the now familiar marvelous/magical realist narrative technique of combining European and African cultural practices with discursive neutrality. More marvelous/magical realist techniques follow. After witnessing this ritual, a missionary recounts to the narrator-protagonist the history of Santiago de los Aguinaldos: "ruined by the Wars of the Barons, smitten by the plague" (118). The medieval quality of the town evinces the historic heterogeneity characteristic of the marvelous American real. However, in another temporal disjuncture that immediately follows, *Los pasos perdidos* evokes a deep history of global cosmopolitanism that relativizes the New World's sensational *métissage*: "Guitar-players, whom Rosario had asked to entertain us with some music, began to pluck their instruments. Suddenly their song carried me much farther than the scenes I had been evoking. Those two black jongleurs were singing ballads telling of Charlemagne, of Roland, the Bishop Turpin, the treachery of Ganelon, and the sword that cut down the Moors at Roncesvalles" (118). The "black jongleurs'" performance of *The Song of Roland* ironically renders them as the bearers of a European chivalric epic that recounts European efforts to repel the advance of Arab/North African armies deeper into Europe. This quiet irony matches the muted racial cues of this section of *Los pasos perdidos*, marking a distinctive deployment of

African diasporic performance in Carpentier's work following *¡Écue-Yamba-Ó!* and *El reino de este mundo.* The narrator's temporal vertigo upon recognizing the epic seemingly owes more to the perseverance of *The Song of Roland* in the remote jungle interior of Latin America than it does to the blackness of the performers. In fact, what is notable about this scene is that blackness might just be incidental to the performance. Rather than relying on blackness as a "Faustian" underwriter of the marvelous real, or as the authentic ground of a New World identity, Carpentier quietly puts the reader in the position of interrogating the significance of blackness here for the white spectator.

Los pasos perdidos continues to distance itself from the sensationalistic appropriation of blackness as the narrator-protagonist travels farther into the jungle. Instead, the novel stages the self-serving, sensationalistic discursive tropes through which the white intellectual processes racial difference. This strategy shifts the question of American cultural identity away from ethnographic phenomena and toward the racialized phenomenology that structures perception of racial difference in the New World. In classic primitivist fashion, recalling hemispheric and transatlantic modernisms' "Negro vogue," the narrator-protagonist frames his journey as one that brings him closer to the originary sources of human expressive culture. His contact first with Rosario, then black musicians, and finally indigenous tribes rejuvenates his own creative impulses, dissipated by a career spent in New York composing marketing jingles. Nestled in this heart of darkness, with Rosario as his common-law wife, he furiously scribbles a symphonic magnum opus on a desperately short supply of paper and must stop composing when he runs out. On forced hiatus from his creative furor, he looks over his work and sees that, in fact, it is nothing special, that he had put himself under an illusory spell of an imagined creative renewal. The narrator-protagonist's journey to the dark sources of human vitality turns out to be a journey instead that exposes the desire of the white subject to find rejuvenation and renewal by crossing the color line.

This self-reflexive critique of whiteness speaks directly not only to Carpentier's *minorista* past and his promotion of the marvelous real in *El reino de este mundo* but also to the moment of world-literary production represented by the transatlantic modernist engagement with blackness and its mid-century aftermath. Carpentier's developing practice of marvelous or magical realism seeks to ground New World artistic innovation not in appropriations of racial difference but through explorations of how that difference is framed. The moment in *Los pasos*

perdidos where the black musicians perform *The Song of Roland* ironically touches upon one of the key framing devices: the focus on black
musical and oral traditions. This focus, as explored in the previous two
chapters and discussed above with respect to white modernists such as
Gertrude Stein, Ezra Pound, and T. S. Eliot, often limits black expressive
culture to musicality and orality. Branche similarly includes Carpentier
in his denunciation of the overwhelming reliance of *negrista* literature
on "a multileveled neobozalic oral register," a register that attempts to
authenticate a primitive Afro-Hispanic subject circumscribed by African orality.[19]

While Carpentier, as we have seen, partakes of his fair share of primi-
tivizing "racial ventriloquism," even in his early works he marks out a
scribal register of blackness. Not only does Carpentier go against the
grain by attempting in *¡Écue-Yamba-Ó!* to make Afro-Cubans icons of
national culture, but he refuses to represent black characters as figures
exclusively of orality. The latter refusal undermines an impulse in ethnographic treatments of African and diasporic cultures that isolates those
cultures from technologies of literacy. Such isolation is an effect generated by the valuable oeuvre of anthropologist and literary ventrilo-
quist Lydia Cabrera, one of Carpentier's white Cuban contemporaries
and the author of texts such as *Cuentos Negros de Cuba* (*Negro Stories
from Cuba*; 1940) and *Refranes de negros viejos* (*Old Negro Proverbs*;
1955). In addition to destabilizing the exclusive affiliation of blackness
with orality, the articulation of an Afro-Cuban scribal register inscribes
it into world narrative systems linking the Caribbean to transhistorical
linguistic networks in the Mediterranean and West Africa. This mapping echoes Zora Neale Hurston's efforts, explored in the previous chapter, to insert African diasporic culture into interwoven processes of oral
and textual transmission that cut across languages, races, nations, and
eras. Plumbing the recursive worldliness of New World culture, Carpentier makes recourse to such processes in order to dismantle the assumptions that structure Caribbean nationalist discourses about race, writing, and orality.

In *¡Écue-Yamba-Ó!*, even within the disenfranchised Afro-Cuban
milieu, writing plays a crucial role in sustaining the community's
oral and performative traditions, as we see at the following *ñáñigo*
meeting:[20]

> While the initiates reclined on the floor, the elders [*antiguos*] began to
> caress the drums. The moment had arrived to stage a "language" contest

[*competencia de lengua*], keeping up dialogues of the *ñáñigo* formulas recorded by the grandfathers in the Notebooks of the Game [*las "libretas" del Juego*]. Scanning sentences with muffled beats, Dominguillo began the proper liturgy:

"Take off your hat, for a wise-man from the land of Efó has arrived."

Over bass rhythms, Antonio approached the old man:

"I am like you because I kill roosters."

"Now that I taught you you want to gouge out my eyes?"

"You only castrate a goat once."

"My House is a college of design."

"One tree alone doesn't make a forest." (164)

The "Notebooks" contain the association's secret liturgical formulas and proverbs—"brought to Cuba by black slaves" and recorded by the "elders" (203). The elders oversee and enforce verbal mastery of "the most up-to-date ritual formulas and expressions of the *ñáñigo* dialect" through the language contest, verbal duels with younger members (204). Such verbal dueling emerged as an ethnographic meme in the early twentieth century, not only discussed repeatedly by Hurston but also featured in Leo Frobenius's studies of West African expressive culture that Carpentier read. The latter conjoins this oral practice to a technology of literacy and sidesteps ethnographic commonplaces isolating black folk culture from writing.

Carpentier develops the link between Afro-Caribbean and West African oral-literate traditions in *El reino de este mundo* through the character Mackandal, the Mandingo precursor of the Haitian Revolution. He emerges as a character with strong resemblances to the vernacular figures encountered in Du Bois and Hurston, as the language in the following passage indicates:

Mackandal rhapsodized [*psalmodiaba*] at the sugar-mill [about] deeds that had occurred in the great kingdoms of Popo, of Arada, of the Nagós, of the Fulas. He spoke of vast migrations of peoples, of century-long wars, of prodigious battles in which animals came to the aid of men. He knew the story of Adonhueso, the King of Angola, of King Dá, incarnation of the Serpent, that is the eternal principle, never ending, who mystically rests with a queen who was the Rainbow, Lady of water and every birth. But, above all, Mackandal made himself eloquent with the epic [*gesta*] of Kankán Musa, the proud Musa, maker of the invincible Malian empire. (103–4; my translation, as much of this section was excised from the English edition)

The reader meets Mackandal as a creole and creolizing griot, cross-hatching the overlapping legends, myths, religions, and royal histories of West Africa throughout the sugar plantations of eighteenth-century Saint-Domingue. The language surrounding Mackandal—specifically the words "psalmodiaba," which translated as "rhapsodized" loses the biblical connection to the songs of David, and "gesta," which translated as "epic" loses the specific connection to medieval Spanish epic song, that is, *cantar de gesta*—points to that conjunction of oral and written narrative practices constitutive of the networks and archives of world literature's *longue durée*.

Mackandal's own access to and figuring of these networks and archives become plain after he has retreated to a mountain hideaway to plot his insurrection against the French colonists:

> On a log stripped of its bark by machete slashes lay an account book [*libro de contabilidad*] stolen from the plantation's book-keeper, its pages showing heavy signs drawn in charcoal. . . . In letters legible only to himself, Mackandal had entered in his register the name of Bocor of Milot, and even of drovers who were useful for crossing the mountains and making contact with the people of the Artibonite region. (19–21)

Here the reader encounters Mackandal the scribe, who has filled his ledger with the names of insurrectionary contacts "in letters legible only to himself." A revolutionary settling of accounts, perhaps these are Arabic characters, for, as Haitian historian Carolyn Fick writes, "he was supposedly brought up in the Moslem religion and apparently had an excellent command of Arabic."[21] Mackandal, whose transit through "the Plaine, establishing direct contact" recalls Delany's Blake and Du Bois's Zora, represents another surrogate of the cosmopolitan past mediating between the spoken and the written word in the service of a revolutionary agenda. Like the *libretas ñáñigas*, Mackandal's *libro de contabilidad* forms part of an opaque, hermetic black knowledge that carries forth Old World weavings of the oral and the textual.

With these *libretas* and *libros*, Carpentier locates a scribal tradition in Afro-Caribbean culture bearing traces of a cosmopolitan Old World past. The *ñáñigo* rituals and griot-like functions of Mackandal allow the reader to conjure an ancestral African culture whose oral and scribal traditions are linked to the diverse flows of world literature's antiquity. Carpentier's staging of African and diasporic cultural expressions at the intersection of textuality and performance gains even more significance alongside his frequent evocations of the *cantar de gesta* and the related *libro de caballería*, epic renderings of knightly adventures. In his essays, lectures, and the short story "The Highroad of Saint James," Carpentier practices a revisionist literary historiography of these quintessentially "Spanish" and "European" genres, whose oral and textual lines of descent invite readers to conjure a world-systemic moment "before European hegemony," outside the hierarchical racial parameters of the current world system. Through the *libro de caballería*, Carpentier invokes a baroque, racially creolized world literature that his development of marvelous realism aspires to channel. The local history of the *libro de caballería* reveals a repressed cosmopolitanism in this Spanish form that establishes a world-literary precedent for Carpentier's marvelous realist strategies for mediating racial difference.

So turning a folkloristic, ethnographic gaze upon late medieval and early modern European culture, Carpentier writes: "*Amadis of Gaul* and other novels that are mentioned in the *Quijote* were in reality the poetic magnification of a folklore that traveled orally."[22] This seminal literary genre emerging from the oral tradition persists as an oral tradition even after textual codification, structurally echoing the role of the *ñáñigo* notebooks. Well after the rise of the printing press and of the popularity of the novel, it was still common to find in Spain "the general custom of reading [the *libro de caballería*] out loud as a social activity, in small groups, whether at the roadside inn around the hearth, at night in the family home, in the town square or even in the taverns."[23] In early modern Europe, through ballads, public readings, and other performances, the *libro de caballería* circulated both textually and orally and informed the popular consciousness so widely that even the conquistadors view their experiences of the New World through the lens of the *libro de caballería*. Carpentier quotes Bernal Díaz de Castillo's *Historia de la conquista de la Nueva España*: "We were astonished and said that these lands, temples, and lakes resembled the enchantments of which Amadís spoke."[24] Such testimony reminds us that, as González Echevarría writes:

> The discovery of America was a rediscovery, the revelation of a world already conjured up by the European imagination. In this sense, the discovery of America was the actualization of a fiction, the founding of a world that had its origins in books before it became a concrete and tangible *terra firma*: thus the mythical and literary names in American topography, from the Antilles to California.[25]

In light of Carpentier's ethnographic gaze upon Spanish folklore, we could add that this double sense of discovery, or rediscovery, depends not only on books, as González Echevarría suggests, but on an oral tradition that precedes and succeeds the *libros de caballería*, conjuring up topoi such as the Antilles and California.

Furthermore, the status of this oral tradition as "conjured up by the European imagination" needs to be qualified. Foundational philological scholarship has shown the place of the Spanish *cantar de gesta* and other epic forms in the mix of Germanic and Romance traditions reaching from Spain and Italy to France, Germany, and Scandinavia.[26] At the same time, the marvelous topoi that fill Arthurian legend, the Niebelungen saga, and *Amadís de Gaula* equally recall the voyages of Sindbad and the adventures of *A Thousand and One Nights*, a central trope of which—marvels, or *'aja'ib* in Arabic—resonates profoundly with Carpentier's oeuvre.[27] Arabic narrative crucially interacted with Germanic and Romance narrative since Arabs arrived in Iberia in 711.[28] As the Introduction's discussion of the *maqamat* established, Arabic narrative and narrative elements circulated orally and textually throughout the Spanish peninsula, well into the heyday of the *libro de caballería*.[29] Through the figure of Cidi Hamete Benengeli, Cervantes parodies the common practice of attributing knightly adventures to Arabic manuscripts or informants. This attribution itself resembles, and suggests a familiarity with, the Arab scholarly practice of *isnad*, which, as Timothy Mitchell writes, testifies to "an unbroken chain of recitation leading back to the original author": "Only such chains of recitation could overcome the inevitable absence of the author within the text. . . . The entire practice of Arab scholarship revolved around the problem of overcoming the absence in writing of the author's unequivocal meaning."[30] The practice of *isnad* indicates a distinctive configuration of the relationship between speech and writing: citation and recitation, interweaving the oral and the written word, becomes the guarantor of authority. Arabic narrative practice often exhibits a similar dynamic, merging the courtly imperative to record while taking for granted the ceaseless proliferation of oral recirculation. Tales from the *Nights* frequently conclude with the king insisting that this noteworthy event or delightful story be committed to writing, so that storytellers far and wide can know of it and spread it orally.[31] Writing, rather than replacing orality, becomes a relay in a ceaseless process of oral transmission, recalling both the *ñáñigo* notebooks and the recursive circulation of *libros de caballería*—in transit from "folklore that traveled orally" to large printed tomes back to the public orality of "small groups, whether at the roadside inn around the hearth, at night in the family home, in the town square or even in the taverns." This creolized itinerary evokes a literary historiography outside racialized parameters of orality and literacy that constrain the African and diasporic subject to an abjectly primitivist relationship to the spoken word. It also imbues local Spanish narrative practices with far-flung and racially miscegenated cultural traces. Finally, it imaginatively conjures the legacy of al-Andalus as the site of a heterotopic world narrative system encompassing an Africa anterior to the rupture of New World slavery.

Carpentier's picaresque short story "El camino de Santiago" rewrites Golden Age imperial Spain from the perspective of this heterotopic world narrative system, formally appropriating its utopian precedent in a gesture that seeks to upend European artistic hegemony in the Americas. The story's protagonist, Juan de Amberes, based on a military drummer whose death notice Carpentier found while researching in European archives, contracts a grave illness in Flanders. Believing himself cured by the grace of St. James, he undertakes a pilgrimage to Santiago de Compostela. As his health and spirits recover, his commitment to the holy route wavers. During a market fair in Burgos, he hears a troupe of busking blind balladeers singing *romances* about America, its fabulous beasts and its lands of riches. As the crowd breaks up to avoid paying for the street entertainment, Juan finds himself in an alleyway with two colorful *indianos*, people who have been to the Americas, stock characters of sixteenth- and seventeenth-century Spanish narrative:

> An indiano *recently returned* from the West Indies was offering for sale with exaggerated gestures two alligators stuffed with straw that he said came from Cuzco. He had a monkey on his shoulder and a parrot perched on his left hand. He blew into a large pink conch, and a black slave emerged from a crimson box, like Lucifer in a miracle play [*auto sacramental*], proffering strings of pitted pearls, stones that would cure headaches, belts made of vicuña wool, tinsel earrings, and other tawdry finery from Potosí.[32]

The black *indiano*'s sensational appearance advertises the marvelous wonders brought back from the New World; at the same time, from the narrator's perspective he evokes the performative tradition of the *auto sacramental*, the medieval morality play that entertained and educated the largely illiterate audiences of medieval and early modern Spain. This telling duality plays a crucial role in the story: the lore the *indianos*

circulate about the New World depends as much upon a European narrative lens as it does upon direct reportage from the Americas.

Tantalized and encouraged by the *indianos*, Juan himself sets sail for
the Americas. Unable to reach the mainland directly, he disembarks in
Cuba and encounters provincial misery: "They found nothing except
gossip there, nothing but scandal and scheming, letters going to and
from, mortal hatreds, and boundless envy, all contained within eight
stinking streets deep in mud the whole year round" (30). One miser-
able night, humid and sticky, drunk on bad wine, Juan quarrels with a
Genoan and mortally stabs him. He flees to the mountains and joins a
palenque, a maroon community composed of escaped African slaves, as
well as persecuted Huguenots and Jews. Eventually, Juan tires of life in
the *palenque*, and along with an African named Golomón, a Huguenot,
and a Jew, they flag down a ship that will carry them back to Europe via
the Canary Islands.

Cursing his misadventures, Juan repents for having abandoned *el
camino de Santiago* and repledges himself to the pilgrimage. The story's
next section, though, nearly duplicates a previous scene:

> One market day, Juan the *indiano* stood at the end of a blind alley, loudly
> offering for sale two alligators stuffed with straw, which he claimed to have
> brought from Cuzco, though he had actually bought them from a pawnbro-
> ker in Toledo. He had a monkey on his shoulder and a parrot on his hand.
> He blew into a large pink conch, and Golomón emerged from a crimson box,
> like Lucifer in a miracle play, proffering strings of pitted pearls, stones that
> would cure headaches, belts made of vicuña wool, tinsel earrings, and other
> tawdry finery from Potosí. (51; translation modified)

Juan has abandoned once again his pilgrimage to Santiago de Compostela, and he has taken up the costume of the *indiano*, responding to
European expectations rather than his own experiences in the Indies.
The repetition extends itself when Juan, now *el indiano*, meets a new
Juan, *el romero*, a pilgrim to Santiago de Compostela: "The *indiano*
ordered wine and began telling the pilgrim cock-and-bull stories" (116,
51). However, Juan *el romero* informs Juan *el indiano*:

> Nobody now had any faith in Springs of Eternal Youth, nor did the story of
> the American Harpy, sold on broadsheets by blind men, have any founda-
> tion in fact. The burning subject of the moment was the city of Manoa in the
> Kingdom of the Omeguas, where there was more gold to be had for the tak-
> ing than the fleets had brought back from New Spain and Peru. (53)

El romero effectively hands *el indiano* a script, the updated folklore about the Americas circulating by word of mouth in Spain. This reversal reads as an allegory of European hegemony and New World narrative dependency: rather than bringing back marvelous tales from his voyages in the New World, the *indiano* learns the urban legends that Europe wants to hear about America. This predicament echoes Carpentier's discussion about the lateness and derivativeness of Latin American narrative, a predicament that "The Highroad of Saint James" addresses in its concluding moments. Tantalized and encouraged by the promised marvels and riches to be found, both Juans decide to set sail for the Americas. To beseech good fortune, they kneel before a statue of the Virgin:

> They looked such a pair of rogues that the Virgin of Navigators frowned when she saw them kneeling before her altar.
>
> "Let them pass, Holy Mother," said St. James, son of Zebede and Salome, thinking of the hundreds of new cities he owed to similar scoundrels. "Let them go; they will keep their promise to me over there." (57)

Years before writers such as the Cuban American Dolores Prida and the Brazilian Jorge Amado would feature speaking saints in their magical realist texts *La botánica* (1991) and *The War of the Saints* (1993), Carpentier employs it here to definitively sidestep an American predicament shaped by European artistic hegemony and the sensationalistic lure of black alterity. The device of making the saints speak formally replicates the baroque and racially creolized world narrative system that yields the *libro de caballería*. Just as that genre derives from Arabic, Germanic, and Greek sources, "The Highroad of Saint James" foregrounds its own creolized narrative sources: the *autos sacramentales*, the performative tradition in which characters from Scripture take the stage and speak; Greek myth, drama, and epic, in which the gods on Mt. Olympus discuss and determine the fates of men and women; and finally the animated Catholic saints of Yoruba-derived New World religious systems such as *santería*, *candomblé*, and *vodun*. Bringing together the literary strategies that give the title to his 1975 essay "The Baroque and the Marvelous Real," Carpentier's narrative pluralism reflects his conviction that "all symbiosis, all *mestizaje*, engenders the baroque":

> The baroque, a constant of the human spirit that is characterized by a horror of the vacuum, the naked surface, the harmony of linear geometry, a style where the central axis, which is not always manifest or apparent . . . is surrounded by what one may call "proliferating nuclei." . . . It is an art in

motion, a pulsating art, an art that moves outward and away from the center, that somehow breaks through its own borders.[33]

With its "proliferating nuclei" that "move outward and away from the center, that somehow break through its own borders," the baroque constitutes a formal strategy of intertextuality that evokes an elusive, decentered world literature not premised on European hegemony but retrospectively located in a heterotopic al-Andalus, in classical antiquity, and surrogated by Carpentier's Havana.

The baroque intertextuality of "The Highroad of Saint James" joins the staging of racialized perception in *The Lost Steps* as crucial frames for the presentation of the marvelous American real. The hemispheric consciousness Carpentier seeks resides, on the one hand, in the mutually constituting yet heterogeneous and stratified phenomenologies of racial difference specific to the history of the Americas and, on the other, in the overdetermined sources of local cultures produced through endlessly recursive processes of narrative creolization extending backward across the Atlantic and Mediterranean down through the deep history of world literature. Heralded as both "precursor and theorizer" of the *boom* in translation and distribution of Latin American writing for North American and European audiences, it is not surprising that other writers share Carpentier's revisionist investment in the marvelous, magical, and fantastic terrain of America's racialized narrative genealogies. Gabriel García Márquez's *One Hundred Years of Solitude* (1967) claims its origins as a Sanskrit, rather than an Arabic, manuscript of the gypsy Melquíades, evoking baroque, pluralist, diasporic itineraries consonant with Carpentier's intertextual gamesmanship in "The Highroad of Saint James." A racially self-reflexive play with perspective structures Julio Cortázar's renowned short story "Axolotl" (1956), that disorienting parable about the relationship of the white intellectual to racial difference, signaled here through the eponymous Nahuatl creature. The floating focalizations of Carlos Fuentes's *The Death of Artemio Cruz* (1962) that collectively document the betrayal of the revolution's egalitarian promise in the end poignantly turn on Cruz's surrogate father, the Afro-Mexican Lunero. These collective revisions of sensationalistic modernist appropriations of racial difference make legible the resonance between the Latin American boom and the contemporaneous revisionist modernism of, for example, Ralph Ellison's *Invisible Man*. Yet, of all the techniques that Latin American literature of the marvelous, the magical, and the fantastic has been commonly perceived to bring to the United

States, self-aware modalities for presenting white negotiations of racial difference rarely get a mention.

As numerous critics have noted, the decontextualization of Latin American writing encourages US readers to overlook such critiques of (neo)colonial hierarchies at work in the texts. Jean Franco has documented Emir Rodriguez Monegal's role, as editor of the Central Intelligence Agency–financed *Review*, in offering the literature of the boom through the depoliticized lens of an aestheticized high modernism.[34] In "The 'Oprahfication' of Literacy," R. Mark Hall analyzes the apolitical discourse of self-help that frames the Oprah book club selections, which have included two García Márquez titles and one by Isabel Allende.[35] Yet perhaps it is the stubborn racialization of Latin America in the United States' market-mediated imagination that contributes most forcefully to obscuring the legibility of Carpentier's critique of white mediations of racial difference. A recent event in US publishing circles indicates the misrecognition of Latin American racial formations that shape the circulation of Latin American literature on this side of the Río Grande/Río Bravo. Alberto Fuguet and Sergio Gómez, editors of the 1996 pan–Latin American short-story collection *McOndo*, tell the story of US agents and editors shopping for new Latin American talent at prestigious writing programs such as the University of Iowa's:

> Well then, the editor reads the three Hispanic texts and rejects two. Those he casts aside possess the stigma of "lacking magical realism." The marginalized writers think they hear wrong, understanding that their writings are not realistic, that they are not structured. But no, the rejection comes from lacking the sacred code of magical realism. The editor dispatches a polemic arguing that these texts "very well could have been written in any First World country."[36]

The situation recalls that of Juan de Amberes, *el indiano*, returning to the metropole from his adventures in the Americas, being told what stories the market craves. The precarious play of dependency and autochthony that Carpentier wrestles with throughout his career continues in the wake of his and his peers' success. The First World–Third World dichotomy invoked by the editor euphemistically codes a racialized division he recognizes as operative in his potential US readership. Sylvia Molloy dubs this racialization the "fabrication of a Latin American 'South.'"[37]

Sarah Pollack masterfully extends this racialization to "the transition from magical to visceral realism" in her study of the translation and reception of Roberto Bolaño's 1998 novel *Los detectives salvajes*, which has reached English-language readers through Natasha Wimmer's 2007 translation.[38] Despite its break with the magical realist formula, Pollack notes how the marketing and reviews of Bolaño's novel evince a set of racialized assumptions about Latin Americans as a whole, inattentive to the stratified racial realities, consistent with the promotion and reception of magical realism as an engine precisely geared toward re-sensationalizing racial difference. Bolaño's novel draws out these assumptions with an "extravagant cast of characters" who "are perhaps even more fantastic than García Márquez's inventions" for being "real."[39] Their narrative trajectories activate, on the one hand, an "adolescent idealism" linked to discursive tropes of the Latin American South as a Kerouackian land of adventure that code white American privilege. On the other hand, the ultimate failures of this adolescent idealism "inadvertently make a convincing case [to many US readers] for societal conformity and, grudgingly, the superiority of Protestant work ethics and values."[40] Pollack's research demonstrates how publishers and reviewers reinscribe a racialized division between North and South:

> *The Savage Detectives* plays on a series of opposing characteristics that the United States has historically employed in defining itself vis-à-vis its neighbors to the south: hardworking vs. lazy, mature vs. adolescent, responsible vs. reckless, upstanding vs. delinquent. In a nutshell, [Domingo Faustino] Sarmiento's dichotomy, as old as Latin America itself: civilization vs. barbarism. Regarded from this standpoint, *The Savage Detectives* is a comfortable choice for U.S. readers, offering both the pleasures of the savage and the superiority of the[ir] civiliz[ation].[41]

Carpentier's work, in fact, directly responds to Sarmiento's categorical rejection of indigenous American culture and his fear that the darker-skinned inhabitants of Latin America will irreparably contaminate the legacy of European culture. From the explicit position of the white "American" intellectual, Carpentier seeks to fashion an antiracist New World aesthetics by radically worlding the recursive streams feeding its baroque *mestizaje*. However, the disjuncture between his own status as white in a Caribbean and Latin American context and his (and others') racialized reception in the United States as "Latin American" obscures their Pan-American explorations of racial difference and reasserts a textual border as bleak as the fences arising from Tijuana to the Gulf of Mexico.

4 Dialectics of World Literature

Derek Walcott between Intimacy and Iconicity

READERS FREQUENTLY BETRAY exhaustion with the critical debates that frame the work of Derek Walcott. Venerable Walcott critic Edward Baugh, recently reviewing four book-length author studies by four other venerable Walcott critics, writes: "None of the studies under review is unreasonable or startling, and, as the general rule, arguments are based on sound, indeed impeccable scholarship. Each has [its] distinctiveness in terms of changes rung on inevitable topics for Walcott criticism."[1] Despite the "sound, indeed impeccable scholarship" of the works under consideration, Baugh shows a bit of fatigue with the "inevitable topics for Walcott criticism," a series of critical oppositions he dutifully enumerates: Europe and Africa; oral traditions and literary canons; provincialism and cosmopolitanism; poetic myth and positivist history. This exhaustion partly flows from what David Damrosch calls "the hegemony of the hypercanon" in world literature, an increasingly consolidated short list of "celebrity authors" garnering major prizes, multinational publishers, reviews, author studies, and syllabus appearances.[2] From Walcott's earliest poetry and drama, his writing has self-reflexively read, fed, and contested this institutionalization of his oeuvre and its "authorized" meanings. His iconic status as a "prodigy of the wrong age and colour," a postcolonial hybrid of the creole Caribbean, highlights the danger—registered in both Walcott's work and the conversations circulating around it—of literary exemplarity taking on the "interchangeability" that Natalie Melas identifies with "the commodity form in its circuit of exchange."[3] Produced as an examplar of the West Indian or postcolonial or Afrodiasporan poet/playwright, Walcott makes legible the material and intertextual processes by which his representations become representative, his example emblematic. This chapter tracks how he lays bare, as well as fashions his participation in, a commodified field of world literature that constantly threatens to reduce his work to its most exchangeable, emblematic aspects. Nonetheless, Walcott recuperates a recalcitrant intimacy in the *longue durée* of world literature, embodied in practices of recitation recursively shuttling, "from hand to mouth," between elite and vernacular idioms and contexts. This "hand to mouth" intimacy inscribes his oeuvre into a transhistorical, transcontinental chain of poetic transmission that stages a suspension of the hypercanonical dialectics that position Walcott as a diasporic icon, or resolution, of contradictions.

A thoroughly drawn interpretive landscape mapping out Walcott's literary production perennially confronts readers. This is a textual effect of the work itself, part of a design that intervenes in its institutionalization in an emergent canon of twentieth-century literature. Walcott's writing seemingly apprehends one of Pierre Bourdieu's arguments in *The Rules of Art*: "The discourse on the work is not a simple side-effect, designed to encourage its apprehension and appreciation, but a moment which is part of the production of the work, of its meaning and its value."[4] Through quite legible cues, Walcott's poetry and drama frame "the discourse on the work . . . its meaning and its value" in ways that produce both pleasure and ennui. Thus *Omeros*, "as much a poem about writing about the Caribbean as it is a poem about the Caribbean," according to Paul Jay, uses the metafictional device of embedded author figures, Dennis Plunkett and Walcott, to animate an explicit exegetical debate about positivist history and poetic mythmaking, imitation and invention, vernacular styles and classical forms.[5] Within five years of the book's publication, Joseph Farrell could survey an extensive body of criticism already rigidly sorted into a set of positions with respect to the question of *Omeros*'s "generic register," an interpretive landscape that returned a weary critical community to an all-too-familiar precipice: "The epic element in *Omeros* threatens to reopen an old debate over Walcott's relationship to the European and African elements in his personal heritage and in the culture of the West Indies as a whole."[6] However, Farrell notes that Walcott "invites such scrutiny" through his consistent use of the "twin motifs of dichotomy and indeterminacy."[7]

Critics thus find themselves ensnared hermeneutically, maneuvered into iterations of the choices imposed upon the poet, staged as early as "A Far Cry from Africa": "Where shall I turn, divided to the vein? / I who have cursed / The drunken officer of British rule, how choose / Between this Africa and the English tongue I love?"[8] The poetry transfers an authorial exhaustion with the "dichotomies and indeterminacies," the

contradictions and their (ir)resolutions, handed down by colonial history and postcolonial ideology. Weariness with these becomes a trope
of the work and of the "discourse on the work." Subsequently, the trope
of stepping outside these dialectics becomes a corollary to the trope of
discursive weariness. Paul Breslin locates this outside literally outside:
"Placed on the scale of nature, the exchange of picong between hegemonic and counterhegemonic discourses appears grotesquely comical,
too petty and obsessed to justify such frenetic gestures."[9] Melas wor-
ries, however, that the scale of nature has become the terrain of a newer,
more urgent "picong between hegemonic and counterhegemonic," that
of tourism. The context of tourism, she argues, supplants the tired "colo-
nial/anticolonial opposition" that has heretofore underwritten Walcott
criticism.[10] Instead, "the interchangeability that tourism's commodification of place endows upon St. Lucia, Greece, and Hawaii," as well as
"the tourist's presence and particularly his or her depropriating gaze,"
makes it "necessary to commemorate a disappearing life in a place that
is on the brink of forgettability."[11]

Melas's avenue of issue from critical exhaustion with the colonial/anti-
colonial dichotomies and indeterminacies "marshals the opacity [and]
incommensurability" of the local, specific, and vernacular in the face of
their tourism-mediated erasure.[12] Ironically, however, Walcott's strategy
to resist the commodified consumption of West Indian landscape and
culture reproduces his approach, articulated since the beginning of his
career, to culturally capitalized metropolitan circuits of world literature.
In his autobiographical poem *Another Life* (1973), Walcott recounts
how in their youth he and the painter Dunstan St. Omer made an oath:

> We swore,
> disciples of that astigmatic saint,
> that we would never leave the island
> until we had put down, in paint, in words,
> as palmists learn the network of a hand,
> all of its sunken, leaf-choked ravines,
> every neglected, self-pitying inlet
> muttering in brackish dialect.[13]

Walcott conceives his poetic vocation as an imperative to "put down,"
with relentless accuracy, the terrain of St. Lucia, which, "self-pity-
ing . . . muttering in brackish dialect," takes on decidedly personified
characteristics. "I looked for some ancestral, tribal country," he writes
in the same poem. "I heard its clear tongue over the clean stones / of the

river."[14] Articulating an ideal marriage of landscape and language that provides a model for his poetry, the punning visual presence of "ton" in both "tongue" and "stones" conjures the French Creole (*ton*, French for "tone") that distinguishes St. Lucia from the other Anglophone islands.[15] Walcott's bardic responsibility to the tones and terrain of St. Lucia—and the *entrée* this formula provides to world literature—frames his early play, *The Sea at Dauphin* (1954). The play's vernacular representation of St. Lucian fishermen engages Irish Revival playwright J. M. Synge's Greek-inspired *Riders to the Sea* (1903), about which Walcott comments:

> Certainly, *The Sea at Dauphin* is modeled completely on *Riders to the Sea*. I have to explain that. As a young writer coming out of the Caribbean, all those models which are obvious, self-evident models didn't bother me because what I had was the same thing Synge had: a totally new language, a totally new set of rhythms, a totally new people in a sense.[16]

Walcott asserts that *The Sea at Dauphin* presents, for the first time, the distinctive vernacular rhythms of the hardscrabble fisherfolk of St. Lucia, the language, landscape, and labor that Melas reads *Omeros* to "commemorate" before tourism's depropriating commodification of place.

Yet the relationship to Synge indicates how Walcott's own "commemoration" participates in a form of cosmopolitan standardization that raises questions about the capacity of these literary representations to preserve a resistant local "incommensurability." Scrutinizing Walcott's claim to have "the same thing Synge had," Michael Malouf argues: "It might be that what he and Synge both 'have' is a similar social position as bourgeois artists working with an impoverished, local culture which has not yet been represented in metropolitan terms."[17] In class terms that lay bare the specifically economic character of this overlap, Malouf points to the definitive transaction productive of Pascale Casanova's world republic—and market—of letters. Tracing this transaction back to the late eighteenth-, early nineteenth-century romantic nationalism inspired by the German theorist and collector of oral traditions Johann Gottfried von Herder, she writes: "The first impulse of writers influenced by Herder's ideas was to embrace a popular definition of literature and to collect specimens of the popular cultural practice of their countries in order to convert them into national capital."[18] What Goethe called *Lokalität* held a latent value that could be rendered into forms recognizable to the centers of literary production, and thereby within the totality of *Weltliteratur*.[19]

The very gesture by which Walcott taps the distinctive language, landscape, and labor of St. Lucia for literary commemoration becomes the transaction that produces the author as yet another iteration in a world-literary series, an emblematic poet of a "disappearing life" caught up once more in the dialectics of influence and emergence. This effort to register singularity that produces a displaced commonality embodies the chiastic structure of repetition and reversal that marks Walcott's entire oeuvre, as David Farrier points out, and also bedevils its apprehension.[20] The rhetorical figure of chiasmus mediates and exposes the critical oppositions, the "dichotomies and indeterminacies," framing Walcott's work. Yet the chiasmus, despite its signifying power in the "picong of hegemonic and counterhegemonic," also exposes aporia that interrupt interpretations of the poet as an emblematic turn in the dialectical reel of world-literary formation.

In other words, Walcott stages the chiastic structure of literary repetition and reversal as part of his hermeneutic snare, a vexing invitation that holds out the possibilities of some sort of dialectic synthesis, sublimation, or resolution; however, local detail ultimately prompts a w(e)ariness toward the whole comparative, dialogic, dialectical endeavor. Two well-known Walcott poems in particular stage the shortcomings of chiastic efforts to address and redress the canon of world literature, "Ruins of a Great House" and "Sea Grapes." In the former, the poet walks the dilapidated grounds of a formerly grand lime plantation:

> Ablaze with rage I thought,
> Some slave is rotting in this manorial lake,
> But still the coal of my compassion fought
> That Albion too was once
> A colony like ours, "part of the continent, piece of the main."
>
> . . . .
>   All in compassion ends
> So differently from what the heart arranged:
> "as well as if a manor of thy friend's . . ."[21]

In these lines, the author weaves fragments of John Donne's "For Whom the Bell Tolls" sermon into his reenactment of Marlow's ruminations on Albion in the opening scene of Joseph Conrad's *Heart of Darkness*: "I was thinking of very old times, when the Romans first came here, nineteen hundred years ago. . . . Sandbanks, marshes, forests, savages,—precious little to eat fit for a civilized man."[22] For the poet of "Ruins of a Great House," the repetitions and reversals of imperial history fan the "coal of compassion," which "fought / That Albion too was once / A colony like ours." The "f" of "fought"—which, following St. Lucian speech patterns, may also signify the "th" of "thought"—marks with an ambiguous local inflection the speaker's conflict between anger and compassion. While the speaker seems to begrudgingly accede to Donne's assurance that "all mankind is of one author, and is one volume," the elliptical ending extends the lingering indeterminacy between "fought" and "thought," rejection and acceptance.[23] The irruption of the vernacular disrupts the resolution offered by the chiastic play of the consolations of philosophy.

Written nearly twenty years later, "Sea Grapes" returns to the consolations of philosophy, this time with Homer mediating the comparison between Old World and New. A prelude to the "Homeric shadow" he would develop and debate more fully in *Omeros*, "Sea Grapes" opens with the poet imagining that "a schooner beating up the Caribbean // for home, could be Odysseus, / home-bound on the Aegean."[24] Alas, "This brings nobody peace. The ancient war / between obsession and responsibility / will never finish and has been the same // for the sea-wanderer or the one on shore." With these lines, the poet self-reflexively stages how and whether the wisdom of the classics should be deterritorialized. As the fates of sacrificed Iphigenia and abandoned Penelope testify, the Achaean leaders' obsession with war abroad violates their responsibilities to families and subjects at home. Likewise, the poet's obsession with the shadow of the Aegean threatens to subordinate aesthetically his responsibility to the Caribbean. Homer, another "blind giant" like his creation Polyphemus, may map out this "ancient war," yet "the great hexameters come / to the conclusions of exhausted surf." The "great hexameters" that name the war between obsession and responsibility "do not bring peace" but reiterate their exhaustion with a war now transferred to the field of prosody. The formal resolution of the poem into a concluding one-line stanza in iambic pentameter betrays a rift between the consoling power of classical forms and the patent weariness with their fraught legacy: "The classics can console. But not enough." Here the poet, who has "learnt to suffer / In accurate iambics,"[25] stages the residual aporia that the chiasmus cannot close between form and content, the Aegean shadow and the Caribbean, Homer and Walcott, Odysseus's ship and "a schooner beating up the Caribbean."

Failure to note such weary aporia falls into the snare Walcott stages, allowing him to be caught up as an abstract, formal entry in a world-literary dialectic, and his work a mere "compromise," as Franco Moretti writes, "of western formal influence and local materials."[26] Returning to *The Sea at Dauphin*, and Walcott's larger appropriation of the Irish Revival, we can see how his work stages and refuses the alienation of "local material" into exchangeable placeholders in a dialectical play of form and precedent. The play represents one day in which Hounakin, an old East Indian widower and friend of the fisherman-protagonist Afa, ends his life while Afa is at sea. When Afa returns to shore and learns the news, he "tears a scapular from his neck and hurls it to the ground," declaiming in a blend of Francophone and Anglophone vernaculars to the priest and all assembled:

> *Mi! Mi!* Pick it up, *père*, is not ours. This scapular not Dauphin own! Dauphin people build the church and pray and feed you, not their own people, and look at Dauphin! *Gadez lui!* Look at it! You see? Poverty, dirty woman, dirty children, where all the prayers? Where all the money a man should have and friends when his skin old? Dirt and prayers is Dauphin life, in Dauphin, in Canaries, Micoud. Where they have priest is poverty. [*The people leave*] Go home! *Allez-la-caille 'ous!* . . . *Allez!* Idiots, *garces!*

To which Père Lavoisier the priest responds:

> You fishermen are a hard race. You think we cannot help you? You are wrong. It is a sacred profession, Afa, the first saints followed your profession, Saint Pierre, Saint Jean. They were hard-headed men too.[27]

Afa bitterly disavows his scapular and the Church as "not Dauphin own," neither of nor for its people. Père Lavoisier doubly refuses Afa's call for local autonomy, not only offering him the Church's succor and comfort, but subsuming Dauphin's Afa to the foreign forms of "the first saints." Overlooking the self-reflexive thrust of Afa's monologue, Bruce King, a preeminent authority on Walcott's theatrical career, reproduces critically the priest's refusal, arguing: "*The Sea at Dauphin* is Walcott's attempt to give St. Lucian life the qualities of Greek drama."[28] This comment leaves aside the aporetic distance, what Melas similarly identifies as the "dissimilation," that Walcott stages between his characters and their literary precedents, a distance that exceeds the dialectical contest between cosmopolitan shadow and local detail.[29]

Walcott seeks discourses of world literature, and world-literary formation, outside such dialectics of influence and overcoming. For instance, he couches his own artistic development in an economic metaphor drawn from a prior mode of production: "I have always believed in fierce, devoted apprenticeship. I have learned that from drawing. You copy Dürer; you copy the great draftsmen because they themselves did. I have always tried to keep my mind Gothic in its devotions to the concept of master and apprentice."[30] Walcott "apprentices" himself to Greek and Irish traditions in order to make himself fit to represent St. Lucian fishermen, not to make St. Lucian fishermen fit to be represented. As an appropriation of Herderian romantic nationalism, the Irish Revival spearheaded by William Butler Yeats provided both strategies and warnings for Walcott's poetics. As Declan Kiberd notes, "In emphasizing locality, Yeats, Synge and Lady Gregory were deliberately aligning themselves with the Gaelic bardic tradition of *dinnsheanchas* (knowledge of the lore of places)."[31] For Walcott, this tradition resonates with the geography of St. Lucia and its local culture. In the essay "Meanings" (1970), he writes:

> There is another strange thing for me about the island of Saint Lucia; its whole topography is weird—very conical, with volcanic mountains and such—giving rise to all sorts of superstitions. Rather like what Ireland was for Yeats and the early Irish poets—another insular culture. Whether you wanted to accept them or not, the earth emanated influences that you could either put down as folk superstition or, as a poet, accept as a possible truth.[32]

Walcott translates the bardic responsibility of *dinnsheanchas*—bearing witness to the symbolic geography of Ireland—to St. Lucia and the West Indies, seen both in his and Dunstan St. Omer's oath cited above and in a section of *Another Life* about Sauteurs, a city in Grenada from which one looks north to St. Lucia. Walcott here demonstrates his "knowledge of the lore of places":

> The leaping Caribs whiten,
> in one flash, the instant
> the race leapt at Sauteurs,
> a cataract! One scream of bounding lace.[33]

In 1650, a thousand Caribs leapt to their deaths from this cliff rather than submitting to European rule. Yet whereas Walcott's hemispheric interlocutor Pablo Neruda, throughout the *Canto General* and particularly in the section "The Heights of Macchu Picchu," uncomplicatedly assumes the role of *portavoz* of the pre-Columbian cultures of the Americas, Walcott questions his own poetic appropriation of place: "Yet who am I, under / such thunder, dear gods, under the heels of the thousand / racing towards the exclamation of their single name, / Sauteurs!"[34] He thus advertises his ambivalence toward the bardic vocation "to put down . . . in words . . . some ancestral, tribal country." Walcott instead represents his calling as an individual agon with local divinities and histories. As Rita Dove comments: "His insistence on the particular and personal precludes any suggestion that he'd like to be seen as a statesman-poet in the tradition of Neruda."[35]

Similarly, Walcott identifies something troubling in the Revival's bardic self-fashioning, namely, its remediation of Gaelic orality. In the work of James Joyce, as Charles W. Pollard and Michael Malouf have documented, Walcott found a model skepticism toward the pieties of cultural nationalism, in particular the attempts to suture Irish identity to precolonial Irish language, folklore, and mythology, which in an essay on the Irish Literary Theatre established by Yeats and Lady Gregory, later to become the Abbey Theatre, Joyce described as "fetichism and deliberate self-deception."[36] We hear echoes of this critique of the fetishization of the folk when Walcott expresses frustration with Yeats's "heraldic and emblematic postures" in his cultural nationalist mythmaking.[37] "Evok[ing] an idyllic peasantry as the repository of the 'national spirit,'" as Casanova puts it, Yeats turns individuals into icons, the latest placeholders in a reterritorialized Herderian practice of sublimating folk orality into national and global literary value.[38] Thus in an interview Walcott warns against "the risk of submitting to the arrogance, to the spiritual vanity of transforming his own people into 'emblems,' of taking a fisherman who may be walking along the beach in Gros-Islet and turning that person, because of one's gift, because of the authority of one's gift, into an 'emblem,' . . . [an] 'epitaph.'"[39] The project of broadcasting local culture through literary form, Walcott recognizes, can too easily liquidate that culture into a cast of transferable fetish objects, emblems, and epitaphs—or, as Melas might have it, souvenirs.

In his efforts to avoid the "heraldic and emblematic postures" of a Yeats or a Neruda, Walcott also attempts to avoid rendering himself as a bardic icon, abstracted from "the particular and the personal." Critics run a similar risk of transforming the poet into an emblem. Evaluating what Baugh calls Walcott's "ongoing fiction of himself," Sarah Phillips Casteel writes: "Walcott's refusal of an inward-looking individualism which values singularity underpins his belief that the artist must represent the collective. As an autobiographer, he sees himself not as unique but as representative."[40] David Hollinger fashions Walcott as a model "rooted cosmopolitan," resolving contradictions and indeterminacies into a "postethnic perspective."[41] Similarly, Jahan Ramazani dubs Walcott "neither a Eurocentric nor an Afrocentric poet but an ever more multicentric poet of the contemporary world."[42] In rendering him an emblem of the West Indian "collective," of "rooted cosmopolitanism," or of postcolonial transcendence, these critics generalize a Walcott for global circulation.

Walcott recognized how the cultural politics of Irish nationalism lamentably fostered Yeats's "heraldic and emblematic postures." As the revived practice of *dinnsheanchas* indicates, the icons of Irish nationalism fashioned and incarnated by Revival writers claimed continuity with a Gaelic orality systematically outlawed and repressed by British colonial rule. While Walcott embraces *dinnsheanchas* in his poetry, he may have found in Joyce's skepticism a sounding board for his own frustrations with the emblematic politics of orality in the milieu of 1970s Black Power–infused Caribbean cultural nationalism. As Laurence Breiner outlines, orality was "doubly privileged by intellectuals": "Creoles (despite their essential hybridity) were associated with the pristine authenticity of the folk, the segment of society least tainted by colonialism. Moreover, orality was regarded as a link to African cultural roots, which were predominantly oral rather than scribal."[43] For Walcott, as for Joyce, notions of "the pristine authenticity of the folk" belie the complex historical mediations by which orality and literacy mutually constitute one another and the symbolic geographies of the nation. In the "Cyclops" episode of Joyce's *Ulysses*, the Citizen touts the grandeur of precolonial Ireland while betraying how his own bardic performance turns on colonial textuality. He passionately and pointedly invokes Ireland's symbolic geography: "the giant ash of Galway and the chieftain elm of Kildare with a fortyfoot bole and an acre of foliage."[44] And later, touching the theme of political economy, he declaims: "Our harbours that are empty will be full again, Queenstown, Kinsale, Galway, Blacksod Bay, Ventry in the kingdom of Kerry."[45] His handkerchief transforms into an "intricately embroidered ancient Irish facecloth" representing "Glendalough, the lovely lakes of Killarney, the ruins of Clonmacnois, Cong Abbey, Glen Inagh and the Twelve Pins, Ireland's Eye, the Green Hills of Tallaght . . ."[46] As Joyce points out through the narrator's pseudo-philological commentary on this performance of *dinnsheanchas*, the resuscitated bardic rite was fueled and enabled by imperial print culture, in particular the mapping of Ireland resulting from the 1824–46 Ordnance Survey. Eric Bulson elucidates this paradox: "The intrusive process of mapping reaffirmed the realities of colonial rule, while simultaneously generating an unprecedented interest in Irish language, culture, history, and custom. . . . Indeed, the ethnological sector of the Ordnance Survey was indirectly responsible for the cultural and national awakening of Young Ireland in the 1840s and into the later nineteenth century."[47] The Citizen's catalogues demonstrate how the cartographic work of the colonial administration has crossed over from antiquarian book knowledge to the raw materials of patriotic oral performance. They point less toward the Citizen as a "pristine" incarnation of Irish orality and more toward the structural position he shares with figures such as Yeats and Lady Gregory, who simultaneously depend on and paper over their debt to colonial textual projects such as the Ordnance Survey.

We hear echoes of Joyce's critique in Walcott's essay "The Muse of History" (1976), similarly exposing how the cultural nationalist aesthetics of orality depend upon the institutions of print culture: "The polemic poet, like the politician, will wish to produce epic work, to summon the grandeur of the past. . . . Yet the more ambitious the zeal, the more diffuse and forced it becomes, *the more it roots into research. . . .* These epic poets create an artificial past, a defunct cosmology without the tribal faith."[48] And elsewhere in the same essay he writes: "It should have become clear, even to our newest hybrid, the black critic who accuses poets of betraying dialect, that the language of exegesis is English, that the manic absurdity would be to give up thought because it is white."[49] Walcott points to the inescapable textuality, from archival research to exegesis, informing even those projects most committed to Caribbean folk culture, a textuality that indexes both the historical tragedies and detours formative of colonial and postcolonial discourse. With his sense that "it should have become clear," he betrays a familiar exhaustion with the reductive oppositions framing Caribbean literary projects. Rather than conceiving them as opposed forces and racialized emblems, it is precisely the sinuous detours, the interwoven dynamics of Caribbean orality and textuality, that enable a worldly cultural practice, a world literature, outside the dialectical play of African/European, colonial/anticolonial, provincial/cosmopolitan, and folk/elite oppositions. As J. Michael Dash writes: "The ultimate aim of Walcott's imaginative enterprise is the dissolution of [such] categories."[50]

For Walcott, the West Indian vernacular context always already bears traces of a cosmopolitan past, muddying up any notion of the Caribbean as the site where pristine origins get creolized. The "archaeology of fragments lying around, from the broken African kingdoms, from the crevasses of Canton, from Syria and Lebanon, vibrating not under the earth but in our raucous, demotic streets" bears witness to verbal itineraries that traverse eras, continents, and media.[51] In *Ti-Jean and His Brothers*, a 1958 play originally produced at the Little Carib

Theatre in Port-of-Spain, Trinidad, a chorus of animals takes the opening stage:

FROG

> Greek-croak, Greek-croak.

CRICKET

> Greek-croak, Greek-croak.

> [*The others (firefly and bird) join*] . . .

FROG

> . . . Well, one time it had a mother,
> That mother had three sons . . .[52]

This scene typifies Walcott's allusiveness. The chorus of animals and insects, the use of vernacular syntax, and the pun "Greek-croak" conjoins the African-derived, Caribbean krik-krak storytelling tradition to the ancient Greek satiric theater of Aristophanes. Often critics stop right there, arguing that Walcott thereby posits "the doubleness of the Caribbean cultural heritage, both classical and folk."[53] Referring to Walcott's play *Dream on Monkey Mountain*, another critic writes:

> Voodoo, song, dance and masquerade contribute both to the sense of an African heritage and help to fulfill demands that Trinidadian arts make use of local props and atmosphere. If the surface characteristics of the play are consciously West Indian, it should be realised that the masquerading, changes of identity, rapid dissolutions of scene and fantasy world owe as much to the example of Jean Genet and conventions of the modern western theatre as they do to a search for authenticity. Walcott remains a cosmopolitan while contributing to the search for a regional theatre.[54]

Both critics praise Walcott's joining together of supposed opposites, the folk and the classical, the regional and the cosmopolitan. Walcott goes even further. He directs us to processes of cultural transmission and exchange that make it impossible to set the folk and the classical, the regional and the cosmopolitan against one another as opposites to be joined. The animal tales that Aristophanes alludes to in plays such as *The Frogs* and *The Wasps* participate in a flow of oral and literary animal narratives reaching from Sub-Saharan Africa through the Near East and all the way to India, recounted throughout in both humble and courtly settings. The legendary lives of Aesop describe him variously as an Egyptian, Ethiopian, Greek, or Syrian slave. Diverse fables associated with Aesop recur in West African traditions as well as in the Sanskrit

Panchatantra and its Arabic version *Kalila wa Dimna*. The history of this latter collection illustrates just how interwoven the folk and the cosmopolitan, the oral and literary can be. Ibn al-Muqaffaʻ translated *Kalila wa Dimna* from Persian into Arabic in the eighth century. It belonged to the *adab* genre, a textual and performative field of wisdom literature entailing "a knowledge of protocol, history, geography, poetry, proverbs, good jokes and entertaining stories."[55] At the Abbasid court in Baghdad, despite their "lowly" origins as orally circulated folk tales, "the prestige of *Kalila wa-Dimna* was immense, and every courtier and court functionary was expected to be familiar with its stories and adages."[56] Upwardly mobile, non-Arab subjects of the caliphate who aspired to be courtiers and court functionaries learned Arabic from *Kalila wa Dimna* and would orally recite relevant stories from the collection at court. The famous classical Arabic poet Abu Nuwas, Persian by birth, rose to the position of *nadim*, or cup companion, through the hybrid oral-scribal performativity of *adab* and subsequently entered *A Thousand and One Nights* as court jester to Harun al-Rashid, recirculating orally and textually from Morocco to Persia as a beloved folk figure.[57]

Walcott, then, does not elevate Caribbean culture through references to Aristophanes. Instead, his references place Caribbean drama in a performative tradition reaching back to the ancient world in which animal stories belong as much to humble evenings around the fire as to the gilded courts of Baghdad or the drama festivals of ancient Greece. Walcott's punning reference to Aristophanes and animal tales demonstrates not only how Walcott's mode of allusion claims for the Caribbean's rightful heritage the folk and the classical, the local and the cosmopolitan, the oral and the written. In what recalls the surrogation of antiquity in Du Bois's rendering of the US South, Walcott demonstrates that often the folk is classical, the local is cosmopolitan, and the oral is irretrievably intermeshed with the written. Walcott's intertextual practice suspends the dialectical contest between such categories, conjuring a world literature made out of the relays between them, out of the way each recursively deposits traces in the other in a *longue durée* of relays across seas and oceans, a multioceanic network that was legible in Hurston as well.

The Sea at Dauphin is instructive for the way it sets textuality and performance, local and cosmopolitan relations to mutually extending work. Walcott faced the challenge of translating the French Creole speech of St. Lucian fishermen into patois for audiences first in Jamaica, then throughout the West Indies and beyond. Breslin cites Jamaican reviewer

Slade Hopkinson's comment that the hybrid patois of the early production he watched is "difficult for the non–St. Lucian."[58] Breslin then notes: "The version of the script that appeared in 1970 in *Dream on Monkey Mountain and Other Plays* goes noticeably lighter on the patois than the version published ten years earlier in *Tamarack Review.* . . . Apparently, Walcott had concluded in the intervening years that foreign readers needed a few more concessions than the earlier version had given them."[59] Multiple aesthetic and political forces shaped Walcott's attention to these "foreign readers" and audiences. Breiner sets the language of *The Sea at Dauphin* within the context of West Indian cultural nationalism, where "the orality movement participated in the politics of independence by reinforcing the promotion of distinctive—and insular—national languages." Rather than "nation language," however, Walcott—in keeping with his support for the West Indian Federation— sought a federation language, a pan-"Caribbean grapholect . . . which balances accuracy with accessibility."[60] As Walcott explains:

> But since one considers the Caribbean—the English-speaking Caribbean—as a whole, as sharing one language with various contributory sources, one must try to find, using syntaxes from various dialects if necessary, one form that would be comprehensible not only to all the people in the region that speak in that tone of voice, but to people everywhere. It is like making an amalgam, a fusion, of all the dialects into something that will work on stage.[61]

In reworking the script of *The Sea at Dauphin*, then, Walcott sets textuality to work to fashion a federationist performance language that would "synthesize a local, island identity with an abstract regional identity which it was in the process of inventing," as Malouf argues.[62]

Walcott's Caribbean grapholect, disseminated on stages throughout the West Indies and the world, models and influences a federation language already in formation by way of interisland migration and the convergence of West Indian speech patterns in the diaspora. Walcott thereby participates in a recursive relay of speech, writing, and performance that echoes the global dissemination of animal stories discussed above. In these hybrid circuits, orality and literacy confront each other not as ideologically freighted dialectical antitheses but as mutually propelling technologies of narrative and linguistic transmission. While Walcott recodes Caribbean orality for worldly itineraries, he does not, after the fashion of a folklorist-ethnographer or world-literary neophyte, transmute a fading vernacular culture into a commodity for metropolitan consumption.

Rather, he operates as an individual node in a non-teleological, recircu-latory verbal network of textuality and performance.

Reading Walcott's poetic function this way brings us closer to that space outside the dialectics of influence and chiasmus, what Vilashini Cooppan calls the "uncanny space" of world literature, "one in which we can understand literary history not in terms of agon's teleological plot of struggle and overthrow between Great Men (and the odd Great Woman, or Great Other), but in the more circular rhythms of a story's 'serial incarnations' and repetitive returns across a global terrain."[63] For as Walcott brings textuality into the service of a federation performance language whose spiritual aims endure beyond the political life of that sabotaged entity, Isidore Okpewho helps us see how Walcott himself appears as a "serial incarnation" of Homer, "with the language of his epics, with their intricate layering of dialects": "This palimpsest arose from an itinerant Homer adjusting his performances to the dialects of many host peoples, or from a harmonization of episodes performed by rhapsodes across regions . . . and especially their [scribal] standardiza-tion for performance at regional or national festivals."[64] Thinking about Walcott as a similarly itinerant rhapsode harmonizing the West Indian dialects gets us out of "agon's teleological plot of struggle and over-throw" and into an uncanny space of "circular rhythms and repetitive returns." He inhabits and carries forth an ancient poetic mediation in the ceaseless relay between textuality and performance.

Such poetic labor resonates with what Walcott has called his "medi-eval mind": "If I were working as a stonemason in a guild, that would be my contribution to the cathedral."[65] Once again Walcott shifts the scale of poetic labor from the hypercanon to the craftsman's guild. A similar shift inflects his reading of Homer: "The *Odyssey* is basically a domestic poem. We have ascribed epic attributes to it because of where we are today, but actually it is a domestic novel about a very small local reality."[66] Similar to Hurston's "neither reverent nor epic" rendering of Moses, Walcott looses the generic guidelines of his source text: "where we are today," he posits, erroneously assigns a white-marble grandeur to ancient Greek culture. As Walcott says elsewhere: "You wouldn't want to believe that Greek statues were painted in the way that Catho-lic icons are painted, or that they had eyes and simulations of lips, and flesh colour, or bright clothes. But Greek statues were not Victorian: they were Asian objects, painted brightly, simulations, in proportion, of actual human figures."[67] Provincializing ancient Greek culture as part of a centuries-long history of the eastern Mediterranean world with its own shifting boundaries, allocations of power, and cultural exchanges taps into that revisionist stream of classical historiography outlined in Chapter 1. It also intensifies our intimacy with ancient Greek culture, bringing us into close, colorful, domestic contact with "a small [but 'bright'] local reality." This craftsman's intimacy transforms the tasks of poetic labor from an iconic shouldering of hypercanonical burdens to a local, individualized layering of stones.

Offering an archive of world literature amassed and assembled through such local, individualized layering, Walcott articulates an artisanal approach to poetic transmission and accumulation in his essay "The Muse of History":

> Each new oral poet can contribute his couplet, [. . .] there is no beginning but no end. The new poet enters a flux and withdraws, as the weaver continues the pattern, hand to hand and mouth to mouth, as the rockpile convict passes the sledge:
>
>> Many days of sorrow, many nights of woe,
>> Many days of sorrow, many nights of woe,
>> And a ball and chain, everywhere I go.[68]

In this metaphor for world-literary accumulation, the canon depends on artisanal and unpaid labor, both of which stand outside the commodified circuit of literary value structuring Casanova's world republic of letters. This "hand to hand and mouth to mouth" poetic labor anatomically implies a relay of textuality and performance, which Walcott stages again in his poem "Forest of Europe." Set in a wintry cabin of Oklahoma, temporary residence of Walcott and the exiled Russian poet Joseph Brodsky, the scene presents two men reciting remembered lines of poetry:

> What's poetry, if it is worth its salt,
> but a phrase men can pass from hand to mouth?
>
> From hand to mouth, across the centuries,
> the bread that lasts when systems have decayed,
> when, in his forest of barbed-wire branches,
> a prisoner circles, chewing the one phrase
> whose music will last longer than the leaves.[69]

The poem evokes the years of Brodsky's Soviet imprisonment, where recollected lines of Osip Mandelstam served as the bread and salt of spiritual sustenance. Such are the key sites of world-literary transmission, intimate "hand to mouth" recitations in a totalitarian prison camp or an isolated cabin in frozen Oklahoma. Apprehending poetry's ongoing relay between printed text and spoken word and back, Walcott works within a discourse of orality and literacy outside the nationalist dialectics limned by Breiner. Orality here sustains the intimacy of poetry, and intimacy sustains the orality of poetry. Walcott says in an interview: "I just hope that I've written a couple poems that someone might recite to someone else. It would be wonderful if somebody, however many years from now, was taking his girlfriend out for a walk on the beach and said a couple of lines that I wrote . . . and that helped him. You know."[70] Even as it may betray a certain sexual politics of transmission, the intimate recitation of verse offers a vision of poetry and orality that eschews nostalgic evocations of the folk or other metropolitan coins of authenticity. Walcott holds to the face-to-face scale of literature, an intimate scale "that lasts when systems have decayed." He comments: "The recitation element in poetry is one I hope I never lose because it's an essential part of the voice being asked to perform."[71] Recitation sustains a recalcitrant intimacy in world literature, not only between lovers, friends, and aficionados, but between textuality and performance, and their uncanny itineraries along which world literature accumulates.

5 Material Histories of World Literature

Intertextuality and Maryse Condé's
Historical Novels

VERONICA MERCIER, the Guadeloupean protagonist of Maryse Condé's first novel, *Hérémakhonon* (1972), announces at the end of her sojourn in an unnamed West African country: "Je me suis trompée . . . d'aïeux [I got my ancestors wrong]."[1] From the very beginning, Condé's literary career foregrounds the vexations of genealogy. Throughout her work, characters track down lost relatives, seek dubious ancestral homelands, and compose uncertain family histories. Meanwhile, her writing discloses multiple sources: autobiography, *faits divers*, historical records, oral and literary traditions. Genealogy thus serves as a preoccupation of the characters and a formal concern of the novels. The genealogical investments, desires, and entanglements at play in Condé's work chart African diasporic writing's revisionist engagement with world literature's own Eurocentric origin story. As metaphor and mode of reading, genealogy propels a demystifying and decentering attention to the narrative itineraries that have drawn African/diasporic culture into scenes of global narrative circulation and translation. Echoing Du Bois in her elaboration of a diasporic world-literary reading protocol attentive to the oscillatory and fragmentary processes of memory and transmission, Condé's work similarly suggests the improvisatory, open-ended possibilities for resignifying genealogical traces and networks. This chapter analyzes how Condé's West African historical saga *Ségou* and *La migration des coeurs*, a Caribbean retelling of *Wuthering Heights*, stage the material histories of Africa and the Caribbean in order to explore two local cultures' imbrication into the *longue durée* of economic and literary world systems. This world-systemic mapping revises both Eurocentric and black nationalist genealogies that repress the overdetermined, multi-directional exchanges shaping what nonetheless remain sharply local articulations of world literature, whether they emanate out of France, Guadeloupe, or Mali. Like Hurston and Walcott, Condé will acknowledge how systemic market forces weigh upon her own local articulations of world literature, laying these bare as part of the deep historical dialectical fabric staged by her writing and reception.

Maryse Condé left Guadeloupe for Paris in 1953 to continue her studies first at the Lycée Fénelon and then at the Sorbonne. She remained in Paris until 1959, when she moved with her first husband to his native Guinea. Subsequently, she lived in Ivory Coast, Senegal, and Mali. After residing in the United States she returned to Guadeloupe in 1986, since that time spending part of the year teaching at American universities and traveling extensively. Her years in West Africa provide the setting for her early novels *Hérémakhonon* and *Une saison à Rihata* (1981) and the two volumes of *Ségou* (1984, 1985). *Ségou* recounts the decline of the Bambara kingdom in the late eighteenth and early nineteenth centuries, in what is now Mali. These two volumes, best sellers in France and commonly taught in the US academy, follow the progeny of Dousika Traoré through the turmoil of religious wars, encroaching European colonialism, the slave trade, and the countless smaller events that shape the lives of its characters. The descendants of Dousika get scattered throughout North and West Africa, England, Brazil, and Jamaica. Some remain in or return to Ségou, the capital city of the Bambara kingdom; many do not. The story of the Bambara kingdom, though, does not simply paint the decline of a static ancestral homeland suddenly shaken out of its equilibrium. If *Ségou* offers a partial, metonymic genealogy of modern Africa and the African diaspora, it does so without leveraging what Edouard Glissant calls "a return to the dream of origin, to the immobile Oneness of Being."[2]

For Condé, as for Glissant, genealogizing always begins in the middle of things, not at a mythical point of origin. For throughout *Ségou*, and her oeuvre as a whole, genealogy is not a thing people have; it is a process they participate in. In her novels, Condé doubles this process at the formal level, where genealogizing involves a creolizing bricolage of disparate cultural materials, "providing," in Emily Apter's reading of Condé's *Creolité*, "new ascriptions of literary genesis, genealogy, and genetic criticism."[3] Misdirection and disorientation mark these new ascriptions, reflecting an irreverent, diasporic poetics attuned to the ostensible hegemony of European literary forms and markets. In an interview with

Françoise Pfaff, Condé frankly (if somewhat coyly) discloses *Ségou*'s sources and principles of composition:

> FP: A historical saga like *Segu* is rather fashionable as a genre. Did you write it to please your readership?
>
> MC: Yes, since it was also a commissioned work. I followed the rules for that type of novel: coincidences, sensational developments, dramatic turns of events, and unexpected encounters. Like everyone else, I had read Alexander Dumas's works, such as *The Three Musketeers* and *Twenty Years After*, as well as many cloak-and-dagger novels. In French literature there is a whole tradition of adventure novels with surprise happenings. . . . I didn't read a single French epic, but I did read a lot of African ones. . . . I also consulted archives and military reports as well as narratives by missionaries and travelers.[4]

Condé's list of sources paradoxically suggests both the artifice and the precision behind her writing: intertextuality troubles claims that *Ségou* is an authentic African narrative; research authenticates the accuracy of her representations. Condé's comment mischievously begs the question of how a market-oriented novel that supposedly relies on the armature of European genres—cloak-and-dagger adventure novels, replete with "coincidences, sensational developments, dramatic turns of events, and unexpected encounters"—could provide such a textured mimesis of African life and history. For critics and teachers agree that *Ségou* is convincing as an African historical recreation. The Cameroonian scholar Cilas Kemedjio chides the French anthropological establishment's self-serving efforts to suggest otherwise.[5] VèVè Clark, Chinosole, and Jean Ouédraogo find Maryse Condé so convincing that they all label her a "griot."[6] And yet, this earnestly awarded title of respect overlooks the implications of her narrative bricolage, depriviliging as it does authenticating sobriquets such as "griot." Condé works to destabilize the logic of authenticity attached to heroic notions of culture. As she says in an interview: "The role of *griotte* just does not apply, because what does a *griotte* do? Praise a given situation, some leaders and their achievements; it seems to me that I am doing just the opposite."[7]

As part of the novels' project of demystifying Africa as a mythical place of origin outside of History, Condé begins materializing the griot in the opening pages of *Ségou*.[8] Dousika Traoré has been called to the palace of the Mansa, the Bambaran king: "At the risk of lowering his dignity he hurried along, waving away the griots always lurking in the streets ready to sing the praises of well-born men."[9] This quotidian portrayal of the griot's praise-singing in the very opening pages of the novel signals a realist, rather than a heroic, approach to representing the griot. In the second volume of *Ségou*, Condé situates this unromantic portrayal within the popular imagination. Complaining about their Toucouleur occupiers, the townspeople protest: "Every day the *talibes* humiliate us and help themselves to our most beautiful women. Our taxes are now so high that if this keeps up, we'll have to start behaving like *guesseres*, like Sarakole griots who obtain gold only through base flattery!"[10] Rather than culture heroes, griots are represented here as base flatterers who sell their insincere words for gold. Griots also appear as court functionaries "who conveyed the Mansa's words to the assembly" (*Segu*, 9). And in another scene: "Lounging on his oxhide, his elbow resting on a leather pillow adorned with arabesques, the Mansa listened with boredom to a griot explaining the problem of two plaintiffs" (*Ségou II*, 325; my translation). Condé portrays the griot in his quotidian functions. This diurnal functionality, along with the ambiguous status of his profession in the popular imagination, deromanticizes the griot and shifts the grounds of African historiography. Condé's revindication of African/diasporic participation in world literature will rely instead on its everyday, material involvement with world narrative systems, rather than a heroic, revisionist historiography.

In the same way that the griot emerges as a material historical figure, *Ségou* embeds the Bambara kingdom in a dynamic material history that contradicts "the immobile Oneness of Being" Glissant warns against. Through the novel's free indirect style, we read thoughts of the Mansa that project the shifting, heterogeneous constitution of the Bambara kingdom:

> He was temporizing because he knew the kingdom of Segu was becoming every day more like an island; an island surrounded by other countries won over to Islam. Yet the new religion had advantages as well as disadvantages. To begin with, its cabalistic signs were as effective as many sacrifices. For generations the mansas of Segu had availed themselves of the mori of the Somono families—the Kane, Dyire and Tyere—and they had resolved the kings' problems just as satisfactorily as the priests. Furthermore, these signs made it possible to maintain and strengthen alliances with other peoples far away, and created a kind of moral community to which it was a good thing to belong. On the other hand, Islam was dangerous: it undermined the power of kings, according sovereignty to one supreme god who was completely alien to the Bambara universe. (*Segu*, 41)

Evoking a dynamic and heterogeneous Bambara history, the Mansa refers to a time frame of multiple generations, during which the various Mansas have depended upon generations of Muslim *"moris"* drawn from generations of Somono families who have called Ségou home. In terms of political history, the "cabalistic signs" of the Arabic alphabet have allowed Ségou to "consolidate alliances" and to join a "moral community to which it was a good thing to belong." The interaction of Bambara life with Islam also marks the body of the Mansa, who was decorated with "amulets made by marabouts—finely worked little leather pouches containing verses from the Koran" (*Segu*, 8; translation modified). Despite this fact of historical transculturation, in the second volume of *Ségou*, we encounter the urge to proclaim "the immobile Oneness of Being" in the descendants of Dousika Traoré. Take Olubunmi, Dousika's grandson: "Olubunmi sensed that the peace and harmony of yesteryear [*la paix et l'équilibre des jours d'antan*] were gone forever, that Segu would no longer be Segu: robbed of a part of herself, she would assimilate a thousand foreign elements imposed on her by her conquerors and end by believing them to be truly her own" (*Children of Segu*, 41). This passage is laden with irony, as Olubunmi's life already embodies precisely the sort of historically produced heterogeneity he prognosticates. To begin with, while he is a Traoré by his father's lineage, his Yoruba mother gave him a name inspired by the promise of a Yoruba *babalawo*: "God will provide" (*Segu*, 311). He was born in Dahomey and "returned" to Ségou after the death of his parents. Olubunmi's nostalgia for a past he never experienced, his evocation of "la paix et l'équilibre des jours d'antan," furthermore, contradicts the historical vision of mixity at work throughout the books, as well as the history of Ségou itself:

> A hundred or a hundred and fifty years earlier, Segu was not numbered among the cities of the Sudan. It was only a village where Ngolo Kulibaly took refuge, while his brother Barangolo settled further north. Then Biton, his son, made friends with the god Faro, master of water and knowledge, and with his protection transformed a collection of daub huts into a proud city at whose name the Somono, Bozo, Dogon, Tuareg, Fulani and Sarakole people all trembled. Segu made war on them all, thus acquiring slaves who were either sold in its markets or made to work in its fields. War was the essence of Segu's power and glory. (*Segu*, 7)

Rather than peace and equilibrium, Ségou's history consists of flight and refuge, war and expansion, and now war and defeat. As we have seen, the foundational construction of "les murailles de terre [the walls of earth]" around the capital does not keep the outside world out: Somonos, Bozos, Dogons, Tuaregs, Fulani, and Sarakoles; Muslims, polytheists, and slaves have entered the walls of Ségou, settled there, borne mixed children, drawn converts, worked in the fields and at court. By contrast, Olubunmi's historiographical desire for the "immobile Oneness of Being" resonates with a more recent one, against which the critic Chinosole contextualizes the revisionary historical outlook of *Ségou*: "By declining to romanticize Segu in all its glory or victimize it in its collapse, Condé departs from her earlier male Négritude models."[11]

Condé foregrounds the instability and flux, the multiplicity and diversity within any particular local genealogy. The multiplicity and diversity at the local level results from imbrication in the networks of material exchange that shape cultural genealogies. Thus, when the book opens, Mungo Park waits on the other bank of the Niger/Joliba River, minarets rise from within the walls of Ségou, and Qur'anic verses decorate the body of the Mansa. Furthermore, Siga, Dousika's son, who has moved from Timbuktu to Morocco, participates in an economic and communicative system reaching from Sub-Saharan Africa to the Mediterranean shores of North Africa and all the way to the Levant:

> Abdallah had recently put him in charge of his dealing in salt. Twice a month he went to Teghaza or Taoudenni with a caravan to be laden with bars of salt, seeing to it that they were properly bound together so that they didn't suffer damage in transit. At those times he ruled over a whole company of slaves, who carried the bars to and from and marked them with black lines or diamonds to indicate to whom they belonged. Then he brought the bars back to Timbuktu and sold them to merchants from Morocco, or even from the Middle East and North Africa. It was hard work, but he liked it. As he supervised the slaves and bargained with the merchants he had a feeling of usefulness, if not of power. He was part of a great system, a grand network of exchanges and communications that extended across the universe [*Il était part d'un grand système, d'un grand courant d'échanges et de communications qui s'étendait à travers l'univers*]. (*Segu*, 120; *Ségou* I, 121; translation modified)

Siga's role in the salt trade echoes his narrative role in *Ségou*, suggested by the doubly significant statement: "He was part of a grand network of exchanges and communications that extended across the universe." The text emphasizes that not only commodities are being exchanged, but communications as well. Siga's plotline dramatizes processes of narrative exchange that knit North and West Africa to Europe and the Levant. He leaves his brother Tiekoro in Timbuktu and moves to Fez, where he works in the bazaar shop of Abdallah, the cousin of the Timbuktu merchant he worked for previously. Fatima, the daughter of Zaïda Lahbabiya, a wealthy and immensely powerful *marieuse* (a woman who prepares high-born brides for their nuptials) falls in love with him, and he with her. Under the irresistible pressure of her mother, though, Siga ends up involved in a sexual affair with both mother and daughter, dangerous liaisons that, were either to learn of the other, could jeopardize his life. In the midst of apprehending this danger, "an old man sat down beside him, dressed poorly in an old burnous and a cap without earflaps." A dialogue ensues, and the old man grabs him and says:

> "Run away! That's the only thing you can do!"
>
> Siga sat down again.
>
> "But what about Fatima?"
>
> "Take her with you. Abduct her. Put the Sahara between you and the mother.". . .
>
> . . . He realized it was an ancestor in disguise who had come to show him what he should do, and a great calm swept over him. (*Segu*, 190–91)

Advised by his ancestor, Siga plots with his friends to abduct Fatima and flee by boat to the other side of the Sahara. These happenings surely provide the "coincidences, sensational developments, dramatic turns of events, and unexpected encounters" that Maryse Condé claims to have drawn from the nineteenth-century French novel. At the same time, however, another source should come to mind, what with the bazaars, the merchants, the lurid escapades, the djinn-like intervention of the ancestor, and the escape by sea—*A Thousand and One Nights*. This compendium of oral-derived tales mediates between Condé's African saga and its supposedly European narrative devices. *Ségou* directly links this mediation to the way merchants like Siga mediate "un grand courant d'échanges et de communications qui s'étendait à travers l'univers." Condé's conjunction of material history and intertextuality channels the crucial role Robert Irwin assigns merchants in the proliferation of "the sea of stories" that traverses Africa, Europe, and Asia. Walter Benjamin, too, mentions the "by no means insignificant share which traders had in the art of storytelling. . . . They have left deep traces in the narrative cycle of *The Arabian Nights*."[12] Condé places Ségou in the thick of this network of economic and narrative exchange, further proliferating the interplay of sources that inform this historical saga.

Condé, we remember, comments: "Like everyone else, I had read Alexander Dumas's works, such as *The Three Musketeers* and *Twenty Years After*." As scholars from Muhsin Jassim al-Musawi and Roger Allen to Roland Barthes and Peter Brooks note, Dumas in turn, as well as his peers and heirs, had read and drawn upon *A Thousand and One Nights*.[13] However, Condé does more than simply show that the European narrative tradition leans on an expansive archive of world literature. The insertion of *A Thousand and One Nights* as a third term, mediating between her African subject matter and her supposedly European narrative devices, decenters the African/European dichotomy. It suggests an overdetermined narrative genealogy that reflects the heterogeneity of Ségou and West Africa that the novels' rigorous historicization announces as well. Furthermore, rather than subsuming diverse narrative traditions into a deterritorialized, universal literary history culminating in the French novel, the novels stage at the formal level a local resistance to such assimilation that refracts Ségou's historical predicament.

By integrating West African religion into its formal and thematic exploration of genealogy, *Ségou* troubles the appropriation of world-literary archives by the European novel, an appropriation that threatens to flatten local narrative traditions into a deterritorialized universalism. *Ségou* challenges the dynamics of plot, character, and mortality often invoked in universalizing attempts to theorize the novel and narrative in general. In *Reading for the Plot*, for example, Peter Brooks writes: "Plot is the internal logic of the discourse of mortality."[14] Reading classic nineteenth-century English and French novels as ciphers for a universalist narratology, Brooks ties narrative dynamics to Benjamin's discussion in "The Storyteller" of reading as a desire for and an encounter with death. Brooks argues that this process reproduces psychically the process of sexual arousal and satisfaction outlined in Freud's *Beyond the Pleasure Principle*. In response to Brooks's influential book, Susan Winnett reads how *Frankenstein* serves as a critique of and alternative to this "Masterplot's reliance on male morphology and male experience." Winnett offers female counterexamples of "arousal and significant discharge" that structure *Frankenstein*, namely, childbirth and breast-feeding.[15] As these acts "force us to think forward rather than backward" because they are life-giving,[16] they question Brooks's proposition that plot necessarily reflects "the internal logic of the discourse of mortality." *Ségou* likewise offers an "alternative model" to the Masterplot of nineteenth-century European fiction.[17] While its attention to the heterogeneity of oral and literary traditions counters monolithic myths of cultural

origins, through an engagement with West African principles of reincarnation *Ségou* also insists that such heterogeneity disrupts the assimilation of local oratures into the European novel form. This mark of
what Melas, following Glissant in her discussion of Walcott, called "the
opacity and incommensurability" of the local, jams its integration into a
"depropriating" universalist narratology and renders instead the specificity of its abundant world-literary relations.

In *Ségou*'s intertextual drama, the djinn-like intervention of Siga's
ancestor constitutes part of the ensemble of narrative devices that links
Siga's plotline to *A Thousand and One Nights*. This narrative intervention belongs to another discourse active in the novels as well: the manifest involvement of the ancestors in the lives of the Segoukaw (people of
Ségou). Chinosole writes:

> [Condé] creates a plot with an intricate system of traps that cyclically enact
> parallel sets of intergenerational and cross-cultural relationships. In this way
> she folds into the narrative the principle of reincarnation—a bad transla-
> tion of a complex belief—described by many scholars as integral to West
> African gnosis. Tiekoro and Muhammad have parallel conflicts with their
> servant brothers, Siga and Malobali, while Nya, Fatima and later Ayisha are
> in conflict with the tragic concubines, Sira, Nadie and Awa. Parallel mis-
> understandings, bitterness, and jealousy get re-enacted in each of the four
> generations depicted.[18]

We could read this "intricate system of traps and parallels" as yet
another way *Ségou* blurs the distinctions between its sources, for as
well as reflecting the principle of reincarnation, not unlike the novelistic devices of Dumas, Dickens, and Emily Brontë, devices that also
recall the "intricate system of traps and parallels" in the series of embedded narratives making up *A Thousand and One Nights*. Intertextuality with the *Nights*, and the structural incorporation of reincarnation,
though, generates a readerly effect not anticipated by Benjamin's discussion of reading novels as an encounter with death. Benjamin writes:
"But the reader of a novel actually does look for human beings from
whom he derives the 'meaning of life.' Therefore he must, no matter
what, know in advance that he will share their experience of death: if
need be their figurative death—the end of the novel—but preferably their
actual one. . . . The meaning of life is revealed only in death."[19] Brooks
comments: "Benjamin thus advances . . . the necessary retrospectivity of
narrative: that only the end can finally determine meaning"[20] By assimilating the *Nights* and the principle of reincarnation into the genealogical

structure of *Ségou*, on the other hand, Condé writes two volumes across which readers cannot know in advance that they will share the characters' experience of death—for what exactly does death signify in a context where characters may choose to reincarnate themselves in a descendant or to reappear as recognizable ancestors-in-disguise? Like the counterexamples that Winnett poses as alternatives to masculine theories of narrative sense-making, reincarnation "forces us to think forward rather than backward." Tzvetan Todorov's structuralist analysis of the *Nights*, "a marvelous story-machine" written under the sign of Scheherazade, similarly yields an "incessant proliferation" of narratives: "Every narrative must create new ones."[21] *Ségou* highlights what can get lost when deterritorializing the *Nights* and other oral-derived "story-machines." For if the "origins" of narrative forms are overdetermined, so too are their futures. Appropriation of the *Nights* into nineteenth-century European fiction constitutes but one of its possible futures: in Condé's historical saga, alternatively, it takes its place alongside the narrative mechanics of reincarnation without either one being subordinated to Brooks's logic of termination.

As if to emphasize a local specificity resistant to appropriation, Condé creates a privileged reader of reincarnation, Koumaré, the fetish-maker (*forgeron-féticheur*) of the Traorés. He interprets the dreams, consults the ancestors, and fashions the totems and taboos of the clan. The totem of the Traorés is the crowned crane, "les oiseaux divins générateurs du langage [holy birds, the sources of language]" (*Ségou I*, 76; *Segu*, 72). Kemedjio thus notes of the Traoré clan: "Their origins and those of the spoken word are conjoined."[22] In this light, Koumaré emerges as a figure of orality who reads the signs of the Traorés to guide and protect them. He plays a crucial role in the process of reincarnation, as we learn after Dousika's son Naba dies in Brazil:

> The *urubu* of death, invisible to the eyes of ordinary mortals, alighted on a tree in the compound and flapped its wings. It was exhausted. It had flown over miles and miles of sea, fighting against spray and air currents, then over dense forests swarming with a thousand different forms of fierce and violent life. Finally it had seen a tawny stretch of sand below and realized that its journey was nearly over. Then the walls of Segu appeared.
>
> The *urubu* had a mission to perform. Naba had died far from home. His body lay in foreign soil and had not received the proper funeral rites. So his people had to be told he was in danger of having to wander forever in the desolate waste of the damned, unable to find reincarnation in

the body of a male baby or to become a protecting ancestor, later a god. (*Segu*, 217)

It is Koumaré who will see "the *urubu* of death" and carry out the necessary rites for Naba, enabling him to reincarnate himself in a male infant or to become a protective ancestor. This mechanism of reincarnation puts us in a strange position as readers whom over the course of the *Ségou* saga Condé has made sensitive to the operation of patriarchal hierarchies. Through her techniques of focalization, readers come to identify with the Traorés; we hope for their individual success and the endurance of their line, seemingly threatened by the historical changes around them. As readers, then, we become invested in the reproduction of male heirs, even as this is achieved through uncomfortable "seductions" that often border on rape or incest.

Ségou repeatedly builds such tense genealogical desires into its narrative fabric. The plotline of Samuel, the great-grandson of Dousika Traoré, offers another example of this. His mother, Emma, proudly proclaims their descent from Nanny's Jamaican Maroons, and in a neat diasporic reversal Samuel leaves Africa to find his roots in Jamaica. Chased out of the Maroon settlement, disillusioned by its material squalor and moral corruption, he is offered food and shelter from an old woman:

> How he would have liked the old woman to recognize him formally and recite [*décline*] his genealogy to him, as in the biblical text: "And A begat B, who begat C, who begat Emma, who had two sons, Samuel and Herbert."
>
> But things happen differently in real life, where genealogies are riddled with uncertainty and error, so that one must sometimes simply choose one's ancestors and stick with them. (*Children of Segu*, 264)

Samuel longs for the genealogical certainty of the biblical text. The narrator's comments mediate between this impossible longing and the privileged genealogical reading of Koumaré, the *forgeron-féticheur*. For not only do individuals engage in a continuous process of "choosing their ancestors," but according to the processes of reincarnation, ancestors engage in a continuous, elusive process of choosing to inhabit their descendants. Desires to read "les récits d'origine"—be they cultural nationalist historiographies, family genealogies, or narrative theories—are necessarily "riddled with uncertainty and error." In the intertextually rich *Ségou*, significantly, only Koumaré knows how to follow the transmigration of souls. Characters like Samuel, who long for the genealogical certainty of the biblical text, remain ignorant of their true genealogies.

So while it is a historical saga, *Ségou* overdetermines narrative genealogies and disrupts genealogical narratives. By placing the Bambara kingdom in a dynamic material context, Condé's novels deromanticize the griot and a heroic historiography of Africa. This move to materially historicize Ségou, by contrast, enacts Condé's efforts—through attention to the far-reaching mercantile systems of Africa and the Mediterranean basin—to include West Africa in world literature's history of circulation and translation. However, *Ségou* dramatizes how West African genealogical practices, both narrative and familial, disrupt the assimilation of local storytelling into a deterritorialized, universal narratology of world literature. The narrative structures of reincarnation stage the cloudiness of retrospection and emphasize the active, impromptu processes of genealogizing we presently participate in: "part d'un grand système, d'un grand courant d'échanges et de communications qui s'étendait à travers l'univers."

Condé's *La migration des coeurs* (1995; English translation, *Windward Heights*, 1998) reincarnates Emily Brontë's *Wuthering Heights* (1847), its title evoking the transmigration of souls folded into the narrative structure of *Ségou*. Like *Ségou*, *La migration des coeurs* allows Condé to comment on genealogical processes, both through the concerns of its characters and through the formal construction of the novel. Also like *Ségou*, *La migration des coeurs* conjoins material history and intertextuality to disrupt genealogical expectations and desires. However, whereas *Ségou* rigorously historicizes the Bambara kingdom, the more recent novel revels in anachronism. Condé writes a novel not just set in but often from within the perspective of the turn of the twentieth century. This antiquated perspective recasts not only *La migration des coeurs'* "postcolonial" relationship to *Wuthering Heights* but also the genealogical relationship of Caribbean and English gothic traditions. Leaning on the same sort of overdetermined, multidirectional narrative traffic encountered in *Ségou*, and excavating the gothic's diffuse and worldly provenance, Condé's text reroutes lines of narrative influence along the lines of global economic exchange and complicates nation-based as well as dichotomous metropolitan-provincial models of literary exchange prevalent in theorizations of literary world systems.

The dedication of *La migration des coeurs* salutes the author of its source text: "A Emily Brontë qui, je l'espère, agréera cette lecture de son chef-d'oeuvre. Honneur et respect! [To Emily Brontë. Who I hope will approve of this interpretation of her masterpiece. Honour and respect!]."[23] This enthusiastic salute anticipates the way "Conde's fiction," as Apter notes, "downplays the ethics of reversal" characteristic of, for example, Jean Rhys's *Wide Sargasso Sea*.[24] Condé's treatment of *Wuthering Heights*, precisely a novel about Heathcliff's revenge, stages a disruption of the narrative logic of vengeance. By not offering "satisfaction" to Razyé, Heathcliff's counterpart, the novel directs readers away from seeking meta-narrative revenge plots between source texts and reversals/revisions. Instead, a spatial and temporal remapping of these texts and their genealogies emerges that decenters and displaces rivalrous analytical axes such as metropole and colony, Europe and its others, offering, like Carpentier and Walcott, a world literature operating through deep historical decenterings and displacements rather than the binary oppositions of recent centuries' colonial discourse.

Conde's protagonist Razyé, named after the barren landscape of the section of Guadeloupe where Hubert Gagneur found him, feels he has much to avenge:

> Why didn't he have a maman like all the other human beings? . . . How could he explain his abandonment? Razyé was suffering agony. There was a time when Cathy had been a papa, a maman and a sister to him [*tout à la fois: de papa, de maman, de soeur*]. Her body had protected him. When he curled up against her he found the softness of the breast and the womb he had never known. (38)

His adoptive sister, Cathy, provides the orphaned Razyé with an entire genealogy: "tout à la fois: de papa, de maman, de soeur." However, after Hubert dies and Justin, Cathy's brother, takes over the estate of L'Engoulvent, he complies with the color-sorting exigencies of plantation society and banishes the dark-dark-skinned Razyé from the house and from the company of Cathy, putting him to work in the fields. Justin hires tutors to refine Cathy and make her a marriageable mulatto. When Aymeric de Linsseuil, a wealthy planter, asks for her hand, he completes Razyé's dispossession. So Razyé pledges to avenge himself on those who took Cathy away from him:

> I must take my revenge. On the man who took the woman I loved and the man who made me unworthy of her love. My plan is all worked out. I've toiled three years in Cuba to have enough money to put it into effect. I'll bring the second man to his knees and if I have to kill the first with both hands, I will. (15)

Razyé focuses his animosity on Aymeric and Justin. Cathy, though, plays a part in the turn of events that dispossesses him of "the softness of the breast and the womb he had never known." She drops Creole, practices her French, and becomes enamored of Belles-Feuilles, the *habitation* of the de Linsseuils corresponding to the Linton's manor house, Thrushcross Grange, in *Wuthering Heights*. Cathy chooses a gilded future with Aymeric de Linsseuil over the wild joys of her youth with Razyé. She describes these two tendencies in her personality as the product of her mulatto psychology: "It's as if there were two Cathys inside me and there always have been, ever since I was little. One Cathy who's come straight from Africa, vices and all. The other Cathy who is the very image of her white ancestor, pure, dutiful, fond of order and moderation. But this second Cathy is seldom heard, and the first always gets the upper hand" (40). Throughout *La migration des coeurs*, Cathy uses nineteenth-century racial discourses to account for her split personality, opposing her atavistic African blood to her dignified white blood. So do the other characters, from her black *mabo* to her dark-skinned daughter. The narrator never intervenes to complicate this psychology, to ironically remind the reader how anachronistic these attitudes are. In fact, *La migration des coeurs* revels in antiquated ways of talking about race. In a novel full of oversexed black men and anemic white ones, where black women are either "Aunt Jemimas" or "Jezebels," Carine Mardorossian observes that the characters in this novel "are notable precisely because their characterization seems to fit rather than disallow conventional stereotypes."[25]

The exaggerated stereotypes of *La migration des coeurs*, though, along with the exaggerated passions, evocations of the supernatural, and bloody violence inscribe a Caribbean gothic continuous with a European, and especially English, gothic tradition. Condé's *"lecture"* of *Wuthering Heights*, rather than "mak[ing] explicit what is latent, invisible, or otherwise suppressed in [the] canonical text," points out what was there all along in plain sight.[26] Susan Meyer's "'Your Father Was Emperor of China, and Your Mother an Indian Queen': Reverse Imperialism in *Wuthering Heights*," Maja-Lisa von Sneidern's "*Wuthering Heights* and the Liverpool Slave Trade," and Terry Eagleton's *Heathcliff and the Great Hunger* read very present "racial scripts" in Brontë's novel. Mardorossian likewise reads a plurality of racial identifications in *Wuthering Heights*, "revealing that it was often through 'racial hybridity' that the Victorian middle class configured and reconfigured the crossings of class, gender, and religious boundaries that they both feared and fetishized."[27] The outrageous racial content of Condé's novel, then, sharpens our vision of the racial content of *Wuthering Heights*.

La migration des coeurs incorporates numerous devices of English gothic fiction and stages their overlapping topographies and mutually constitutive genealogies. By aligning the Caribbean *habitation* with the European castle, manor, or country house, Condé invites us to read common histories of terror and violence. On her wedding night, Cathy ruminates on the history of Belles-Feuilles, her new home:

> Under the crystal chandeliers she waltzed with Aymeric over a floor that generations of slaves, her ancestors, had polished, and the music sounded in her ears like the tears of a requiem. For the house of Belles-Feuilles was filled with the sighs and sorrows of black, mulatto and white women united in the same subjection. Slaves raped by sadistic planters. Mistresses poisoned by a rival and dying in unspeakable suffering at the banquet table. Virgins sold to old men for money and parcels of land. Sisters lusted after by their brothers. Mothers by their sons. A week after her marriage, one bride had thrown herself headfirst from the second-floor circular gallery, and the flagstones in the hallway were still stained with her blood. The servants covered it up with pots of flamingo flowers and red ginger. After slavery was restored by the infamous Richepanse, some Mandingo women strangled themselves rather than go back into irons. And discerning these walls and sighs amidst the echoes of the wedding feast, Cathy realized she was taking her place of her own accord in a long procession of victims. (49–50)

Rather than reading the Caribbean *habitation* as uniquely steeped in blood, these gothic elements recall the sadistic impulses given free rein at Wuthering Heights. And just as *La migration des coeurs* highlights how Caribbean economics ("Virgins sold to old men for money and parcels of land") form part of this gothic weave of sex and blood, Condé's mode of referentiality prompts us to identify the same trends in the English gothic. Indeed, Raymond Williams has tracked the shifting legibility of violence in the English literature of the country house since the sixteenth century. He writes: "It is not easy to forget that Sidney's *Arcadia*, which gives a continuing title to English neo-pastoral, was written in a park which had been made by enclosing a whole village and evicting the tenants. The elegant game was then only at arm's length—a rough arm's length—from a visible reality of country life."[28] In the work of poets such as George Crabbe, Williams finds an attack (albeit limited) on this mystifying exorcism of violence within the English literary tradition. The gothic novel, from Horace Walpole's *The Castle of Otranto* (1764) to Mary Shelley's *Frankenstein* (1818) and J. W. Polidori's *The Vampyre* (1819), goes much further in showcasing the potential for violence in castles, manors, and country houses. Franco Moretti has brilliantly illuminated the role of the economic in what he calls this "literature of terror":

> The fear of bourgeois civilization is summed up in two names: Frankenstein and Dracula. . . .
> Frankenstein and Dracula lead parallel lives. They are two indivisible, because complementary, figures; the two horrible faces of a single society, its *extremes*: the disfigured wretch and the ruthless proprietor. The worker and capital . . . The literature of terror is born precisely *out of the terror of a split society*, and out of the desire to heal it.[29]

La migration des coeurs evokes this European literature of terror and acknowledges the critical scripts, economic and racial, present in that tradition. However, the misdirecting and disorienting diasporic sensibility of Condé's novel also involves key displacements that reorient the lines of influence that would exclusively find in the European tradition the origins of the Caribbean gothic.

Condé situates her novel in a particular moment of Guadeloupean history, the late nineteenth and early twentieth centuries. To execute his revenge against Aymeric de Linsseuil and the entire planter class he holds responsible for separating him from Cathy, Razyé allies himself with the revolutionary Socialist party founded by Hégésippe Jean Légitimus (1868–1944), who would go on to become mayor of Pointe-à-Pitre and Guadeloupe's *député* to the Assemblée nationale in France. Popular, black, socialist agitation against the white and mulatto planter class and crises in the sugar market have generated a state of emergency at the time in which *Les migration des coeurs* is set:

> For over a year it had been one strike after another. . . . The previous week in Morne-à-l'Eau, the workers from the Dubost factory had held their boss hostage for two days and two nights. In Belle-Plaine, the gendarmes had had to use their clubs and left three men as good as dead on the distillery flagstones. Justin-Marie carefully cut out all the articles that dragged Razyé in the mud, calling him the creature of Jean-Hilaire Endomius and Monsieur Légitimus's Socialists, and likening him quite simply to the Devil himself. (134; translation modified)

The newspaper's language echoes the language of *Frankenstein*: Razyé, like the monster, "belongs wholly to his creator."[30] In the anachronistic language of *La migration des coeurs*, furthermore, his blackness makes him, as Moretti writes, "a disfigured wretch" who seeks vengeance against the class that so disfigured him.[31] Through Razyé's racially and economically inflected monstrousness, then, we see the consonance of Condé's text with the English gothic forms that precede it. This consonance once again confounds desires, stoked by both the textual context of revolutionary politics and the paratextual context of postcolonial revision, for reversal.

These contexts, in other words, make legible a narrative logic of revenge, a narrative desire for "satisfaction," that *La migration des coeurs* frustrates. After weeks of strikes and arson led by Razyé, the Socialists under Endomius and Légitimus reach a tenuous entente with the planters. Razyé's refusal to abide by these terms suggests another parallel with Frankenstein's monster:

> "Get the horses ready and take a few men. We're leaving for Petit Canal. I want all that's left of Aymeric de Linsseuil's land to go up in flames this very evening."
>
> Nelson looked surprised.
>
> "That's not what the boss told us. With the capital-labour agreement he ordered us to lie low."
>
> "Yeah, yeah!" Razyé said angrily. "The capital-labour agreement is a load of rubbish. The Socialists are quarelling about it amongst themselves . . . Everything must go up in smoke tonight, I'm telling you." (150)

Razyé disregards his "creator's" entente. He wants his revenge. He will see the cane burn:

> Razyé whipped his horse then set off again at a gallop. Morne-à-l'Eau, with its string of cabins like so many cowpats strung out on a savanna after the rain, was quickly swallowed up by the sugar-cane fields. This was the former land of the Linsseuils, sold to the Crédit Foncier some years before. Their remaining estates covered a loosely drawn square around Port-Louis. (152)

The language here makes something about Razyé's revenge underwhelming. In fact, he seems a bit late. Metropolitan finance has steadily dispossessed the *békés* across the period when *La migration des coeurs* takes place. De Linsseuil lands have shrunk to a pittance of their former expanse, "sold to the Crédit Foncier." In their attacks on the planter class, the Socialists merely exploit the opening that metropolitan monopoly capital had already made. Economics have displaced the scene of revenge. Even Razyé derives no satisfaction from his vengeance: "Since Aymeric had passed on, the revenge he had hankered after was meaningless and he no longer saw a reason for living" (252). As the *békés* migrate in large numbers to France, perhaps he too recognizes the social and economic restructuring that undercuts the revolutionary enterprise of the Socialists, the revolutionary enterprise that would have allowed him to avenge himself on the whole planter class:

> The Socialists clung on to the municipality of La Pointe and won the major towns. They also held the General Council. But the lot of the black folks was no sweeter. The cane-fields continued to go up in flames. The Lebanese hawkers were now making a fortune. Italians off the steamships were chiselling jewels in the back of their shops and the Indians were demanding the right to vote. (342)

Despite extending their electoral reach, in the face of a restructuring of the economic world-system, the Socialists fail to fundamentally reorganize Guadeloupean society, let alone mitigate the suffering of the black population. Refracting both the troubled history of Socialist agitation in Guadeloupe and the ambiguous status of Guadeloupe's own "post"-colonial status, Condé's anachronistic *"lecture"* of *Wuthering Heights* denies readers and characters the satisfactions of a revolutionary revenge plot.

If *La migration des coeurs* frustrates the plot's narrative logic of revenge, it also frustrates a literary historiographical logic of revenge. While situating the Caribbean gothic in dialogue with European forerunners, the text makes clear that it does not depend on the European gothic to derive its exaggerated passions, supernatural beings, and records of violence and bloodlust. Five hundred–odd years of Caribbean history have offered plenty, and *La migration des coeurs* paints popular oral traditions as the bearer of this history. As Françoise Lionnet observes: "Like the Yorkshire author, [Condé] is at pains to represent an oral culture."[32] Echoing the housekeeper Nelly Dean's role as primary narrator in *Wuthering Heights*, a series of *récits* structure the novel that belong primarily to the *mabos*, the fishermen, and the peasants whose lives intersect those of Razyé, Cathy, Aymeric, and their offspring. The novel thereby offers a popular oral commentary on its action, filtering the plot through Guadeloupean gossip and public opinion. In the context of Latin America, Francine Masiello has written:

> It is impossible to narrate the *fin de siglo* without the structures of melodrama, whose voice is found in public opinion and gossip. . . . Melodrama has been described by its linguistic extravagance in the field of realist representation.

In nineteenth-century fiction, it inserts a hyperbolic register into discourse. Because of its extreme bipolarity, it discovers the limits of language and marks the very essence of theatricality . . . it shakes the world of feelings, awakens the audience's taste for horror and exploits its passion for violence.[33]

The context of Latin America is not irrelevant to situating *La migration des coeurs* historically. Not only does the novel open in Cuba, but Lionnet also argues for reading the novel as part of a *"transcolonial* historical circuit connecting distinct but comparable sites of conflicts in which racial borderlines and borderlands have constantly been crossed."[34] With a gesture of spatial genealogizing, Condé uses popular supernatural beliefs to integrate this transcolonial circuit. Mahdi, Razyé's *kimbwazè*, recalls a "reunion" of "the greatest masters of the invisible": "Melchior, who worked in Cuba, . . . Ciléus Ciléas, the Elder, who worked here on Grande-Terre, Déméter the Wise from Fonds-Saint-Jacques in Haiti, Escubando the First from Santo Domingo, and many others" (216). *La migration des coeurs* articulates a trancolonial Caribbean context that presents gothic as a form of racial melodrama, with its "taste for horror" and "passion for violence," proper to the *fin de siglo.* Using gossip, public opinion, and popular supernatural philosophies to mark gothic and melodrama as local forms, the novel unsettles the genealogical indebtedness of Caribbean gothic to the English gothic tradition.

In fact, *La migration des coeurs* suggests that the lines of indebtedness run both ways. We recall Cathy's wedding night and the litany of horrors Belles-Feuilles has witnessed: "At night the old house groaned and shook and resonated with all the sounds of its secrets locked in its dressers and cupboards. Rapes, murders and theft of all sorts" (58–59). This architectural memory of terror does not remain secret, though. This terror has woven itself into the popular oral culture of Guadeloupe, as we see at the manor of L'Engoulvent:

Surely spirits and werewolves [*esprits et volans*] were haunting the room, surely under the bedcovers the people in league with the devil [*les jans gajé*] had folded up their skins and flown through the attic windows with a great beating of wings. Hosannah had only been able to calm the children down by chanting one of those old slave laments [*ces vieilles mélopées*] that the children of Africa used to sing in memory of everything they had lost. (279; translation modified)

The phantasmagoric pantheon of the Caribbean—"esprits et volans," "les jans gajé"—demarcates a local tradition of revenants, of the undead, that antedates the gothic literature of Frankenstein and Dracula. Condé suggests that the experience of slavery produced a gothic imagination, and oral traditions—"ces vieilles mélopées"—constitute a popular mode of explanation and defense. Joan Dayan, in fact, argues that the phantasmagoric pantheon of the Caribbean and Europe derives from oral and written discursive contests in the West Indies over the illogical and contradictory system of racial taxonomy developed under colonial slavery: "The figures of blackness imagined by the white colonialist exposed how unnatural became the attempt to sustain 'natural' distinctions between races of men. This kingdom of grotesques would resonate in later supernatural 'fictions,' rooted quite naturally in the need for racist territoriality: Bronte's Heathcliff, not 'a regular black'; the blood taint lurking in Dracula's not-quite-right white skin."[35] Addressing the popular counter-discourse that inverted the values of the white colonialist taxonomy, she writes: "The gods, monsters, and ghosts spawned by racial terminology redefined the supernatural. What colonists called sorcery was rather an alternative philosophy. The most horrific spirits of the Americas came out of the perverse logic of the master reinterpreted and exposed by slaves who had been mediated to their bones by the colonial myths."[36] Caribbean society produced a host of gothic figures ("gods, monsters, and ghosts spawned by racial terminology") that traveled the lines of exchange and communication from Havana, Point-à-Pitre, and Port-au-Prince to New Orleans, New York, Liverpool, and Bordeaux. Both the legal taxonomies and their vernacular reinterpretations in the Caribbean, Dayan argues, fed the gothic literary imagination.

For this reason, Condé does not need to enact a reversal of her literary predecessor. *La migration des coeurs* does not seem driven by a sense of belatedness, of not having had the first word, of needing to set the record straight. The novel, so fond of anachronism and historical reorderings, prompts us to recognize parallel and intersecting narrative genealogies of the gothic: from Slavic vampire legends to the duppies, zombies, and *jans gajé* of the Caribbean basin that likewise fired transatlantic popular and literary imaginations. Multiple histories of "split societies" soaked in blood draw *La migration des coeurs* and *Wuthering Heights* together. Rather than seeking revenge, Condé's novel asks us to attend to those histories with "honneur et respect." Rather than narrowing lines of filiation, in her hands the genealogical impulse opens outward toward multiplicity and possibility.

6 "Healing" World Literature

Toni Morrison's Conflicts of Interest

IN *LA MIGRATION DES COEURS*, the *récits* of fishermen and nannies provide a popular commentary on the novel's melodrama while connecting up formally with *Wuthering Heights*, prominently marked by Nelly Dean's Yorkshire vernacular. Yet as the Caribbean vernacular reveals itself to be caught up in the world-literary formation of the gothic by inflecting a transatlantic discursive contest over racial taxonomy, the novel points to ways the vernacular exceeds its role as a mark of the local. Its imbrication in global generic and racial formations recall the ways Du Bois and Hurston, Carpentier and Walcott, constitute the vernacular as a site of cosmopolitan accumulation. By treating it primarily as an authenticating local marker, cultural nationalist ideologies of the vernacular—from *negrismo* to Black Power—often serve these authors as a hostile interlocutor threatening their freedom to trace the diaspora's discursive relations scattered across space and time, worldly relations congealed within and indexed by the vernacular.

Similarly, Maryse Condé's 1993 anti-manifesto "Order, Disorder, Freedom, and the West Indian Writer" rejects a prescriptive series of "commands decreed" for Francophone Caribbean writing, from *Négritude* to *Creolité*.[1] Condé positions herself as a writer who introduces chaos to the recognizable order of French Antillean literature. By avoiding sacred tropes of messianic masculinity, contesting mythical geographies of Africa and the native land, and foregrounding women's sexuality and psychology, she claims to strike a note for artistic freedom against restrictive identitarian protocols. Toni Morrison, in her own 1983 *ars poetica*, "Rootedness: The Ancestor as Foundation," by contrast, acknowledges her conformity to "the major characteristics of Black art."[2] These textual markers of blackness include an "oral quality" (343); "the affective and participatory relationship between the artist or the speaker and the audience" (341); "the real presence of a cho-rus[, m]eaning the community or the reader at large, commenting on the action as it goes ahead" (341); and "the presence of an ancestor" (343). And she concludes by noting that "the work must be political" (344). Whereas Condé expresses exasperation at "the tedious enumeration of the elements of popular culture which . . . leaves very little freedom for creativity," Morrison advocates for the cultural nationalism of the Black Arts movement.[3] She expresses an urgent social need to infuse the characteristics of popular black art into the novel due to the loss of "exclusive rights" to black music, on the one hand ("Other people sing it and play it; it is the mode of contemporary music everywhere" [340]), and to the demise of oral storytelling, on the other ("We don't live in places where we can hear those stories anymore; parents don't sit around and tell their children those classical, mythological archetypal stories that we heard years ago" [340]). The African American novel, for Morrison, is a "healing" and "didactic" substitute for the waning functions of oral and performative traditions (340). By these terms, as well as those of the market and the Nobel Prize committee, Morrison, with her well-distributed dreadlocked image, has emerged on the world-literary stage as an avatar of the very ancestor she theorized: "benevolent, instructive, and protective . . . provid[ing] a certain kind of wisdom" (343).

As a world-literary figure, then, Morrison ostensibly embodies the communitarian cohesiveness that "Rootedness" claims for black art, working on the terrain of what Farah Jasmine Griffin refers to as "textual healing."[4] And yet while Morrison's image and texts circulate far and wide as a symbol of what La Vinia Delois Jennings, building off Morrison's essay, calls that "elusive but identifiable Blackness," her novels expansively imagine their kin and kind.[5] While their plots frequently dramatize the quest for a restorative sense of communal rootedness, her formal engagements frequently work counter to the notion of linear, singular descent implicit in the metaphor of rootedness. Morrison's work traverses the vernacular with highly trafficked lines of descent indexing multiple histories and geographies. These formal engagements turn the vernacular toward a different sort of healing than organic rootedness in the local, instead situating African American culture in long-lived itineraries of narrative circulation, translation, and exchange.

In *Song of Solomon* (1977) and *Paradise* (1998), local identitarian textual markers get pulled into geographies of transmission by which the specter of far-flung times and places complicate and disrupt contemporary politics of the vernacular and its modalities of healing. As an instance of what Madhu Dubey calls a postmodern "southern folk aesthetic," *Song of Solomon* has typically been read as the genealogical quest of its protagonist through a cultural nationalist African American symbolic geography aligning the North with literacy, disenchantment, and alienation and the South with orality, magic, and authenticity.[6] This chapter identifies those threads of the novel that not only confound this nation-based aesthetic cartography but radically globalize it. Following textual clues to Africa, Europe, and the Middle East, an alternative to the cultural nationalist paradigm emerges that firmly plants the novel, and African American vernacular culture, in the shuttling, swirling history of world literature's networks and archives. Written twenty years after *Song of Solomon*, *Paradise* explicitly engages that novel's cultural nationalist aesthetics and politics at formal and thematic, as well as local and global, levels. A generational divide amongst the inhabitants of an increasingly sterile all-black town in Oklahoma poses one model of black solidarity against another, pitting nation-based political allegiances against Pan-African spiritual ones. When the town consolidates and regenerates itself through a stunning act of violence that effectively dismisses diasporic spiritual commitments, the novel limns the tragic incommensurability of identity-based ethics, politics, and aesthetics. So while *Song of Solomon* holds out the restorative promise of a nation-based vernacular community but instead unfurls a rhizomatic worldliness, *Paradise* holds out the promise of a creolizing Pan-African spiritual community only to retract into the boundaries of the nation. This ebb and flow between nation and world stages a persistent tension in the literary articulations of the vernacular tracked in this study, caught between its traditional function as a cipher of the local and its reinvention as a nodal archive of the global.

Set primarily in the 1940s through the early 1960s, *Song of Solomon* tells the story of Milkman Dead, the only son of a wealthy black family in an unnamed Michigan city. Prompted by his father, Macon Dead, he sets off to find a horde of gold supposedly hidden many years ago by Macon's sister, Pilate. Following in reverse the path of migration that brought the Deads to Michigan, a twentysomething Milkman visits for the first time the small town of Danville, Pennsylvania, where after Emancipation his grandfather established a farm, Lincoln's Heaven, before being murdered by local whites: "It was a good feeling to come into a strange town and find a stranger who knew your people. All his life he'd heard the tremor in the word: 'I live here, but my *people* . . .' or: 'She acts like she ain't got no *people*,' or: 'Do any of your *people* live there?' But he hadn't known what it meant: links."[7] On the first stop of Milkman's quest for the gold, where he is warmly received by folks who remember his grandfather with admiration, he appears to learn the meaning of a vernacular usage: people. This foreshadows the future of his quest, in which he will piece together clues gleaned from the oral traditions of people he meets along the way and discover, not gold, but his family history and genealogy. It is worth noting the undecidability in the quoted passage above, though: "All his life he'd heard the tremor in the word [*people*]. . . . But he hadn't known what it meant: links." The "it" here refers ambiguously to "the tremor in the word" or "the word" itself. A casual reading (of this scene and the novel as a whole) suggests that Milkman finds comfort in having "links" to his "people." However, the novel will also lead us to wonder whether having links doesn't also cause a tremor, whether these links may not be an ambivalent source of discomfort.

On the face of it, though, Milkman's reverse migration evokes an intimate imagination of his family history, an intimacy rarely achieved in his loveless home in Michigan. Here the old men of Danville reminisce about Lincoln's Heaven: "The more the old men talked—the more he heard about the only farm in the county that grew peaches, real peaches like they had in Georgia, the feasts they had when hunting was over, the pork kills in the winter and the work, the backbreaking work of a going farm—the more he missed something in his life" (234). These old-time memories of agricultural labor and leisure, when measured next to his own occupation of collecting rents for the slum dwellings his father owns, provoke the recognition of an absence in his life, what Susan Willis calls "a meaningless void of bourgeois alienation."[8] Milkman's journey offers him the possibility of a sense of connectedness to language, to kin, and to work. His next destination, the town of Shalimar (pronounced *Shalleemone*), Virginia, will even offer the possibility of a sense of primeval connectedness. The old men of the town invite him along for a nighttime bobcat hunt. Exhausted and out of breath as he listens to the purposeful barking of the hunting dogs, he thinks:

> It was not language; it was what there was before language. Before things were written down. Language in the time when man and animals did talk to one another, when a man could sit down with an ape and the two converse; when a tiger and a man could share the same tree, and each understood the other; when men ran *with* wolves, not from or after them. And he was hearing it in the Blue Ridge Mountains under a sweet gum tree. (278)

Once again, Milkman's voyage south counteracts his sense of existential alienation, providing a deep communion with the natural world. It also extends the drive toward human communion that the novel aligns with his southward movement, allowing him to empathize with his estranged best friend, Guitar: "This was what Guitar had missed about the South— the woods, hunters, killing" (278). The reiterated alignment of the Southern geography with a sense of connectedness leads Willis to argue: "The problem at the center of Morrison's writing is how to maintain an Afro-American cultural heritage once the relationship to the black rural south has been stretched thin over distance and generations."[9]

However, as we will see, Milkman's journey south questions precisely what the contours and contents of that cultural heritage are. *Song of Solomon* signals in multiple ways against reading Milkman's trajectory exclusively as a "return to the source." Thus the critic Wes Berry asks of Milkman's rather outlandish discourse on the hunting trip: "To what extent is Milkman's 'regenerative moment' in the Virginia woodlands a sincere expression of natural mysticism or, conversely, a parody of the American gesture of escaping into the wilds to soothe the wounds of the soul?"[10] *Song of Solomon* is riddled with just these sorts of ambiguities. As Geneviève Fabre says about Milkman:

> Morrison's protagonist is entrusted with the task of putting bits and pieces together, of de/ re/ constructing chronology and genealogy. The use of Milk- man is ironic; this male hero is unimaginative and uncommitted, a reluctant confidant, a poor listener who does not pay attention to words, asks the wrong questions, and offers erroneous interpretations. He is ill equipped for the quest: an imperfect inquirer into a heritage that is cumbersome to him.[11]

Morrison's novel, by fashioning such a problematic protagonist, casts doubts on the entire discourse of returning to the rural South to locate an authentic African American cultural heritage. Thus Gerry Brenner insinuates that the desire to retrieve this heritage is nothing more than bourgeois wish-fulfillment: "Milkman's discovery of his lineage is little more than an intoxicant to gratify his wish for some grandiose illu- sion—that in his gene pool lies the birdlike ability to soar."[12] Yet as Dubey has persuasively argued, the point here is not to suggest that *Song of Solomon*, and the "southern folk aesthetic" more generally, is simply a fantasy of connectedness produced by a postmodern heritage industry. Instead, Milkman, the ironically fashioned mock hero, is peculiarly well suited to revisit the very serious genealogical tropes of African American cultural discourse precisely because he is so productively and comically "unimaginative and uncommitted." An ambiguous character on the threshold of irony and commitment, his anatomy subtly suggests that he derives some of his hermeneutical power from West Africa. Consider Milkman's legs of unequal length:

> By the time Milkman was fourteen he had noticed that one of his legs was shorter than the other. . . . It bothered him and he acquired movements and habits to disguise what to him was a burning defect. He sat with his left ankle on his right knee, never the other way around. And he danced each new dance with a curious stiff-legged step that the girls loved and other boys eventually copied. (62)

And now consider Nathaniel Mackey's description of

> the Fon-Yoruba orisha of the crossroads, the lame dancer Legba. Legba walks with a limp because his legs are of unequal lengths, one of them anchored in the world of humans and the other in that of the gods. . . . Legba presides over gateways, intersections, thresholds, wherever different realms or regions come into contact. His limp a play of difference, he is the master linguist and has much to do with signification, divination, and translation . . . he is the master musician and dancer. . . . The master of polyrhythmicity and heterogeneity, he suffers not from deformity but multiformity, a "defective" capacity in a homogeneous order given over to uniform rule. Legba's limp is an emblem of heterogeneous wholeness, the image and outcome of a peculiar remediation.[13]

While the "curious[ly] stiff-legged" dancer Milkman may be an "imperfect inquirer," he nonetheless clumsily delves into a heritage in which, as we will see below, "different realms or regions come into contact." His mock-heroic quest will uncover a heritage marked by a "heterogeneous wholeness," and it is the heterogeneity of this heritage that constitutes *Song of Solomon*'s "peculiar remediation" of genealogical tropes of rootedness, authenticity, and healing in the Southern folk aesthetic.

Milkman leaves Michigan to find a horde of gold that his father believes Pilate must have left in a cave near Danville. Finding nothing there, he deduces that Pilate must have taken the gold and gone to where she had people. So he heads for Shalimar, Virginia, and is directed to Susan Byrd, an old woman of the town who might know something about them. While trying to glean clues from her about where Pilate may have stashed the gold, Milkman hears instead the fantastic story about his great-grandfather Solomon and the less fantastic story about his great-grandmother Ryna:

"[Solomon j]ust stood up in the fields one day, ran up some hill, spun around a couple of times, and was lifted up in the air. Went right on back to wherever it was he came from. There's a big double-headed rock over the valley named for him. It like to [have] killed the woman, the wife. I guess you could say "wife." Anyway, she's supposed to have screamed out loud for days. And there's a ravine near here they call Ryna's Gulch, and sometimes you can hear this funny sound by it that the wind makes. People say it's the wife, Solomon's wife, crying. Her name was Ryna." (323)

Milkman's genealogy is preserved in the "gossip, stories, legends, speculations" of Shalimar and monumentalized in its landscape (323). Between Susan Byrd's recitations and a local ring-around-the-rosy children's song (the Song of Solomon, to be discussed below), Milkman pieces together his descent from Solomon and Ryna's son, Jake, the first Macon Dead. Milkman's immersion in the landscape and vernacular culture of the African American rural South pays off, not in gold, but in a fabulous genealogy. This use of the legend of the flying Ibos/Africans, as well as the portrait of African American orature as a repository of the cultural memory of the oppressed, has led many critics to argue that the book thus sets up a conflict between black oral culture and white written culture. Gay Wilentz writes:

> In the weaving of this tale, Morrison can be seen as an Afrocentric tale teller who overturns Western Biblical and cultural notions by revealing the legends and folkways of her community. From the double entendre of the title to the mythical, contradictory ending, Morrison bears witness to "that civilization that existed underneath the white civilization," a society in which the fathers soared and the mothers told stories so that the children would know their names.[14]

In a similar vein, Joyce Irene Middleton writes:

> In *Song of Solomon* . . . Morrison's readers observe how literacy, a means to success and power in the external, material, and racist world, alienates Macon Dead's family from their older cultural and family rituals, their inner spiritual lives, and their oral memories.[15]

These critics read *Song of Solomon* as a schematic conflict between Afrocentricity and orality, on the one hand, and Eurocentricity and literacy, on the other. This schema, though, seems to leave no room for the ambiguities of a mock-heroic trickster's tale. For example, the polarized reading of these two critics aligns African American culture with orality more tightly than the novel, neglecting the rich role of literacy in Morrison's representation of African American vernacular culture. Similarly, this reading ironically privileges Euro-American culture in a way that the novel does not. Rather than setting up a monolithic and overbearing white culture that comes to structurally define black culture through negation, *Song of Solomon* provincializes and decenters white culture. The novel thereby opens up a terrain of intertextuality and narrative syncretism—or, in Mackey's terms, "heterogeneity" and "multiformity"—that interweaves the oral and the scribal as well as the secular and the enchanted, in a perhaps more radical gesture than the reversal advocated by the critics above.

Wilentz argues that "Morrison bears witness to 'that civilization that existed underneath the white civilization,' a society in which the fathers soared and the mothers told stories so that the children would know their names." Despite borrowing the quoted phrase from Morrison, the civilizational discourse provides dubious grounds for novelistic exegesis. It entails a discourse of modernity that generalizes black culture as open to enchantment and white culture as decisively secular. Thus, considering the role of flight in the African American imagination, Wilentz writes: "This motif markedly augments the alternative reality of an Afrocentric world view presented in the novel."[16] One problem with proposing "the alternative reality of an Afrocentric world view" lies in the implicit projection of a disenchanted worldview onto white/European civilization and, by extension, readers. Scholars including Gauri Viswanathan, Robert Darnton, Susan Gillman, and Alison Winter have revised the totalizing alignment of European modernity with secularism and disenchantment. Even at the height of the Enlightenment, Darnton writes:

> The progressive divorce of science from theology in the eighteenth century did not free science from fiction, because scientists had to call upon the imagination to make sense of, and often to *see*, the data revealed by their microscopes, telescopes, Leyden jars, fossil hunts, and dissections. That the eye alone could not decode nature seemed clear from scientific observations of mermaids and little men talking in rocks; and that machines need not improve perception followed from reports of fully developed donkeys seen through microscopes in donkey semen.[17]

Rather than uniformly purging the fantastic, the discourses of secularism and science shift—at the level of the individual, ultimately—the negotiated (imaginary) line where reality ends and enchantment begins. Writing about mesmerism in Victorian England, another classic site of white modernity, Winter comments: "Mesmerism was not only ubiquitous but challenging within Victorian intellectual culture, as experiments became catalysts for competing assertions about the nature and seat of intellectual authority."[18] The persistence of occultism throughout the so-called period of modernity, the ordinariness of it even into the present day, should warn us against reading novels through the eyes of an imaginary readership whose racial configurations preassign their relationship to enchantment and disenchantment.[19]

Furthermore, while segregation indelibly marks the social and political histories of white and black in the United States, the realm of the imagination was certainly not impermeable to crosscurrents. In our discussion of the Caribbean gothic in the previous chapter, we saw how Maryse Condé suggests a transatlantic genealogy of the gothic imagination drawing on everything from Slavic vampire legends to the duppies, zombies, and *jans gajé* of the Caribbean, narrative elements that fired popular and literary imaginations. A similar traffic marks the regional culture of the South, where stories of ghosts, night riders, and supernatural animals traversed the oral traditions of whites and blacks alike.[20] This regional oral culture, discussed at length with respect to Zora Neale Hurston in Chapter 2, troubles efforts to align "alternative realities," to use Wilentz's term, exclusively with black vernacular culture.

Neither does Morrison exclusively portray literacy as a force that alienates African Americans "from their older cultural and family rituals, their inner spiritual lives, and their oral memories," as Middleton suggests. The very opening pages of *Song of Solomon* demonstrate how the literate practices of the African American population are consistent with their angular, vernacular parodies of authoritative white discourses. Thus after the "city legislators . . . had notices posted in the stores, barbershops, and restaurants" that "Doctor Street" "had always been and would always be known as Mains Avenue and not Doctor Street," black folks "called it Not Doctor Street" (4). The community stubbornly revises and retains its own nomenclature, not only in speech, but also in writing, in the addresses specified in letters sent via the postal service and in forms registering young black men for the draft (4). Morrison locates the vernacular will to contest authoritative discourse in black speech and black writing. Often, furthermore, this will to contest appears in acts that intertwine orality and literacy. Still during the opening scene of the novel, with a crowd gathered around (No) Mercy Hospital to watch Robert Smith take flight, a bossy nurse orders the young black character Guitar to go fetch the security guard:

"Listen. Go around to the back of the hospital to the guard's office. It will say 'Emergency Admissions' on the door. a-d-m-i-s-i-o-n-s." . . .

"You left out a *s*, ma'am," the boy said. The North was new to him and he had just begun to learn he could speak up to white people" (7).

In this instance, black backtalk relies on a mastery of literacy.

Elsewhere in the novel too, acts of outwitting and evading white authority conjoin a mastery of oral and scribal traditions. Milkman and Guitar get arrested for burglarizing Pilate's house, the first place where Macon suspected she hid the gold (the sack turns out to contain human bones and not gold). At the police station, Pilate dons the minstrel mask and performs a crazy routine "verifying Milkman's and Guitar's lie that they had ripped off the sack as a joke on an old lady" (206). She makes up a story about how the bag contained her late husband's bones, how she could not afford the funeral costs, "so she just carried what was left of Mr. Solomon . . . and put it in a sack and kept it with her. 'Bible say what so e'er the Lord hath brought together, let no man put asunder—Matthew Twenty-one: Two. We was bony fide and legal wed, suh" (207). This biblical reference "astonishes" Milkman: "He thought Pilate's only acquaintance with the Bible was the getting of names out of it, but she quoted it, apparently, verse and chapter" (207). The ruse of the pious, batty, and submissive old black lady dupes the police officers and allows Milkman and Guitar to go home with no further repercussions. The success of this ruse depends on Pilate's minstrel speech as well as her self-portrait as a devout reader. It is worth noting that Pilate had the right Gospel, and she was only off by a couple of chapters; the passage occurs in Matthew 19:6. No one at the police station seems to have had a mastery of the biblical text great enough to contest Pilate's authority, which perhaps comments obliquely on the status of white textual mastery in the novel. Similarly, white textual incompetence results in Milkman's grandfather Jake Solomon obtaining the ludicrous name Macon Dead, the product of a drunken Union soldier's clerical error (18).

The cultural heritage that Milkman's mock-heroic quest pursues, then, does not take shape by defining black orality against white literacy or black magic against white disenchantment. Nor do the novel's references to an ostensibly European narrative heritage dilute the novel into a sort of melting-pot universalism. Instead, the novel's mode of allusion engages cultural diversity through a palimpsestic play of difference rather than through Manichean polarities. This emerges quite clearly in *Song of Solomon*'s, and Morrison's own, dialogue with ancient Greek culture. The Homerically named character Circe worked as a maid for the Butlers, the family responsible for murdering Milkman's grandfather and incorporating his farmland into their extensive holdings. After the crime, Circe hid and fed Milkman's father, Macon, and his aunt Pilate, who were only adolescents at the time. Intertextually figured as an avatar of the sorceress of the *Odyssey*, she lives in the decaying Butler mansion with a pack of dogs, recalling the Greek Circe, who surrounds herself with the beasts that used to be Odysseus's crew. Like her antecedent, this Circe too is supernatural; Milkman recognizes her as an undead "witch": "She *had* to be dead. Not because of the wrinkles, and the face so old it could not be alive, but because out of the toothless mouth came the strong, mellifluent voice of a twenty-year-old girl" (240). The allusion to ancient Greek narrative gains purpose as Milkman and Circe's conversation progresses. Milkman, of course, cannot reveal the real reasons for his visit. He feigns to be merely getting in touch with his family history. Circe knows a fair amount about it. She knows for example that his grandfather's body was dumped in a cave. She also knows about his father and aunt's feud: "Hurt me to hear they broke away from one another" (244). In the context of this story of sibling strife and unburied relatives, Milkman tries to glean the location of the cave, the supposed site of the gold, by lying about his motives:

> "I'd like to see that cave. Where he's . . . where they put him."
> "Won't be anything left to see now. That's been a long time ago."
> "I know, but maybe there's something I can bury properly."
> "Now, that's a thought worth having. The dead don't like it if they're not buried." (245)

Milkman effectively takes up the role of Antigone, aiming to settle a family feud over the remains of a dead relative. The Antigone plot thus functions to foreshadow the transformation of his quest for gold into the resolution of a genealogical mystery that will bring a modicum of intimacy and decorum to the Dead family.

In Shalimar, *Song of Solomon* rewrites another classic scene from the Greek tradition. After the bobcat hunt, Milkman joins in the merriment over his panic in the woods (he was actually fighting off Guitar, who tracked him down and tried to strangle him): "Really laughing . . . , he found himself exhilarated by simply walking the earth. Walking it like he belonged on it; like his legs were stalks, tree trunks, a part of his body that extended down down down into the rock and soil, and were comfortable there" (282). This laughter deepens Milkman's sense of rootedness in the world, and his connection to this community, for it prompts the men to offer him one of their women, Sweet. Pretty and available, Sweet draws Milkman a bath: "What she did for his sore feet, his cut face, his back, his neck, his thighs, and the palms of his hands was so delicious he couldn't imagine that the lovemaking to follow would be anything but anticlimactic" (285). After she bathes Milkman and tends his wounds, he readies to leave to go meet Susan Byrd and inquire about his people: "She said please come back. He said I'll see you tonight" (285). In light of Milkman's increasing sense of rootedness in Shalimar, in light of his wounds, and in light of his being offered a home to return to, the bath scene resonates with the bath scene of Odysseus's homecoming and his childhood nursemaid's recognition of his scar. This scene of homecoming and recognition from the *Odyssey* intensifies the reader's sense of imminent discovery in *Song of Solomon*. For just as Milkman's quest resembles a detective story, in which he attempts to piece together clues about his genealogy and his ancestral landscape, the novel drops intertextual clues for the reader. The allusions to Greek culture help frame and advance the reader's own interpretive detective work about Milkman's genealogical relationship to Shalimar, while also fashioning *Song of Solomon* as a palimpsestic text suturing a rigorous localism to overdetermined, cosmopolitan traces.[21]

And once again ancient Greek narrative provides world-literary intertexts privileged precisely for their own disorienting capacities. Du Bois drew from Greek culture a model of aesthetics and cultural development that rejected European philosophies aligning African American orality with cultural infancy and aesthetic naïveté and European American literacy with cultural advancement and aesthetic sophistication. Building off this revision, Derek Walcott drew on a historical portrait of Homer as a bard from the margins of Egyptian and Semitic empires, fashioning ancient Greece not as the birthplace and centerpiece of Western civilization but as a small place with a *bricoleur*'s big imagination. The character Circe partakes of this bricolage, too, for not only is she a portal to the multiple ancient Greek narratives inflecting *Song of Solomon*, but Jennings has also decoded the textual signs that render her an "African sorceress."[22] This coded Africanization of the *Odyssey*'s Circe indicates the ways Morrison also works within the revisionist tradition of literary historiography of antiquity, imagining Greece and Africa in dialogue carried forth to the present day: "A large part of the satisfaction I have always received from reading Greek tragedy, for example, is in its similarity to Afro-American communal structures (the function of song and chorus, the heroic struggle between the claims of community and individual hubris) and African religion and philosophy."[23] Leaning on the work of Martin Bernal's *Black Athena*, Morrison dislodges ancient Greece from a European orientation, seeing it instead "as Levantine—absorbed by Egyptian and Semitic culture."[24] This recontextualization of ancient Greece sheds light on the overdetermined intertextuality of *Song of Solomon*. We should read references to ancient Greece, or the fairy tales of England and Germany—Rumpelstiltskin (14), Jack and the Beanstalk (180, 184), Hansel and Gretel (219)—not as an appeal to universality, but through a decentered mapping of cultural geographies that have palimpsestically congealed traces in the gestures, rituals, and recitations of the rural South. The novel thus figures African American vernacular culture as one node rhizomatically linked to a sprawling global array.

This decentered, rhizomatic mapping of circum-Mediterranean anteriority opens up broader genealogical terrains of African American heritage than those charted in conventional readings of *Song of Solomon*. Throughout the novel, scenes give way to a certain odor: "this heavy spice-sweet smell that made you think of the East and striped tents and the *sha-sha-sha* of leg bracelets" (184); "a sweet spicy perfume[, l]ike ginger root," (239); "a spicy sugared ginger smell" (335). Alongside Morrison's recontextualization of Greek narrative in an African and Semitic milieu, alongside the very *A Thousand and One Nights*–like plot of a quest for gold hidden in caves, the explicit evocation "of the East and striped tents and the *sha-sha-sha* of leg bracelets" definitively connects *Song of Solomon* to an Arab-Islamic context. Even the title of the book provides a jolt of Semitic recognition and opens up increasingly heterogeneous genealogical prospects for the novel. In fact, Milkman's discovery of his flying African forebear, Solomon, his genealogical detective work that sifts vernacular clues, leads ultimately to an ancestral scene of writing. As Nada Elia's own detective work into Morrison's sources reveals, the Song of Solomon sung by the children of Shalimar rewrites the genealogy of the family of Belali Mahomet of the Georgia Sea Islands. Here is a verse from the Song of Solomon, that is, the ring-around-the-rosy children's song Milkman hears in Shalimar:

Solomon and Ryna Belali Shalut
Yaruba Medina Muhammet too.
Nestor Kalina Saraka cake.
Twenty-one children, the last one Jake! (303)

An interview with Katie Brown, Belali Mahomet's great-granddaughter, was conducted by the New Deal–era Georgia Writers Project and collected in *Drums and Shadows: Survival Studies among the Georgia Coastal Negroes*: "Belali Mohomet? Yes, I knows bout Belali. He wife Phoebe. He hab plenty daughters, Magret, Bentoo, Chaalut, Medina, Yaruba, Fatima, an Hestuh."[25] Milkman's ancestor Solomon is modeled after Belali, just as the lyrics of his genealogy borrow the names of Belali's daughters. Elia also notes that "Belali had authored a 'Diary' which, after much research, was revealed to consist in large part of Belali's recollections of an Islamic legal work written in Tunisia in the 10th century. . . . Hausa Muslims in Nigeria . . . recognized the text as part of the curriculum of higher Qur'anic studies in West Africa, written in a mixture of Arabic and Pulaar."[26] Milkman's journey, which has been read as a "cultural immersion in a black, traditional oral culture,"[27] actually leads him to an avatar of a highly literate Muslim ancestor schooled in the tradition Blyden encountered and assimilated during his own Liberian sojourn. This surprising outcome problematizes African American cultural genealogies that work backward from an inauthentic scribal present to an authentic oral past. It also reiterates the gestures staged throughout *Song of Solomon*, in which the African American tradition interweaves orature and literature while projecting geographically decentered narrative filiations and affiliations. Milkman, the unlikely avatar of Legba, in stumbling upon Solomon/Belali's scene of writing, definitively discovers a "multiform" and "heterogeneous" cultural heritage, where "different realms or regions come into contact."[28]

As we have seen in our readings of Maryse Condé, Alejo Carpentier, and Zora Neale Hurston, these writers invoke Africa not as a monolithic source of African diasporic identity but as a decentered site of creolization where oral and scribal narrative, linguistic, and religious traditions intersect and recombine. Morrison also takes up the heterogeneous signifying power of Africa in *Paradise* (1998), a novel that revisits many of the genealogical tropes of *Song of Solomon*. Set in the 1970s, *Paradise* can be read as a commentary on the cultural politics of the period when Morrison emerged as a writer, and on her own earlier literary production and reception, interrogating the symbolic capital of vernacular modes of identity-making and community formation.

In this novel, Reverend Misner has been installed as the new Baptist minister in Ruby, Oklahoma, an all-black town populated by the descendants of fifteen families that founded the town of Haven, Oklahoma, in the late nineteenth century. In addition to a plague of sterility preventing the birth of new children, trouble has been brewing lately between Misner and the youth, on the one hand, and the "grownfolk," led by the twins Deacon and Steward Morgan, on the other. At a town meeting, one youth gives voice to his generation's position, as it is heard by Soane Morgan, Deacon's wife:

> He said they were way out-of-date; that things had changed everywhere but in Ruby. He wanted to . . . have meetings . . . to talk about how handsome they were while giving themselves ugly names. Like not American. Like African. All Soane knew about Africa was the seventy-five cents she gave to the missionary society collection. She had the same level of interest in Africans as they had in her: none. . . .
>
> Yet there was something more and else in his speech. Not so much what could be agreed or disagreed with, but a kind of winged accusation. Against whites, yes, but also against them—the townspeople listening, their own parents, grandparents, the Ruby grownfolk. As though there were a new and more manly way to deal with whites. Not the Blackhorse or Morgan way, but some African-type thing full of new words, new color combinations and new haircuts.[29]

Misner and the younger generation situate their activism in the context of Pan-African identification. However, unlike Milkman Dead's quest for his heritage, the recourse to Africa does not respond to a sense of rootlessness or an ignorance of genealogy and family history. Quite the opposite. Like the generations that came before, the Morgan twins' generation relentlessly promulgates the vernacular history of Ruby and Haven, the tale of the founders' journey out of the Deep South into Oklahoma Territory:

> The Old Fathers recited the stories of that journey: the signs God gave to guide them—to watering places, to Creek with whom they could barter their labor for wagons, horses and pasture; away from prairie-dog towns fifty miles wide and Satan's malefactions: abandoned women with no belongings, rumors of riverbed gold. . . .

The twins were born in 1924 and heard for twenty years what the previous forty had been like. They listened to, imagined and remembered every single thing because each detail was a jolt of pleasure, erotic as a dream, outthrilling and more purposeful than even the war they had fought in. (14, 16)

So rigorously do the people of Ruby tell and retell their history that Reverend Misner notes:

Over and over and with the least provocation, they pulled from their stock of stories tales about the old folks, their grands and great-grands; their fathers and mothers. Dangerous confrontations, clever maneuvers. Testimonies to endurance, wit, skill, and strength. Tales of luck and outrage. But why were there no stories to tell of themselves? About their own lives they shut up. Had nothing to say, pass on. As though past heroism was enough of a future to live by. As though, rather than children, they wanted duplicates. (161)

To Reverend Misner, this devotion to the old stories promises nothing but ruination: "Soon Ruby will be like any other country town," he thinks, "the young thinking of elsewhere; the old full of regret" (306). While a mysterious ailment impedes the reproduction of new generations, *Paradise* also sets up a generational conflict between competing modes of identity-making. The Morgans and their generation hold hard and fast to the old stories in order to make Haven and then Ruby unlike "all the other [all-black towns Steward] knew about or heard tell of [that] knuckled to or merged with white towns" (5). The older generation insists upon a rigorously stable mode of storytelling and exegesis. In order to channel the "endurance, wit, skill, and strength" that made Haven and then Ruby possible, all stories must replay, "duplicate," the foundational "tales about the old folks."

This mode of storytelling and exegesis, however, merges oral and scribal modes of community formation. After a recollection of their education first at school and then in the army, the Morgan twins think:

They had been first to understand everything, remember everything. But none of it was as good as what they had learned at home, sitting on the floor in a firelit room, listening to war stories; to stories of great migrations— those who made it and those who did not; to the failures and triumphs of intelligent [and great] men—their fear, their bravery, their confusion; to tales of love deep and permanent. All there in the one book they owned then. Black leather covers with gold lettering; the pages thinner than young leaves, than petals. (110–11)

The text seems to create a scene of oral storytelling, "sitting on the floor in a firelit room." The reader assumes that once again the twins are listening to stories of the Old Fathers' "great migration." But then one fragmentary sentence reveals the scene as one of reading and recitation: "All there in the one book they owned then." While the reader may at first want to align Ruby/Haven with the contours and practices of an ethnographically rendered primary oral culture, he or she comes to recognize that the older generation's mode of storytelling and exegesis reworks instead the hermeneutics of Christian allegory. For the older generation, an unbroken chain of reading, recitation, and repetition binds Ruby/Haven to the Bible; every sacred story prefigures and explains in advance every story to come.

The Morgans permit no interpretive deviation from the "past heroism" and "tales of love" that make up the biblically authorized sacred history of Ruby and Haven. As Jennifer Terry argues, precisely the desire to "question traditional narrative and reinterpret" is behind the insurgency of Reverend Misner and the younger generation.[30] The generational conflict comes to a head over the inscription on the town's communal oven, built in 1890 by the founders of Haven, dis- and reassembled when the town relocated to Ruby. As Katrine Dalsgård notes: "While originally . . . the Oven held the dual function of nourishing the community as well as monumentalizing its pioneers' accomplishments, now, at a time when all of Ruby's households have long had their own private ovens installed, it has lost its use-value."[31] Absent its use-value, a struggle erupts over the symbolic value of the Oven. All that remains of the original inscription is "the Furrow of His Brow." Upon the authority of Miss Esther's "finger memory," the elders claimed that the inscription read "Beware the Furrow of His Brow." The youth "howled at the notion of remembering invisible words you couldn't even read by tracing letters you couldn't pronounce" (83). Reflecting their desire to innovate the struggle of the race, they propose reconsecrating the oven with the inscription "Be the Furrow of His Brow":

> "Excuse me, sir. What's so wrong about 'Be the Furrow'? 'Be the Furrow of His Brow'?"
>
> "You can't be God, boy." Nathan DuPres spoke kindly as he shook his head.
>
> "It's not being Him, sir; it's being his instrument, His justice. As a race—"
>
> "God's justice is His alone. How you going to be His instrument if you don't do what He says?" asked Reverend Pulliam. "You have to obey Him."

"Yes, sir, but we are obeying Him," said Destry. "If we follow His com-
mandments, we'll be His voice, His retribution, As a people—"

Harper Jury silenced him. "It says 'Beware.' Not 'Be.' Beware means
'Look out. The power is mine. Get used to it.'"

"'Be' means you putting Him aside and you the power," said Sargeant.

"We *are* the power if we just—"

"See what I mean? See what I mean? Listen to that! You hear that, Reverend? That boy needs a strap. Blasphemy!" (87)

Morrison displaces the critical trope of the struggle between oral and
written memory-making and stages instead an interpretive struggle over
exegetical authority. Ultimately, what underwrites the certainty of the
elders over the faded inscription is not Miss Esther's finger memory or
the vernacular consensus it shores up. Instead, it is the elders' interpretive logic that makes it impossible for the inscription to read, or to have
read, "Be the Furrow of His Brow." The debate over the Oven reveals
how *Paradise* refuses to privilege hearing, touch, or vision—the oral or
the scribal—as stable repositories or guarantors of communal memory.

Ruby's grownfolk attempt to maintain the authority of their locally
grounded Christian allegory, and the expansive Pan-African impulse of
the younger generation threatens their interpretive integrity. The great
irony at the heart of *Paradise*, though, is that the youth's efforts to discursively and sartorially affiliate with Africa, while perceived as an adul-
teration, echoes Ruby's savage enforcement of a pure genealogical filiation with Africa.[32] The character Patricia (Pat) Best, by collating the oral
and written histories of Haven and Ruby, uncovers this unspoken regime
of genealogical purity. Her history project "began as a gift to the citizens of Ruby—a collection of family trees; the genealogies of each of the
fifteen families" (187). Pat then explores the biographical details, filling
in the genealogical chart with the dramatic narratives behind the births,
marriages, divorces, and deaths. Yet as an unseen authority modifies the
annual school play that reenacts the journey out of the South and the
founding of Haven, reducing the number of founding families from fifteen to nine, Pat gets increasingly suspicious of the forces at work: "The
town's official story, elaborated from pulpits, in Sunday school classes
and ceremonial speeches, had a sturdy public life. Any footnotes, crev-
ices or questions to be put took keen imagination and the persistence
of a mind uncomfortable with oral histories" (188). As she probes the
genealogies, she observes: "Each and every one of the intact nine families, had the little mark she had chosen to put after their names: 8-R. An

abbreviation for eight-rock, a deep deep level in the coal mines. Blue-black people, tall and graceful, whose clear, wide eyes gave no sign of what they really felt about those who weren't 8-rock like them" (193). Over two hundred years, the 8-rock families have rigorously maintained pure African bloodlines. Under slavery they chose fieldwork; although it "was harder and carried no status, they believed the rape of women who worked in white kitchens was if not a certainty a distinct possibility—neither of which they could bear to contemplate" (99). However, when they set out for Oklahoma Territory, "the sign of racial purity they had taken for granted had become a stain" (194). Bedraggled, hungry, and with some sick members, the band of freedmen and freedwomen arrived at a Negro town ostensibly looking for more homesteaders. They were turned away because they were too black. This becomes known in town lore as the Disallowing. Patricia Best deduces: "Everything anybody wanted to know about the citizens of Haven or Ruby lay in the ramifications of that one rebuff out of many" (189). Subsequent to it, a subtle regime of color prejudice institutes itself that discourages or sabotages relationships which involve a lighter-skinned partner, while lighter-skinned offspring invite censure and suspicion.

The enforcement of genealogical purity reflects the enforcement of discursive purity. A singular line of descent from Africa parallels a singular interpretation of biblical history made manifest in the story of Haven and Ruby. The Pan-Africanism of Misner's camp would actually make Ruby's biological genealogy and its historical discourse not only parallel but integrated. Nonetheless, the older generation radically divorces itself from Africa. For Dalsgård, this indicates their alignment, paradoxically, with the very white discourse of American exceptionalism: "By molding Ruby's self-narrative in the cast of an ancestral heroic commemoration of the success of the community's founding fathers in establishing a covenanted community in an inhospitable western landscape . . . Morrison invites us critically to acknowledge the presence of one of the most canonical European American narratives—that of American exceptionalism, in African American discourse."[33] Not only do the elders of Ruby refuse to integrate their African filiation with an African affiliation, but that refusal reveals a very unpleasant discursive bedfellow: "the European American narrative . . . of American exceptionalism." Here *Paradise* presents an interesting contrast with *Song of Solomon*. Whereas in *Song of Solomon* a trail of vernacular clues bestows recognition of the Deads' African legacy, in *Paradise* Morrison presents a community steeped in vernacular culture that refuses a diasporic consciousness. In fact, through this persistent refusal, the elder generation of Ruby, and *Paradise* itself, asks: Of what use would such a politics of recognition be to Ruby?

Terry reads the answer to this question in the competing spaces of Ruby and the nearby Convent, the abandoned "Christ the King School for Native Girls," where a group of physically and psychologically damaged women have taken refuge with the aging Consolata, the only remnant from the days of the Convent school. Many years before, Sisters from the Convent on a mission to Brazil found Consolata, a poor street urchin, and smuggled her back to Oklahoma. Now she serves as a sort of Mother Superior to the women. To help them heal their bodies and souls, Consolata leads them in rituals derived from Candomblé. Terry writes: "Not only is patriarchal Christianity re-envisioned, but the African Brazilian religious practices of Candomblé . . . formulate a positive model of New World creolization."[34] For Terry, these religious practices offer "new strategies of resistance" superior to the "patriarchal Christianity" of Ruby. Justine Tally agrees: "The reader cannot help but relate the sterility of the isolationist, class-conscious, 'all-black' community of Ruby to the fecund, anarchic but vibrant inclusiveness of the 'raceless' Convent."[35] The reader may like the Convent way of doing things better, yet that does not mean, unfortunately, that they are better for Ruby. Morrison poses a more difficult problem for the reader.

In response to the growing unrest in Ruby, "the men spoke of the ruination that was upon them" (275). Led by the Morgan twins, they direct their ire toward the women of the Convent:

> The women in the Convent were for [Steward] a flaunting parody of the nineteen Negro ladies of his and his brother's youthful memory and perfect understanding. . . . He could not abide them for sullying his personal history with their streetwalkers' clothes and whores' appetites; mocking and desecrating the vision that carried him and his brother through a war, that imbued their marriages and strengthened their efforts to build a town where the vision could flourish. (279)

Soon a great part of the men and women of Ruby come to scapegoat the Convent for all their ills: generational conflict, stillborn children, sibling rivalries. Lone, Ruby's midwife, recognizes a witch hunt when she sees one: "The fangs and the tail are somewhere else. Out yonder all slithery in a house full of women. Not women locked safely away from men; but worse, women who chose themselves for company, which is to say not a convent but a coven" (276). And so a band of men, old and young, head out to the convent to butcher the women. Reverend Misner thinks: "Their selfishness had trashed two hundred years of suffering and triumph in a moment of such pomposity and error and callousness it froze the mind" (306). And yet, in a classic case of "regeneration through violence," this unjust act succeeds in saving the town. While the townspeople of Ruby, as well as the reader, may recognize the horror of the slaughter, and while the moral balance may clearly tilt toward the Convent, a sort of peace settles over Ruby: "the future panted at the gate" and, at long last, births are in store. Despite a few individual consciences being shaken up temporarily, there are no punitive repercussions (in this world). The men's assault was "unbridled by Scripture," yet the massacre not only confirms but also rewards the interpretive paradigm of American exceptionalism Ruby shares with the Puritans of Salem (306).

The alternative discourses that temporarily challenge this nationalist paradigm, those of Pan-Africanism or New World creolization, in the end fade out of Ruby's collective view. By politically and economically rewarding Ruby for abandoning these alternative discourses of African diasporic identity, *Paradise* disavows the healing promised by the assimilative practices of African-derived, New World religions such as Candomblé. In this, *Paradise* reads as a sort of inversion of *Song of Solomon*, which subtly disavows the comforts of cultural nationalist healing. On the one hand, that novel suggests that African American vernacular culture could ameliorate to some degree the effects of racialized subordination and bourgeois alienation by encompassing the individual in a restorative genealogy. On the other hand, precisely the assimilative intertextual practices of the novel radically globalize this genealogy, displacing orality as authentic origin and bringing readers to a primal scene of institutional Islamic writing. Milkman Dead, rather than finding a singular sense of rootedness, inherits a diffuse, cosmopolitan ancestry always already caught up in transnational histories of circulation and translation. What *Paradise* indexes by way of contrast, however, is that being at home in the world may not cover the costs of making a home at home.

Conclusion

In *PARADISE*, the citizens of Ruby prefer not to recognize "the fecund, anarchic but vibrant inclusiveness of the 'raceless' Convent."[1] The town rejuvenates itself, in fact, through its violent rejection of "the positive model of New World creolization" offered by Consolata's Afro-Brazilian *Candomblé*.[2] *Song of Solomon*, furthermore, never explicitly divulges the scene of institutional Islamic writing palimpsestically embedded within Milkman's vernacular treasure, his descent from one of the legendary flying Africans of Black Atlantic lore. Morrison's novels reiterate a hesitation to embrace the worldly filiations and affiliations that irrupt within the frame of what Dubey discusses as ostensibly "organic communities" circumscribed by a "southern folk aesthetic."[3] Locally rooted vernacular commitments trouble a politics of cosmopolitan recognition, questioning genealogies and histories that threaten to temporally and spatially displace the urgency of those commitments, lost as they might become in a haze of palimpsestic, spectral possibilities.

Yet the persistent possibility of encountering the legible sedimentation of the ancient Nile Valley, of classical antiquity, or of Arab-Islamic learning, the reiterations of this possibility from the halls of Liberia College and Atlanta University, from Harlem and Havana, from the Caribbean and the Mediterranean, attests to African diasporic textuality's quest for a world-literary politics of recognition. So when Blyden encounters the legacy of trans-Saharan and circum-Mediterranean networks in West Africa's textual and recitative practices, he subsequently amends Liberia's Anglophone literary curriculum. As readers of al-Hariri's *Maqamat*, generations of repatriated Africans now belong, once more, to a transcontinental community linked by these *séances*. Such ancient literary networks exert a powerful magnetism, resonating down through the works of Blyden's heirs. Du Bois and Hurston find themselves insistently called to recognize and account for the persistence of antiquity embodied in the hybrid oral-scribal verbal arts of the rural South. Beyond what David Scott labels "the ideological desire to supply a foundational past," Du Bois and Hurston embrace the spectral trace, the uncanny echo, as they apprehend the surrogates of world literature's ages past in the New World figures of the African diaspora.[4]

Fashioning a politics of recognition grounded in philological fragments, suggestions, and possibilities, these authors inscribe African diasporic textuality into the networks and archives of world literature's *longue durée*. Thus Alejo Carpentier, confronting the "neobozalic" assumptions of the Spanish Caribbean avant-garde, locates in the obscure revolutionary script of the Haitian Muslim Mackandal and the secret notebooks of Cuba's *ñáñigos*, hybrid techniques of vernacular transmission that link New World creolization to anterior sites of multiculturalism in al-Andalus. As with his African American contemporaries Du Bois and Hurston, Carpentier's New World modernism listens for how African diasporic discursive practices carry forth and inhabit styles of recitation and appropriation from prior literary world systems "which are not, in fact, past," as Baucom writes. From the eastern Mediterranean of antiquity to Islamic rule in al-Andalus, from Monrovia to the Black Belt to the Antilles, the writers in this study excavate recursive processes of hybridization and transculturation rather than monolithic "foundational pasts." The continuities and correspondences between and across these sites of verbal circulation and exchange, their "sedimentation" in twentieth-century texts, offer a vision of contemporary cosmopolitanism historiographically loosened from the tectonic blocks and developmental schema mapped out by colonial discourses of culture and civilization.

The twentieth-century world market for literature inherits these latter discourses, framing writers of the African diaspora through their reified dialectic categories. Derek Walcott's self-narration as a poetic agent of primitive accumulation, newly preparing the singular landscape, language, and labor of St. Lucia for global consumption, stages the discursive power of Eurocentric teleologies of world-literary formation. However, this nation-oriented paradigm of literary alchemy, refining the raw specificities of local traditions into metropolitan cultural capital, paradoxically renders abstract the individual author, making him or her a chiastic icon in a dialectical progression turning around colonial antinomies. In the intimate spaces of recitation, though, in the embodied practice of "hand to mouth" transmission, Walcott designates an alternative logic of world literature, a recognition of poetic form not as emblematic of a political formation, but poetic form as the transhistorical accumulation in "the voice being asked to perform." Traces deposited in even the humblest of voices, in the most autochthonous of performances, reveal cosmopolitan itineraries that radically displace the modern as the moment of worldly arrival or irruption.

These hybrid traces, then, index the long material histories cutting across the "widely dispersed and heterogeneous sociocultural formations" now integrated, Mufti argues, into "a global ensemble" called literature.[5] Maryse Condé embraces the precariousness of this integration, excavating riddles and uncertainties that evacuate the authority of hegemonic discourses of literary history. Archaeologies of the popular, the volumes of *Ségou* and *La migration des coeurs* invite readers to recognize the intertextual, palimpsestic layers of the page-turner's generic devices. From the adventure novel to the gothic romance, Condé's novels foreground the world-economic imbrication of local narrative forms, a helical intertwining of economics and narrative that decenters Eurocentric literary historiography and narratology. As the circuits of world trade disseminate the devices and tropes of *A Thousand and One Nights* and the gothic romance, these material histories supplant chronologies of literary formation that privilege the European novel form as a vehicle of world-literary transcendence, assimilating the world's narrative traditions and authorizing a universal narratology. Condé instead offers a literary historiography attuned to the multiple histories and futures of narrative forms, some recursively deterritorializable but some, like the genealogies Koumaré chronicled, whose recalcitrant specificities insist on their unassimilability.

In Morrison's genealogical novels *Song of Solomon* and *Paradise*, she apprehends the stakes of this tension between deterritorialization and unassimilability as the possibility of a "healing." Staging the hesitation to recognize the call of ex-centric filiations and affiliations, she offers a surface romance of origins whose chronological degree zero is the end of New World slavery. Yet the genre of romance, with its promise of resolution—like epic's generic promise of a stable foundation in *The Quest of the Silver Fleece*, *Moses, Man of the Mountain*, and *Omeros*—undergoes a diasporic reconfiguration.[6] Patterns, codes, and allusions from the Old World haunt her novels, and invitations to Pan-African identification and hemispheric creolization are held out, yet "regeneration" stubbornly transpires on local grounds. Morrison seems to suggest that a further scattering into rhizomatic itineraries holds little promise to redress the displacements of geography her characters must overcome.

At the same time, the subtle pulsings of these rhizomatic itineraries, their suggestions of alternative histories and parallel presents, their methods of writing diasporic subjects into world history, heed a call for recognition as well. In her recuperation of classical antiquity as a narrative interlocutor, an access point to conversations imagined between Greece and Africa, Morrison credits the literary as a space of historiographical possibility responsive to the urgent "healing" and "didactic" demands of the novel. For these calls for world-literary recognition offer histories and geographies attentive to how the New World is inscribed into the ongoing production of what Earl Lewis calls its "overlapping diasporas."[7]

Instructively conjoining the transatlantic African diaspora, the Nubian diaspora, and the Greek diaspora, Nubian-Egyptian author Idris 'Ali's 1993 *Dongola: A Novel of Nubia* reaches spatially across the Atlantic to Richard Wright's *Native Son* while reaching back in history to the Phoenician Heliodorus's fourth-century AD Hellenistic romance *Aithiopika*. These divergent intertextual engagements ground *Dongola*'s heterogeneous solidarity with African and Greek diasporas on world literature's slender networks and far-flung archives outlined throughout this book. In narrating Awad Shalali's story against the drowning of Nubia beneath the "water reservoir for the north" created by Egypt's Aswan High Dam, *Dongola* evokes a host of devices and elements from Wright's life and work.[8] A scribal witness to the rural folk traditions of a population consigned to agriculture and servitude, Shalali, like the Wright of *Twelve Million Black Voices: A Folk History of the Negro in the United States* (1941), chafes at the conflicted politics of a national Communist party that continually sidelines the priorities of its black internal minority, before, again like Wright, seeking exile in Europe. 'Ali, who reappropriates for Nubia the biblical language of "scattering" and "exodus" (*Dongola*, 26, 59) that Wright too uses to link the transatlantic African diaspora to the workers of the world, punctuates Shalali's story with familiar figures from *Native Son*.[9] Simone, the sexually alluring white leftist, recalls Mary Dalton, while Mrs. Dalton's blindness gets transferred to Shalali's mother. Through such correspondences, *Dongola* articulates the Nubian diaspora with the transatlantic African diaspora, a literary call for diasporic recognition across time, space, and language, a call made more difficult to heed after the demise of proletarian literature's global mediating mechanisms, sustained for years by Soviet publishing houses.

If the contingency of world-literary networks obstruct the legibility of *Dongola*'s call to Wright, linguistic and disciplinary borders threaten to obstruct the commonly conjured ancestry of *Dongola* and the New World African diasporic literary tradition shared through Heliodorus's *Aithiopika*. Written in Greek by a Phoenician, covering a geography from Delphi to the Nile Delta, Memphis to Meroë, from a narrative perspective that assumes Homer was Egyptian, *Aithiopika* textually embodies those hybrid networks and archives Du Bois would reclaim sixteen hundred years later.[10] While not nearly as canonical as Homer, "Heliodorus," nonetheless, "was a favourite from Elizabeth's reign to the close of the seventeenth century. Shakespeare knew him, and read him, you may be certain, in Underdowne's version."[11] Lady Anna Letitia (Aikin) Barbauld's 1810 "On the Origin and Progress of Novel-Writing" would prominently inventory Heliodorus in her worldly genealogy of the novel, privileging "The East [as] emphatically the country of invention."[12] Reverend Rowland Smith would offer English readers a new translation in 1855, and in 1902 Pauline Hopkins would begin knitting allusions to Heliodorus into her serialized novel *Of One Blood, or The Hidden Self*. Awad Shalali stumbles into the plot of *Aithiopika* when "Good fortune led him to a rich Greek who was part owner of a beautiful ship. This man [who] had first made money in Alexandria . . . knew the Nubian homeland, and knew some of the Nubian language, and he pronounced it perfectly" (*Dongola*, 72). Displaced and literally at sea, the Greek offers Shalali diasporic recognition by reciprocating a nostalgia for Nubia that also bears witness to "the exodus of the Greek community from Egypt" intensified by the Suez War of 1956 and Gamal Abdel Nasser's Egyptianization laws of 1957.[13] Not merely testifying to the "overlapping diasporas" of recent history, this scene intertextually invokes an ancient diasporic scene of the hybrid eastern Mediterranean. Collapsing historical epochs, this solidarity between Greek and Nubian reanimates the romance of Chariclea, heiress to the throne of Meroë whose mother, Queen Persina, hurried her out of the kingdom upon seeing she was born white, "which couler is strange amonge the Aethiopians": "I knewe the reason, because I looked upon the picture of Andromeda naked, while my husband had to do with me."[14] Adopted by a series of Greek priests, the chaste Chariclea—"How farre she was from her Countrey, and was now called daughter by a false name, whereas shee had lost her naturall Countrey soyle, and royall bloud of Aethiopia!" (109)—lived as a priestess at Delphi, in ignorance of her origins, until the oracle prophesied her homecoming along with her beloved, the noble and chaste Thessalian descendant of Achilles, Theagenes. After "bloodthirsty pirates and armed men, caves and ambushes, dreams and visions, burnings, poisonings, and sudden death, battle and rapine,"[15] the couple arrives as prisoners of war in Meroë, bound to be sacrificed to the gods of the Sun and Moon. When Chariclea unfurls her fascia, in which her mother narrates her true genealogy, and reveals her possession of the magical ring Pantarbe, King Hydaspes "did not onely suffer him selfe to be perswaded that he was a father, but was also affected like a father: so that, when he saw Persina fell with her daughter, hee tooke her up, embraced Cariclia, and with teares, as with an offering, made a fatherly league with her" (271). This story of homecoming and recognition across the color line forms part of the palimpsestic work 'Ali's *Dongola* performs, excavating the histories, genealogies, and solidarities of "a forgotten land, which the world had erased from its map, to serve as a reservoir for its water" (24).

Triangulated between Wright and 'Ali, New World and Nubian diasporas, however, the scattered invocations of Heliodorus retrospectively recuperate a shared terrain of world literature. Dependent on readers or translations that may never come, though, world literature's accumulated archives and fragile networks contend with linguistic, economic, political, and disciplinary forces that constantly threaten to foreclose or dismiss the diasporic recognitions they figure. Yet a world literature attuned to "whoever may chance to receive this paper," a world literature imagined from the historical and historiographical exigencies of overlapping African diasporas, may yet keep them possible.

Notes

Introduction

1. Garvey, "A Talk with Afro-West Indians," 57.
2. Goethe and Eckermann, *Conversations*, 265–66 (translation modified).
3. Ibid., 227; Damrosch, *What Is World Literature*, 3.
4. Quoted in Strich, *Goethe and World Literature*, 32.
5. Quoted in Schulz and Rhein, *Comparative Literature: The Early Years*, 11; Strich, *Goethe and World Literature*, 5.
6. Marx and Engels, *Communist Manifesto*, 476–77.
7. Blyden, "Arabic Manuscript," 71.
8. Trumpener, *Bardic Nationalism*, xiii.
9. Blyden, "Arabic Manuscript," 71.
10. Al-Hariri appears, for example, in Omar ibn Sa'id's 1819 letter. See Hunwick, "I Wish to Be Seen in Our Land Called Afrika," 63–65. Blyden, "Arabic Manuscript," 72.
11. "A Letter from the King of Musadu," 134–35.
12. See Holt, "Narrative and the Reading Public in 1870s Beirut."
13. Blyden, "Arabic Manuscript," 73.
14. Mufti, "Orientalism and the Institution of World Literatures," 465–66. See also Hoesel-Uhlig, "Changing Fields."
15. Blyden, "Arabic Manuscript," 69–70.
16. Ibid., 96.
17. Hoesel-Uhlig, "Changing Fields," 39.
18. Douglass, "Claims of the Negro Ethnologically Considered," 285.
19. Roach, *Cities of the Dead*, 45.
20. Cf. Dimock, *Through Other Continents*, 5.
21. Jameson, *Political Unconscious*, 141.
22. Baucom, *Specters of the Atlantic*, 20.
23. Jameson, *Political Unconscious*, 141.
24. Gilroy, *Black Atlantic*, 197, 212.
25. Benjamin, "Theses on the Philosophy of History," 262; Hartman, "Time of Slavery," 768, 772.

26. Scott, "Archaeologies of Black Memory," vi.

27. Mufti, "Orientalism and the Institution of World Literatures," 466; Glissant, *Poetics of Relation*, 7; Walcott, *The Antilles: Fragments of Epic Memory*, unpaged.

28. Moretti, *Atlas of the European Novel*, 194–95.

29. Moretti, "Conjectures on World Literature," 58.

30. Casanova, *World Republic of Letters*, 21.

31. Hartman, "Time of Slavery," 764.

32. Cf. Edwards, "Uses of Diaspora."

33. Cited in Baucom, *Specters of the Atlantic*, 210.

34. Fabre, "René Maran, *The New Negro*, and Négritude," 340, 341.

35. Egonu, "Le Prix Goncourt de 1921 et la 'Querelle de *Batouala*,'" 539.

36. Hemingway, review of *Batouala*, 2.

37. Locke, "La jeune poésie africo-américaine," col. 2. Translation in Edwards, Practice of Diaspora, 113.

38. Edwards, Practice of Diaspora, 113.

39. Harris and Moleworth, *Alain L. Locke*, 72–78.

40. Dixon, "Toward a World Black Literature and Community."

41. "Je n'ai été là qu'un appareil à enregistrer." Quoted in Edwards, *Practice of Diaspora*, 88.

42. Ibid., 90.

43. Casanova, *World Republic of Letters*, 226.

44. Ibid.

45. Fabre, "René Maran, *The New Negro*, and Négritude," 348–49.

46. Walkowitz, *Cosmopolitan Style*, 1–32; Hart, *Nations of Nothing but Poetry*, 3–25.

47. Roach, *Cities of the Dead*, 11.

48. Glissant, *Poetics of Relation*, 65.

49. Moses, *Afrotopia*, 21.

50. Benjamin, "Theses on the Philosophy of History," 263.

51. Walkowitz, *Cosmopolitan Style*; Hart, *Nations of Nothing but Poetry*.

52. Clark, "Developing Diaspora Literacy and *Marasa* Consciousness," 40.

53. Hurston, "Characteristics of Negro Expression," 830.

54. Denning, *Culture in the Age of Three Worlds*, 5–6.

55. Branche, *Colonialism and Race*, 178.

56. Walcott, *Ti-Jean and His Brothers*, in *Dream on Monkey Mountain, and Other Plays*, 85.

57. Glissant, *Poetics of Relation*, 62.

Chapter 1: World Literature and Antiquity

1. Moses, *Afrotopia*, 22.

2. Pope, "Ägypten und Aufhebung," 184.

3. Damrosch, *What Is World Literature*, 12.

4. Roach, *Cities of the Dead*, 2.

5. Quoted in Schulz and Rhein, *Comparative Literature: The Early Years*, 6.

6. Quoted in Bernal, *Black Athena Writes Back*, 173.

7. Volney, *Ruins*, 16.

8. Walker, *Appeal*, 22, 10.

9. Ibid., 22.

10. Douglass, "Claims of the Negro Ethnologically Considered," 288.

11. Bruce, "Ancient Africa and the Early Black Historians," 685.

12. Keita, *Race and the Writing of History*, 44.

13. Wheatley, "To Maecenas," in *Poems of Phillis Wheatley*, 9.

14. Pope, "Ägypten und Aufhebung," 185.

15. Mudimbe, *Invention of Africa*, 132.

16. Blyden, *Christianity, Islam, and the Negro Race*, 82.

17. Blyden, "Negro in Ancient History," 10.

18. Ibid., 15.

19. Diodorus Siculus, *Library of History*, 2.35–4.58.

20. Blyden, "Negro in Ancient History," 9.

21. Diodorus Siculus, *Library of History*, 2.35–4.58. Partially quoted in Delany, *Principia of Ethnology*, 32.

22. Delany, *Principia of Ethnology*, 46.

23. Ibid.

24. Ibid.

25. Blyden, *Christianity, Islam, and the Negro Race*, 276.

26. Du Bois, *Souls of Black Folk*, 162. Hereafter cited parenthetically.

27. Weheliye, "Grooves of Temporality," 321.

28. Baucom, *Specters of the Atlantic*, 30.

29. Lemert, "Race of Time," 243, 248.

30. Weheliye, "Grooves of Temporality," 336.

31. Baucom, *Specters of the Atlantic*, 342.

32. Moses, *Golden Age of Black Nationalism*, 25.

33. Williams, *History of the Negro Race in America*, 18.

34. Cf. Kirschke, "Du Bois, *The Crisis*, and Images of Africa and the Diaspora"; and Schmeisser, "Ethiopia Shall Soon Stretch Forth Her Hands."

35. Du Bois, *"The Conservation of Races" and "The Negro,"* 22–23.

36. Ibid., 48.

37. Ibid., 49, 57.

38. Ibid., 47.

39. Ibid.

40. Ibid., 43.

41. Ibid., 96.

42. Baucom, *Specters of the Atlantic*, 342.

43. Schrager, "Both Sides of the Veil," 554.

44. Rampersad, *Art and Imagination of W. E. B. Du Bois*, 76.

45. Sundquist, *To Wake the Nations*, 465.

46. Cicero, *Pro Archia Poeta Oratio*, 9.

47. Cowherd, "Wings of Atalanta," 297.

48. Cicero, *Pro Archia Poeta Oratio*, 27.

49. Ibid.

50. Ibid., 27–29.

51. Rampersad, *Art and Imagination of W. E. B. Du Bois*, 75.

52. Sundquist, *To Wake the Nations*, 465.

53. For a fuller discussion of the Afro-Semitic context of classical epic, see Chapter 4.

54. Oliver, "W. E. B. Du Bois' *The Quest of the Silver Fleece* and Contract Realism," 32.

55. Lee, "Du Bois the Novelist," 396; Van Wienen and Kraft, "How the Socialism of W. E. B. Du Bois Still Matters," 68.

56. Moretti, *Modern Epic*, 50.

57. Du Bois, *Quest of the Silver Fleece*, 44. Hereafter cited parenthetically.

58. Rampersad, *Art and Imagination of W. E. B. Du Bois*, 120.

59. Elder, "Swamp versus Plantation," 202.

60. Lee, "Du Bois the Novelist," 396.

61. Delany, *Blake*, 112.

62. Ibid., 114.

63. Nwankwo, "Promises and Perils of US African-American Hemispherism," 583.

64. Locke, "New Negro," 7.

65. Casanova, *World Republic of Letters*, 226.

66. Locke, "Negro Youth Speaks," 51.

67. Ibid., 4; Casanova, *World Republic of Letters*, 226.

68. Eliot, "*Ulysses*, Order, Myth," 177–78.

69. Benjamin, *Arcades Project*, 463.

70. Tate, introduction to *Dark Princess*, by Du Bois, xxv.

71. Baker, *Modernism and the Harlem Renaissance*, xv–xvi.

Chapter 2: World Literature in Hiding

1. Lionnet, "Autoethnography," 256.

2. Colla, *Conflicted Antiquities*, 10–15.

3. While this chapter explores Hurston's rhetoric of familiarity with respect to the reader, in "Insider and Outsider, Black and American: Rethinking Zora Neale Hurston's Caribbean Ethnography," Ifeoma C. K. Nwankwo traces Hurston's shifting rhetorics of familiarity with respect to the communities she investigates in her anthropological work.

4. Hurston, "Florida Negro," 880.

5. Casanova, *World Republic of Letters*, 226.

6. Mullen, "African Signs and Spirit Writing," 674.

7. Ibid., 686.

8. Hurston, *Jonah's Gourd Vine*, 27. Hereafter cited parenthetically.

9. Hemenway, *Zora Neale Hurston*, 155.

10. Gates, "*Their Eyes Were Watching God*: Hurston and the Speakerly Text," 168.

11. Hurston, *Dust Tracks on a Road*, 591. Hereafter cited parenthetically.

12. Boyd, *Wrapped in Rainbows*, 194.

13. Ibid., 99.

14. Hemenway, *Zora Neale Hurston*, 79.

15. Hurston, *Tell My Horse*, 296. Hereafter cited parenthetically.

16. Hurston, *Their Eyes Were Watching God*, 148–49.

17. Hurston, "Florida Negro," 884.

18. Cf. Gruesz, *Ambassadors of Culture*, 1–29.

19. Hemenway, *Zora Neale Hurston*, 276–78.

20. Hurston, "Characteristics of Negro Expression,"

21. Hurston to Burroughs Mitchell, 2 October 1947, in Hurston, *Letters*, 559.

22. Hurston to Burroughs Mitchell, 3 February 1948, in Hurston, *Letters*, 568.

23. Clark, "Developing Diaspora Literacy and *Marasa* Consciousness," 40.

24. Hemenway, *Zora Neale Hurston*, 61.

25. Hurston, "High John de Conquer," 925.

26. Hurston, *Mules and Men*, 63. Hereafter cited parenthetically.

27. Hemenway, *Zora Neale Hurston*, 111.

28. Wall, "Zora Neale Hurston: Changing Her Own Words," 80–81; Washington, "I Love the Way Janie Crawford Left Her Husbands," 98–99.

29. Hurston to Hughes, 20 September 1928, in Hurston, *Letters*, 126.

30. Locke to Hurston, 28 April 1930, quoted in Boyd, *Wrapped in Rainbows*, 194.

31. Hurston to Hughes, 12 April 1928, in Hurston, *Letters*, 116.

32. Boyd, *Wrapped in Rainbows*, 231.

33. Kraut, "Between Primitivism and Diaspora," 444.

34. Kaplan, "The Thirties," 179.

35. The material could make money, though. Hall Johnson would steal Hurston's choreography and costumes in his enormously successful *Run, Little Chillun!* He would also excise the "complex and heterogeneous vision of diaspora." See Kraut, "Between Primitivism and Diaspora," 446.

36. Quoted in Boyd, *Wrapped in Rainbows*, 232.

37. Hurston to Boas, 20 August 1934, in Hurston, *Letters*, 308.

38. Ellis, "Enacting Culture," 159.

39. Reflecting these desires of "Godmother" Mason, Hurston recounts: "I must tell the tales, sing the songs, do the dances, and repeat the raucous sayings and doings of the Negro farthest down. She is altogether in sympathy

with them, because she says truthfully, they are utterly sincere in living" (*Dust Tracks on a Road*, 689).

40. See, e.g., the influential volume *Writing Culture: The Poetics and Politics of Ethnography*, edited by James Clifford and George E. Marcus.

41. Wright, "Between Laughter and Tears," 17. While Wright technically addresses *Their Eyes Were Watching God* here, his perspective on this book can fairly be extrapolated to Hurston's literary aesthetics in general, as many critics have done.

42. Carby, "Politics of Fiction, Anthropology, and the Folk," 79.

43. Ibid., 76.

44. Rowe, "Opening the Gate to the Other America," 122.

45. Mellor, introduction to *Making of the Old Testament*. See also Van Seters, *Abraham in History and Tradition*, 309–12.

46. Shaw, *Oxford History of Ancient Egypt*, 313.

47. Jameson, ed., "Autobiography of Omar ibn Said, Slave in North Carolina, 1831."

48. Hiskett, *Development of Islam in West Africa*, 19–43.

49. Michael Gilsenan presents the complex mediations between orality and literacy characteristic of Muslim practices: "Islam, which means submission to God, is constructed upon what Muslims believe is a direct Revelation in Arabic from God: the Quran. This recitation or reading, for that is what the word *Quran* means, is the miraculous source of the umma, the Islamic community. It is the Word. And the conception and communal experience of the Word in prayer, in study, in talismans, in chanting of the sacred verses, in *zikr* (Sufi rituals of remembrance), in the telling of beads, in curing, in social etiquette, and in a hundred other ways are at the root of being a Muslim." Gilsenan, *Recognizing Islam*, 15–16.

50. Williams, *History of the Negro Race in America*, 66.

51. Marr, *Cultural Roots of American Islamicism*, 1–19.

52. Julien, *African Novels and the Question of Orality*, 24.

53. Hale, *Scribe, Griot, and Novelist*, 1–16, 30–46.

54. Hurston, "Spirituals and Neo-spirituals," 869.

55. Hurston to Hughes, 10 July 1928, in Hurston, *Letters*, 121–22.

56. Hurston, *Moses, Man of the Mountain*, 92.

57. Quoted in Wright, *Moses in America*, 83.

58. On worlding the epic genre, see Dimock, "Genre as World System."

Chapter 3: Whiteness and World Literature

1. Branche, *Colonialism and Race*, 30, 213.

2. Carpentier, "Habla Alejo Carpentier," 52. My translation unless otherwise noted.

3. Hartman, *Scenes of Subjection*, 26.

4. Carpentier, "Conciencia e identidad de América," 162.

5. Carpentier, *¡Écue-Yamba-Ó!*, 11. Hereafter cited parenthetically. The translations are my own unless otherwise specified.

6. Branche, *Colonialism and Race*, 185.

7. González Echevarría, *Alejo Carpentier*, 125.

8. North, *Dialect of Modernism*, 3–36; Hughes, "The Negro Artist and the Racial Mountain," 694.

9. Carpentier, "América ante la joven literatura europea," 55. The article originally appeared in the Havana periodical *Carteles*, 28 June 1931.

10. Alonso, *Spanish American Regional Novel*, 14.

11. Padura Fuentes, "Lo real maravilloso," 80 (my translation).

12. Carpentier, "De lo real maravilloso americano," 118. The translations of this essay are my own.

13. Ibid.

14. Branche, *Colonialism and Race*, 163.

15. Carpentier, "De lo real maravilloso americano," 121.

16. Gruesz, *Ambassadors of Culture*.

17. Carpentier, *Lost Steps*, 107 (translation modified). Hereafter cited parenthetically.

18. Alonso, *Spanish American Regional Novel*, 4.

19. Branche, *Colonialism and Race*, 178.

20. In the novel's glossary, Carpentier defines *ñáñigo*: "Secret mutual-aid associations brought to Cuba by black slaves . . . At their meetings the *ñáñigo*s practice a picturesque and complicated ceremony that includes songs, dances, and beautiful drumming" (203–4).

21. Fick, *Making of Haiti*, 60.

22. Carpentier, "Habla Alejo Carpentier," 33.

23. López de Mariscal and Farré, "El *Quijote*, un acercamiento a las formas de apropiación," n.p. (my translation).

24. Carpentier, "Lo barroco y lo real maravilloso," 148. All translations of this essay are my own.

25. González Echevarría, *Alejo Carpentier*, 28.

26. Cf. Menéndez Pidal, *La "Chanson de Roland" y el neotradicionalismo*.

27. Mottahedeh, "'*Aja'ib* in *The Thousand and One Nights*."

28. Cf. Galmes de Fuentes, *Épica árabe y épica castellana*; and Menocal, *Arabic Role in Medieval Literary History*.

29. For information on the translation into Spanish of Arabic narrative, see Seniff, "Orality and Textuality in Medieval Castilian Prose."

30. Mitchell, *Colonising Egypt*, 149–50.

31. Cf. "The Tale of King Muhammad bin Sabaik and the Merchant" and "Sayf al-Muluk and Badia al-Jamal," in Haddawy, trans., *Arabian Nights*.

32. Carpentier, "Highroad of Saint James," 18–19 (translation modified). Hereafter cited parenthetically.

33. Carpentier, "Lo barroco y lo real maravilloso," 100, 93.

34. Franco, *Decline and Fall of the Lettered City*, 35–45.

35. Hall, "The 'Oprahfication' of Literacy," 655.

36. Fuguet and Gómez, introduction to *McOndo*, 3 (my translation). For a survey of the critiques of *lo real maravilloso* and magical realism, see Faris, "Question of the Other."

37. Molloy, "Postcolonial Latin America and the Magical Realist Imperative," 371.

38. Pollack, "Latin America Translated (Again)," 353.

39. Ibid., 360.

40. Ibid., 361.

41. Ibid., 362.

Chapter 4: Dialectics of World Literature

1. Baugh, "Derek Walcott and the Centering of the Caribbean Subject," 151.

2. Damrosch, "World Literature in a Postcanonical, Hypercanonical Age," 50.

3. Walcott, *Another Life*, in *Collected Poems*, 145; Melas, "Forgettable Vacations and Metaphor in Ruins," 152.

4. Bourdieu, *Rules of Art*, 170.

5. Jay, "Fated to Unoriginality," 546.

6. Farrell, "Walcott's *Omeros*," 251–52.

7. Ibid., 249.

8. Walcott, "Far Cry from Africa," in *Collected Poems*, 10.

9. Breslin, "Derek Walcott's 'Reversible World,'" 14.

10. Melas, "Forgettable Vacations and Metaphor in Ruins," 154.

11. Ibid., 152.

12. Melas, *All the Difference in the World*, xiii.

13. Walcott, *Another Life*, in *Collected Poems*, 194.

14. Ibid., 184.

15. Dominica and small portions of Trinidad still keep up French Creole.

16. Walcott, "Conversation with Derek Walcott," by Hamner, in *Conversation with Derek Walcott*, 24.

17. Malouf, "Dissimilation and Federation," 146.

18. Casanova, *World Republic of Letters*, 306.

19. Cf. Tang, *Geographic Imagination of Modernity*.

20. Farrier, "Charting the 'Amnesiac Atlantic,'" 23–37.

21. Walcott, "Ruins of a Great House," in *Collected Poems*, 20–21.

22. Conrad, *Heart of Darkness*, 102.

23. Donne, "Devotions upon Emergent Occasions," in *Complete Poetry and Selected Prose*, 441.

24. Cf. Davis, "With No Homeric Shadow," 321–33; Walcott, "Sea Grapes," in *Collected Poems*, 297.

25. Walcott, "Prelude," in *Collected Poems*, 3.

26. Moretti, "Conjectures on World Literature," 58.

27. Walcott, *Sea at Dauphin*, in *Dream on Monkey Mountain, and Other Plays*, 73–75.

28. King, *New English Literatures*, 126.

29. Melas, *All the Difference in the World*, 84–112.

30. Walcott, "Thinking Poetry," 183.

31. Kiberd, *Inventing Ireland*, 107.

32. Walcott, "Meanings," 50.

33. Walcott, *Another Life*, in *Collected Poems*, 213.

34. Ibid., 214.

35. Dove, "Either I'm Nobody, or I'm a Nation," 75.

36. Pollard, "Traveling with Joyce"; Malouf, *Transatlantic Solidarities*, 124–72; Joyce, "Day of the Rabblement," 71.

37. Walcott, "On Robert Lowell," 101.

38. Casanova, *World Republic of Letters*, 305.

39. Fumagalli, *Flight of the Vernacular*, 282.

40. Baugh, "Poet's Fiction of Self," 311. He continues: "Walcott's binding theme is Walcott, the pursuit and delineation of a fictive character based on an actual person named Derek Walcott. This writing of the self involves a process of self-address and self-interrogation. No mere egocentricity or self-indulgent display of private angst, it is Walcott's way of engaging with the world, by examining himself-in-the-world" (311). Casteel, "Autobiography as Rewriting," 27.

41. Hollinger, *Postethnic America*, 86, 5.

42. Ramazani, *Hybrid Muse*, 64.

43. Breiner, "Creole Language in the Poetry of Derek Walcott," 32.

44. Joyce, *Ulysses*, 268.

45. Ibid., 269.

46. Ibid., 272.

47. Bulson, "Joyce's Geodesy," 91–92.

48. Walcott, "Muse of History," 43–44.

49. Ibid., 31.

50. Dash, "Psychology, Creolization, and Hybridization," 51.

51. Walcott, *Antilles: Fragments of Epic Memory*, n.p.

52. Walcott, *Ti-Jean and His Brothers*, in *Dream on Monkey Mountain, and Other Plays*, 85–86. For his commentary on animal tales, see Walcott, "Afterword: Animals, Elemental Tales, and the Theater."

53. Burnett, *Derek Walcott*, 149.

54. King, *New English Literatures*, 128.

55. Irwin, *Arabian Nights*, 81.

56. Ibid., 79.

57. Ibid., 124.

58. Breslin, *Nobody's Nation*, 86.

59. Ibid.

60. Breiner, "Creole Language in the Poetry of Derek Walcott," 34.

61. Walcott, "Reflections before and after Carnival," 303.

62. Malouf, "Dissimilation and Federation," 146.

63. Cooppan, "Ghosts in the Disciplinary Machine," 29.

64. Okpewho, "Walcott, Homer, and the 'Black Atlantic,'" 33.

65. Walcott, "Interview with Derek Walcott," by Montenegro, in *Conversations with Derek Walcott*, 148.

66. Walcott, interview, in Fumagalli, *Flight of the Vernacular*, 281.

67. Walcott, "The Sea Is History," 23.

68. Walcott, "The Muse of History," 47.

69. Walcott, "Forest of Europe," in *Collected Poems*, 377.

70. Walcott, "Interview with Derek Walcott," by Burnett.

71. Walcott, interview, in "Art of Poetry," by Hirsch, in *Conversations with Derek Walcott*, 104.

Chapter 5: Material Histories of World Literature

1. Condé, *En attendant le bonheur (Hérémakhonon)*, 244.

2. Glissant, *Discours antillais*, 56 (my translation). Leah Hewitt in her analysis of *Hérémakhonon* similarly explores Condé's critique of Antillean myths of African origin. See Hewitt, *Autobiographical Tightropes*.

3. Apter, *Translation Zone*, 178.

4. Condé, *Conversations with Maryse Condé*, 49.

5. For a defense of Condé against the French anthropological establishment, whose members attacked *Ségou* for its historical fallacies and illegitimate representations of African history, see Kemedjio, *De la négritude à la créolité*.

6. Chinosole, "Maryse Condé as Contemporary Griot in *Segu*"; Clark, in Condé, "I Have Made Peace with My Island"; Ouédraogo, *Maryse Condé et Ahmadou Kourouma*.

7. Condé, "I Have Made Peace with My Island," 107.

8. Chinosole analyzes Condé's demystification of the griot as privileged storyteller, noting the multiple voices (especially Condé's own) that perform the role of African historian. I am interested not so much in Condé's treatment of the griot as narrator but in the griot as culture hero in a heroic historiography of Africa. Chinosole, "Maryse Condé as Contemporary Griot in *Segu*."

9. Condé, *Ségou I*, 15; Condé, *Segu*, 7. Hereafter cited parenthetically.

10. Condé, *Ségou II*, 61; Condé, *Children of Segu*, 58. Hereafter cited parenthetically.

11. Chinosole, "Maryse Condé as Contemporary Griot in *Segu*," 594.

12. Irwin, *Arabian Nights*, 81; Benjamin, "Storyteller," 101.

13. Al-Musawi, *Anglo-Orient*; Allen, "Sindbad the Sailor and the Early Arabic Novel"; Barthes, *S/Z*; Brooks, *Reading for the Plot*.

14. Brooks, *Reading for the Plot*, 22.

15. Winnett, "Coming Unstrung," 144.

16. Ibid.

17. Ibid., 143.

18. Chinosole, "Maryse Condé as Contemporary Griot in *Segu*," 599.

19. Benjamin, "Storyteller," 100–101.

20. Brooks, *Reading for the Plot*, 22.

21. Todorov, "Narrative-Men," 78.

22. Kemedjio, "Curse of Writing," 129.

23. Condé, *Migration des coeurs*; Condé, *Windward Heights*. Hereafter cited parenthetically.

24. Apter, *Translation Zone*, 182.

25. Mardorossian, *Reclaiming Difference*, 50.

26. Yelin, "In Another Place," 84.

27. Mardorossian, *Reclaiming Difference*, 92.

28. Williams, *Country and the City*, 22.

29. Moretti, "Dialectic of Fear."

30. Ibid., 85.

31. "Frankenstein's invention is thus a pregnant metaphor of the process of capitalist production, which forms by deforming, civilizes by barbarizing, enriches by impoverishing—a two-sided process in which each affirmation entails a negation." Ibid., 87.

32. Lionnet, "Narrating the Americas," 54.

33. Masiello, "Melodrama, Sex, and Nation in Latin America's *Fin de Siglo*," 136–37.

34. Lionnet, "Narrating the Americas," 47.

35. Dayan, "Codes of Law and Bodies of Color," 61.

36. Ibid., 66.

Chapter 6: "Healing" World Literature

1. Condé, "Order, Disorder, Freedom, and the West Indian Writer," 152.

2. Morrison, "Rootedness," 341. Hereafter cited parenthetically.

3. Condé, "Order, Disorder, Freedom, and the West Indian Writer," 129.

4. Griffin, "Textual Healing."

5. Jennings, *Toni Morrison and the Idea of Africa*, 1.

6. Dubey, *Signs and Cities*, 144–85.

7. Morrison, *Song of Solomon*, 229. Hereafter cited parenthetically.

8. Willis, "Eruptions of Funk," 270.

9. Ibid., 264.

10. Berry, "Toni Morrison's Revisionary 'Nature Writing,'" 153.

11. Fabre, "Genealogical Archaeology or the Quest for Legacy in Toni Morrison's *Song of Solomon*," 108.

12. Brenner, "*Song of Solomon*," 101.

13. Mackey, "Sound and Sentiment, Sound and Symbol," 613.

14. Wilentz, "Civilizations Underneath," 110.

15. Middleton, "From Orality to Literacy," 24.

16. Wilentz, "Civilizations Underneath," 126.

17. Darnton, *Mesmerism and the End of the Enlightenment*, 12.

18. Winter, *Mesmerized*, 5–6.

19. Viswanathan, "Ordinary Business of Occultism."

20. Harris, *Fiction and Folklore*, 2.

21. Middleton excises the allusiveness of this scene and argues: "In this story the bathing ritual communicates rebirth: Milkman discovers giving and sharing, new meaning in a loving relationship with a woman." While leaving out the homecoming and recognition aspects of this encounter, this seems a bit of a stretch for a three-day affair tenderly mediated through money. Middleton, "From Orality to Literacy," 22–23.

22. Jennings, *Toni Morrison and the Idea of Africa*, 160–77.

23. Morrison, "Unspeakable Things Unspoken," 202.

24. Ibid., 206. For more on Bernal, see Bernal, *Black Athena Writes Back*; Lefkowitz and Rogers, eds., *"Black Athena" Revisited*; and Burkert, *Babylon, Memphis, Persepolis*.

25. Quoted in Elia, *"Kum Buba Yali Kum Buba Tambe, Ameen, Ameen, Ameen,"* 103.

26. Ibid., 184.

27. Middleton, "From Orality to Literacy," 23.

28. Mackey, "Sound and Sentiment, Sound and Symbol," 613.

29. Morrison, *Paradise*, 104. Hereafter cited parenthetically.

30. Terry, "Creolisation and Candomblé," 62.

31. Dalsgård, "One All-Black Town Worth the Pain," 239.

32. On filiation and affiliation, see Said, *The World, the Text, and the Critic*, 21–24.

33. Dalsgård, "One All-Black Town Worth the Pain," 233–34.

34. Terry, "Creolisation and Candomblé," 61.

35. Tally, *Paradise Reconsidered*, 31.

Conclusion

1. Tally, *Paradise Reconsidered*, 31.

2. Terry, "Creolisation and Candomblé," 61.

3. Dubey, *Signs and Cities*, 147.

4. Scott, "Obscure Miracle of Connection," 108.

5. Mufti, "Orientalism and the Institutions of World Literatures," 465–66.

6. Cf. Goyal, *Romance, Diaspora, and Black Atlantic Literature*, 1–24.

7. Lewis, "To Turn as on a Pivot."

8. 'Ali, *Dongola*, 8. Hereafter cited parenthetically.

9. On his participation in the circuits of proletarian literature, for example, Wright commented: "My attention was caught by the similarity of the experiences of workers in other lands, by the possibility of uniting scattered but

kindred peoples into a whole." Quoted in Denning, *Culture in the Age of Three Worlds*, 52.

10. Heliodorus, *Aethiopian Historie*, 75. Hereafter cited parenthetically.

11. Whibley, introduction to *Aethiopian Historie*, by Heliodorus, xxv.

12. Barbauld, "On the Origin and Progress of Novel-Writing," 3.

13. Kazamias, "'Purge of the Greeks' from Nasserite Egypt," 13.

14. Heliodorus, *Aethiopian Historie*, 107.

15. Whibley, introduction to *Aethiopian Historie*, by Heliodorus, viii.

Bibliography

'Ali, Idris. *Dongola: A Novel of Nubia.* Translated by Peter Theroux. Fayette-ville: University of Arkansas Press, 1998.

Allen, Roger. "Sindbad the Sailor and the Early Arabic Novel." In *Tradition, Modernity, and Postmodernity in Arabic Literature,* edited by Kamal Abdel-Malek and Wael Hallaq, 78–85. Boston: Brill, 2000.

Alonso, Carlos. *The Spanish American Regional Novel: Modernity and Autochthony.* New York: Cambridge University Press, 1989.

Apter, Emily. *The Translation Zone: A New Comparative Literature.* Princeton, NJ: Princeton University Press, 2005.

Baker, Houston A., Jr. *Modernism and the Harlem Renaissance.* Chicago: University of Chicago Press, 1987.

Barbauld, Anna Letitia (Aikin). "On the Origin and Progress of Novel-Writing." In *The British novelists; with an essay, and prefaces, biographical and critical by Mrs. Barbauld.* London: F. C. and J. Rivington, 1810.

Barthes, Roland. *S/Z.* Translated by Richard Miller. New York: Hill and Wang, 1974.

Baucom, Ian. *Specters of the Atlantic: Finance Capital, Slavery, and the Philosophy of History.* Durham, NC: Duke University Press, 2005.

Baugh, Edward. "Derek Walcott and the Centering of the Caribbean Subject." *Research in African Literatures* 34.1 (2003): 151–59.

———. "The Poet's Fiction of Self: 'The Schooner *Flight.*'" *South Atlantic Quarterly* 96.2 (1997): 311–20.

Benjamin, Walter. *The Arcades Project.* Edited by Rolf Tiedemann and translated by Howard Eiland and Kevin McLaughlin. Cambridge, MA: Belknap Press of Harvard University Press, 1999.

———. *Illuminations.* Edited by Hannah Arendt and translated by Harry Zohn. New York: Schocken Books, 1968.

———. "The Storyteller." In Benjamin, *Illuminations,* 83–110.

———. "Theses on the Philosophy of History." In Benjamin, *Illuminations,* 253–64.

Bernal, Martin. *Black Athena Writes Back: Martin Bernal Responds to His Critics.* Edited by David Chioni Moore. Durham, NC: Duke University Press, 2001.

Berry, Wes. "Toni Morrison's Revisionary 'Nature Writing': *Song of Solomon* and the Blasted Pastoral." In *South to a New Place: Region, Literature, Culture,* edited by Suzanne W. Jones and Sharon Monteith, 147–64. Baton Rouge: Louisiana State University Press, 2002.

Blyden, E. W. (Edward Wilmot). "Arabic Manuscript in Western Africa." In Blyden et al., *People of Africa,* 69–73.

———. *Christianity, Islam, and the Negro Race.* 1888. Baltimore: Black Classic Press, 1993.

———. "The Negro in Ancient History." In Blyden et al., *People of Africa,* 1–34.

Blyden, E. W., Taylor Lewis, Theodore Dwight, et al. *The People of Africa: A series of papers on their character, condition, and future prospects.* New York: Anson D. F. Randolph and Co., 1871.

Bourdieu, Pierre. *The Rules of Art: Genesis and Structure of the Literary Field.* Translated by Susan Emanuel. Stanford, CA: Stanford University Press, 1995.

Boyd, Valerie. *Wrapped in Rainbows: The Life of Zora Neale Hurston.* New York: Scribner, 2004.

Branche, Jerome. *Colonialism and Race in Luso-Hispanic Literature.* Columbia: University of Missouri Press, 2006.

Breiner, Laurence. "Creole Language in the Poetry of Derek Walcott." *Callaloo* 28.1 (2005): 29–41.

Brenner, Gerry. "*Song of Solomon*: Rejecting Rank's Monomyth and Feminism." In *Toni Morrison's "Song of Solomon": A Casebook,* edited by Jan Furman, 95–112. New York: Oxford University Press, 2003.

Breslin, Paul. "Derek Walcott's 'Reversible World': Centers, Peripheries, and the Scale of Nature." *Callaloo* 28.1 (2005): 8–24.

———. *Nobody's Nation: Reading Derek Walcott.* Chicago: University of Chicago Press, 2001.

Brooks, Peter. *Reading for the Plot: Design and Intention in Narrative.* Cambridge, MA: Harvard University Press, 1984.

Bruce, Dickson D., Jr. "Ancient Africa and the Early Black Historians, 1883–1915." *American Quarterly* 36.5 (1984): 684–99.

Bulson, Eric. "Joyce's Geodesy." *Journal of Modern Literature* 25.2 (2001–2): 80–96.

Burkert, Walter. *Babylon, Memphis, Persepolis: Eastern Contexts of Greek Culture.* Cambridge, MA: Harvard University Press, 2004.

Burnett, Paula. *Derek Walcott: Politics and Poetics.* Gainesville: University Press of Florida, 2000.

Carby, Hazel. "The Politics of Fiction, Anthropology, and the Folk: Zora Neale

Hurston." In *New Essays on "Their Eyes Were Watching God,"* edited by Michael Awkward, 71–94. Cambridge: Cambridge University Press, 1990.

Carpentier, Alejo. "América ante la joven literatura europea." In *La novela latinoamericana en vísperas de un nuevo siglo y otros ensayos*, by Alejo Carpentier, 7–32. Mexico City: Siglo Veintiuno Editores, 1981.

———. "Conciencia e identidad de América." In Carpentier, *Ensayos selectos*, 155–66.

———. "De lo real maravilloso Americano." In Carpentier, *Ensayos selectos*, 101–22.

———. ¡Écue-Yamba-O! 1933. Madrid: Alianza Editorial, 1989.

———. *Ensayos selectos*. Buenos Aires: Ediciones Corregidor, 2003.

———. "Habla Alejo Carpentier." In *Recopilación de textos sobre Alejo Carpentier*, edited by Salvador Arias, 15–55. Havana: Casa de las Américas, 1977.

———. "The Highroad of Saint James." In *War of Time*, translated by Frances Partridge. 1958. New York: Knopf, 1970.

———. "Lo barroco y lo real maravilloso." In Carpentier, *Ensayos selectos*, 123–54.

———. *The Lost Steps*. Translated by Harriet de Onís. 1956. Minneapolis: University of Minnesota Press, 2001.

Casanova, Pascale. *The World Republic of Letters*. Translated by M. B. DeBevoise. Cambridge, MA: Harvard University Press, 2005.

Casteel, Sarah Phillips. "Autobiography as Rewriting: Derek Walcott's *Another Life* and *Omeros*." *Journal of Commonwealth Literature* 34.2 (1999): 9–32.

Chinosole. "Maryse Condé as Contemporary Griot in *Segu*." *Callaloo* 18.3 (1995): 593–601.

Cicero. *Pro Archia Poeta Oratio*. Translated by N. H. Watts. Loeb Classical Library, vol. 11. London: William Heinemann, 1923.

Clark, VèVè. "Developing Diaspora Literacy and *Marasa* Consciousness." In *Comparative American Identities: Race, Sex, and Nationality in the Modern Text*, edited by Hortense Spillers, 40-61. New York: Routledge, 1991.

Clifford, James, and George E. Marcus, eds. *Writing Culture: The Poetics and Politics of Ethnography*. Berkeley: University of California Press.

Colla, Elliot. *Conflicted Antiquities: Egyptology, Egyptomania, and Egyptian Modernity*. Durham, NC: Duke University Press, 2008.

Condé, Maryse. *Children of Segu*. Translated by Linda Coverdale. New York: Viking, 1989.

———. *Conversations with Maryse Condé*. By Françoise Pfaff. Lincoln: University of Nebraska Press, 1996.

———. *En attendant le bonheur (Hérémakhonon)*. 1972. Paris: Seuil, 1989.

———. "'I Have Made Peace with My Island': An Interview with Maryse Condé." By VèVè Clark. *Callaloo* 12.1 (1989): 86–133.

———. *La migration des coeurs*. Paris: Robert Laffont, 1995.

———. "Order, Disorder, Freedom, and the West Indian Writer." *Yale French Studies*, no. 97 (2000): 151–65.

———. *Ségou I: Les murailles de terre.* Paris: Editions Robert Laffont, 1984.

———. *Ségou II: La terre en miettes.* Paris: Editions Robert Laffont, 1985.

———. *Segu.* Translated by Barbara Bray. New York: Ballantine Books, 1987.

———. *Windward Heights.* 1995. Translated by Richard Philcox. London: Faber and Faber, 1998.

Conrad, Joseph. *Heart of Darkness.* 1899. New York: Norton, 1987.

Cooppan, Vilashini. "Ghosts in the Disciplinary Machine: The Uncanny Life of World Literature." *Comparative Literature Studies* 41.1 (2004): 10–36.

Cowherd, Carrie. "The Wings of Atalanta: Classical Influences in *The Souls of Black Folk.*" In *"The Souls of Black Folk" One Hundred Years Later*, edited by Dolan Hubbard, 284–97. Columbia: University of Missouri Press, 2003.

Dalsgård, Katrine. "The One All-Black Town Worth the Pain: (African) American Exceptionalism, Historical Narration, and the Critique of Nationhood in Toni Morrison's *Paradise.*" *African American Review* 35.2 (2001): 233–48.

Damrosch, David. *What Is World Literature?* Princeton, NJ: Princeton University Press, 2003.

———. "World Literature in a Postcanonical, Hypercanonical Age." In *Comparative Literature in the Age of Globalization*, edited by Haun Saussy, 43–53. Baltimore: Johns Hopkins University Press, 2006.

Darnton, Robert. *Mesmerism and the End of the Enlightenment in France.* Cambridge, MA: Harvard University Press, 1968.

Dash, J. Michael. "Psychology, Creolization, and Hybridization." In *New National and Post-colonial Literatures: An Introduction*, edited by Bruce King, 45–58. New York: Oxford University Press, 1996.

Davis, Gregson. "'With No Homeric Shadow': The Disavowal of Epic in Derek Walcott's *Omeros.*" *South Atlantic Quarterly* 96.2 (1997): 321–33.

Dayan, Joan. "Codes of Law and Bodies of Color." In *Penser la créolité*, edited by Maryse Condé and Madeleine Cottenet-Hage, 41–66. Paris: Editions Karthala, 1995.

Delany, Martin. *Blake, or The Huts of America.* 1861–62. Boston: Beacon, 1970.

———. *Principia of Ethnology.* Harper and Brother, 1879.

Denning, Michael. *Culture in the Age of Three Worlds.* New York: Verso, 2004.

Dimock, Wai Chee. "Genre as World System: Epic and Novel on Four Continents." *Narrative* 14.1 (2006): 85–101.

———. *Through Other Continents: America Literature across Deep Time.* Princeton, NJ: Princeton University Press, 2008.

Diodorus Siculus. *The Library of History.* Translated by C. H. Oldfather. Cambridge, MA: Harvard University Press, 2000.

Dixon, Melvin. "Toward a World Black Literature and Community." In Harper and Stepto, eds., *Chant of Saints*, 175–94.

Donne, John. *The Complete Poetry and Selected Prose of John Donne.* Edited by Charles M. Coffin. New York: Random House, 1952.

Douglass, Frederick. "The Claims of the Negro Ethnologically Considered." Address delivered at Western Reserve College, July 12, 1854. In *Frederick Douglass: Selected Speeches and Writings,* ed. Philip S. Foner, 282–97. Chicago: Lawrence Hill Books, 1999.

Dove, Rita. "Either I'm Nobody, or I'm a Nation." *Parnassus: Poetry in Review* 14.1 (1987): 49–76.

Dubey, Madhu. *Signs and Cities: Black Literary Postmodernism.* Chicago: University of Chicago Press, 2003.

Du Bois, W. E. B. *"The Conservation of Races" and "The Negro."* Hazelton: Pennsylvania State University Electronic Classics, 2007.

———. *The Quest of the Silver Fleece.* 1911. New York: AMS Press, 1972.

———. *The Souls of Black Folk.* 1903. New York: Dover, 1994.

Eagleton, Terry. *Heathcliff and the Great Hunger: Studies in Irish Culture.* London: Verso, 1996.

Edwards, Brent Hayes. *The Practice of Diaspora: Literature, Translation, and the Rise of Black Internationalism.* Cambridge, MA: Harvard University Press, 2003.

———. "The Uses of Diaspora." *Social Text* 66 (2001): 45–73.

Egonu, Iheanachor. "Le Prix Goncourt de 1921 et la 'Querelle de *Batouala.*'" *Research in African Literatures* 11.4 (1980): 529–45.

Elder, Arlene. "Swamp versus Plantation: Symbolic Structure in W. E. B. Du Bois' *The Quest of the Silver Fleece.*" In *Critical Essays on W. E. B. Du Bois,* edited by William Andrews, 201–20. Boston: G. K. Hall, 1985.

Elia, Nada. "'*Kum Buba Yali Kum Buba Tambe, Ameen, Ameen, Ameen*': Did Some Flying Africans Bow to Allah?" *Callaloo* 26.1 (2003): 182–202.

Eliot, T. S. "*Ulysses,* Order, Myth." In *The Selected Prose of T. S. Eliot,* edited by Frank Kermode, 175–78. New York: Harcourt Brace Jovanovich, 1975.

Ellis, Juniper. "Enacting Culture: Zora Neale Hurston, Joel Chandler Harris, and Literary Anthropology." In *Multiculturalism: Roots and Realities,* edited by C. James Trotman, 155–69. Bloomington: Indiana University Press, 2002.

Fabre, Geneviève. "Genealogical Archaeology or the Quest for Legacy in Toni Morrison's *Song of Solomon.*" In *Critical Essays on Toni Morrison,* edited by Nellie McKay, 105–14. Boston: G. K. Hall, 1988.

Fabre, Geneviève, and Klaus Benesch, eds. *African Diasporas in the New and Old Worlds: Consciousness and Imagination.* Amsterdam: Rodopi, 2004.

Fabre, Michel. "René Maran, *The New Negro,* and Négritude." *Phylon* 36.3 (1975): 340–51.

Faris, Wendy B. "The Question of the Other: Cultural Critiques of Magical Realism." *Janus Head: Journal of Interdisciplinary Studies in Literature, Continental Philosophy, Phenomenological Psychology, and the Arts* 5.2 (2002): 101–19.

Farrell, Joseph. "Walcott's *Omeros*: The Classical Epic in a Postmodern World." *South Atlantic Quarterly* 96.2 (1997): 247–73.

Farrier, David. "Charting the 'Amnesiac Atlantic': Chiastic Cartography and Caribbean Epic in Derek Walcott's *Omeros*." *Journal of Commonwealth Literature* 38.1 (2003): 23–37.

Fick, Carolyn. *The Making of Haiti: The Saint Domingue Revolution from Below*. Knoxville: University of Tennessee Press, 1990.

Franco, Jean. *The Decline and Fall of the Lettered City: Latin America in the Cold War*. Cambridge, MA: Harvard University Press.

Fuguet, Alberto, and Sergio Gómez. Introduction to *McOndo*, edited by Alberto Fuguet and Sergio Gómez. Barcelona: Grijalbo Mondadori, 1996.

Fumagalli, Maria Cristina. *The Flight of the Vernacular: Seamus Heaney, Derek Walcott, and the Impress of Dante*. Amsterdam: Rodopi, 2001.

Galmes de Fuentes, Alvaro. *Épica árabe y épica castellana*. Barcelona: Ariel, 1978.

Garvey, Marcus. "A Talk with Afro-West Indians: The Negro Race and Its Problems." In *The Marcus Garvey and Universal Negro Improvement Association Papers*, edited by Robert Hill, 1:66–75. Berkeley: University of California Press, 1983.

Gates, Henry Louis, Jr. "*Their Eyes Were Watching God*: Hurston and the Speakerly Text." In Gates and Appiah, eds., *Zora Neale Hurston: Critical Perspectives*, 154–203.

Gates, Henry Louis, Jr., and K. Anthony Appiah, eds. *Zora Neale Hurston: Critical Perspectives Past and Present*. New York: Amistad, 1993.

Gilroy, Paul. *The Black Atlantic: Modernity and Double Consciousness*. Cambridge, MA: Harvard University Press, 1993.

Gilsenan, Michael. *Recognizing Islam: An Anthropologist's Introduction*. London: Croom Helm, 1982.

Glissant, Edouard. *Le discours antillais*. Paris: Editions Gallimard, 1997.

———. *Poetics of Relation*. Translated by Betsy Wing. Ann Arbor: University of Michigan Press, 1993.

Goethe, Johann Wolfgang von, and Johann Peter Eckermann. *Conversations of Goethe with Johann Peter Eckermann*. Edited by J. K. Moorhead and translated by John Oxenford. 1930. New York: Da Capo, 1998.

González Echevarría, Roberto. *Alejo Carpentier: The Pilgrim at Home*. Austin: University of Texas Press, 1990.

Goyal, Yogita. *Romance, Diaspora, and Black Atlantic Literature*. Cambridge: Cambridge University Press, 2010.

Griffin, Farah Jasmine. "Textual Healing: Claiming Black Women's Bodies, the Erotic, and Resistance in Contemporary Novels of Slavery." *Callaloo* 19.2 (1996): 519–36.

Gruesz, Kirsten Silva. *Ambassadors of Culture: The Transamerican Origins of Latino Writing*. Princeton, NJ: Princeton University Press, 2002.

Haddawy, Hussein, trans. *The Arabian Nights*. New York: Norton, 1990.

Hale, Thomas A. *Scribe, Griot, and Novelist: Narrative Interpreters of the Songhay Empire*. Gainesville: University Press of Florida / Center for African Studies, 1990.

Hall, R. Mark. "The 'Oprahfication' of Literacy: Reading 'Oprah's Book Club.'" *College English* 65.6 (2003): 646–67.

Harper, Michael, and Robert Stepto, eds. *Chant of Saints: A Gathering of Afro-American Literature, Art, and Scholarship*. With a foreword by John Hope Franklin. Urbana: University of Illinois Press, 1979.

Harris, Leonard, and Charles Moleworth. *Alain L. Locke: The Biography of a Philosopher*. Chicago: University of Chicago Press, 2008.

Harris, Trudier. *Fiction and Folklore: The Novels of Toni Morrison*. Knoxville: University of Tennessee Press, 1991.

Hart, Matthew. *Nations of Nothing but Poetry: Modernism, Transnationalism, and Synthetic Vernacular Writing*. Oxford: Oxford University Press, 2010.

Hartman, Saidiya. *Scenes of Subjection: Terror, Slavery, and Self-Making in Nineteenth-Century America*. New York: Oxford University Press, 1997.

———. "The Time of Slavery." *South Atlantic Quarterly* 101.4 (2002): 757–77.

Heliodorus. *An Aethiopian Historie*. Translated by Thomas Underdowne. 1587. London: David Nutt, 1895.

Hemenway, Robert. *Zora Neale Hurston: A Literary Biography*. Urbana: University of Illinois Press, 1977.

Hemingway, Ernest. Review of *Batouala* (1921), by René Maran, *Toronto Star Weekly*, 25 March 1922. In *Hemingway and the Mechanism of Fame: Statements, Public Letters, Introductions, Forewords, Prefaces, Blurbs, Reviews, and Endorsements*, edited by Matthew J. Bruccoli and Judith Baughman, 1–2. Columbia: University of South Carolina Press, 2006.

Hewitt, Leah. *Autobiographical Tightropes*. Lincoln: University of Nebraska Press, 1990.

Hiskett, Mervyn. *The Development of Islam in West Africa*. London: George Allen, 1984.

Hoesel-Uhlig, Stefan. "Changing Fields: The Directions of Goethe's *Weltliteratur*." In Prendergast, ed., *Debating World Literature*, 26–53.

Hollinger, David. *Postethnic America: Beyond Multiculturalism*. Boston: Basic Books, 1995.

Holt, Elizabeth. "Narrative and the Reading Public in 1870s Beirut." *Journal of Arabic Literature* 40.1 (2009): 37–70.

Hughes, Langston. "The Negro Artist and the Racial Mountain." *Nation* 122 (1926): 692–94.

Hunwick, John O. "'I Wish to Be Seen in Our Land Called Afrika': 'Umar b. Sayyid's Appeal to be Released from Slavery (1819)." *Journal of Arabic and Islamic Studies* 5.3 (2003–4): 62–77.

Hurston, Zora Neale. "Characteristics of Negro Expression." 1934. In Hurston, *Folklore, Memoirs, and Other Writings*, 830–46.

———. *Dust Tracks on a Road*. 1942. In Hurston, *Folklore, Memoirs, and Other Writings*, 557–808.

———. "The Florida Negro." Previously unpublished [1938]. In Hurston, *Folklore, Memoirs, and Other Writings*, 875–900.

———. *Folklore, Memoirs, and Other Writings*. Edited by Cheryl A. Wall. New York: Library of America, 1995.

———. "High John de Conquer." 1943. In Hurston, *Folklore, Memoirs, and Other Writings*, 922–31.

———. *Jonah's Gourd Vine*. 1934. New York: Perennial, 1990.

———. *Moses, Man of the Mountain*. 1939. New York: Harper Collins, 2010.

———. *Mules and Men*. 1935. New York: Perennial, 1990.

———. "Spirituals and Neo-spirituals." 1934. In Hurston, *Folklore, Memoirs, and Other Writings*, 869–74.

———. *Tell My Horse*. 1938. In Hurston, *Folklore, Memoirs, and Other Writings*, 269–555.

———. *Their Eyes Were Watching God*. 1937. New York: Perennial, 1990.

———. *Zora Neale Hurston: A Life in Letters*. Collected and edited by Carla Kaplan. New York: Doubleday, 2002.

Irwin, Robert. *The Arabian Nights: A Companion*. New York: Tauris Parke, 2005.

Jameson, Fredric. *The Political Unconscious: Narrative as a Socially Symbolic Act*. Ithaca, NY: Cornell University Press, 1981.

Jameson, J. Franklin, ed. "Autobiography of Omar ibn Said, Slave in North Carolina, 1831." *American Historical Review* 30.4 (1925): 787–95.

Jay, Paul. "Fated to Unoriginality: The Politics of Mimicry in *Omeros*." *Callaloo* 29.3 (2006): 545–59.

Jennings, La Vinia Delois. *Toni Morrison and the Idea of Africa*. Cambridge: Cambridge University Press, 2008.

Joyce, James. "The Day of the Rabblement." 1901. In *Critical Writings*, edited by Ellsworth Mason and Richard Ellmann, 68–72. New York: Viking, 1959.

———. *Ulysses*. 1922. Edited by Hans Walter Gabler with Wolfhard Steppe and Claus Melchior. New York: Vintage, 1986.

Julien, Eileen. *African Novels and the Question of Orality*. Bloomington: Indiana University Press, 1992.

Kaplan, Carla. "'I Like Working Hard': The Thirties." In *Zora Neale Hurston: A Life in Letters*, collected and edited by Carla Kaplan, 159–84. New York: Doubleday, 2002.

Kazamias, Alexander. "The 'Purge of the Greeks' from Nasserite Egypt: Myths and Realities." *Journal of the Hellenic Diaspora* 35.2 (2008): 13–34.

Keita, Maghan. *Race and the Writing of History: Riddling the Sphinx*. New York: Oxford University Press, 2000.

Kemedjio, Cilas. "The Curse of Writing: Genealogical Strata of a Disillusion; Orality, Islam-Writing, and Identities in the State of Becoming in Maryse Condé's *Ségou.*" *Research in African Literatures* 27.4 (1997): 124–43.

———. *De la négritude à la créolité: Edouard Glissant, Maryse Condé et la malédiction de la théorie.* Hamburg: LIT Verlag, 1999.

Kiberd, Declan. *Inventing Ireland: Literature of the Modern Nation.* New York: Vintage, 1997.

King, Bruce. *The New English Literatures: Cultural Nationalism in a Changing World.* London: Macmillan, 1980.

Kirschke, Amy. "Du Bois, *The Crisis,* and Images of Africa and the Diaspora." In Fabre and Benesch, eds., *African Diasporas in the New and Old Worlds,* 239–62.

Kraut, Anthea. "Between Primitivism and Diaspora: The Dance Performances of Josephine Baker, Zora Neale Hurston, and Katherine Dunham." *Theatre Journal* 55.3 (2003): 433–50.

Lee, Maurice. "Du Bois the Novelist: White Influence, Black Spirit, and *The Quest of the Silver Fleece.*" *African American Review* 33.3 (1999): 389–400.

Lefkowitz, Mary, and Guy MacLean Rogers, eds. *"Black Athena" Revisited.* Chapel Hill: University of North Carolina Press, 1996.

Lemert, Charles. "The Race of Time: Du Bois and Reconstruction." *boundary 2* 27.3 (2000): 215–48.

"A Letter from the King of Musadu." In Blyden et al., *People of Africa,* 129–38.

Lewis, Earl. "To Turn as on a Pivot: Writing African Americans into a History of Overlapping Diasporas." *American Historical Review* 100.3 (1995): 765–87.

Lionnet, Françoise. "Autoethnography: The An-Archic Style of *Dust Tracks on a Road.*" In Gates and Appiah, eds., *Zora Neale Hurston: Critical Perspectives,* 241–66.

———. "Narrating the Americas: Transcolonial *Métissage* and Maryse Condé's *La Migration des coeurs.*" *Women in French Studies* 11 (2003): 46–64.

Locke, Alain. "La jeune poésie africo-américaine." *Les Continents,* 1 September 1924, 2.

———. "The Negro Youth Speaks." In Locke, ed., *New Negro,* 47–56.

———. "The New Negro." In Locke, ed., *New Negro,* 3–18.

———, ed. *The New Negro: Voices from the Harlem Renaissance.* 1925. New York: Touchstone, 1997.

López de Mariscal, Blanca, and Judith Farré. "El *Quijote,* un acercamiento a las formas de apropiación: De la imprenta a la mascarada." *La Gaceta del Fondo de Cultura Economica Filial Colombia* 20 (April 2005).

Mackey, Nathaniel. "Sound and Sentiment, Sound and Symbol." In *The Jazz Cadence of American Culture,* edited by Robert O'Meally, 603–28. New York: Columbia University Press, 1998.

Malouf, Michael. "Dissimilation and Federation: Irish and Caribbean

Modernisms in Derek Walcott's *The Sea at Dauphin.*" *Comparative American Studies* 8.2 (2010): 140–54.

———. *Transatlantic Solidarities: Irish Nationalism and Caribbean Poetics.* Charlottesville: University of Virginia Press, 2009.

Mardorossian, Carine. *Reclaiming Difference: Caribbean Women Rewrite Postcolonialism.* Charlottesville: University of Virginia Press, 2005.

Marr, Timothy. *The Cultural Roots of American Islamicism.* Cambridge: Cambridge University Press, 2006.

Marx, Karl, and Friedrich Engels. *The Communist Manifesto.* In *The Marx-Engels Reader,* edited by Robert Tucker, 469–500. New York: Norton, 1978.

Masiello, Francine. "Melodrama, Sex, and Nation in Latin America's *Fin de Siglo.*" In *The Places of History: Regionalism Revisited in Latin America,* edited by Doris Sommer, 134–43. Durham, NC: Duke University Press, 1999.

Melas, Natalie. *All the Difference in the World: Postcoloniality and the Ends of Comparison.* Stanford, CA: Stanford University Press, 2007.

———. "Forgettable Vacations and Metaphor in Ruins: Walcott's *Omeros.*" *Callaloo* 28.1 (2005): 147–68.

Mellor, Enid B. Introduction to *The Making of the Old Testament,* edited by Enid B. Mellor, 1–44. London: Cambridge University Press, 1972.

Menéndez Pidal, Ramón. *La "Chanson de Roland" y el neotradicionalismo (origines de la épica románica).* Madrid: Espasa-Calpe, 1959.

Menocal, María Rosa. *The Arabic Role in Medieval Literary History: A Forgotten Heritage.* Philadelphia: University of Pennsylvania Press, 1987.

Meyer, Susan. "'Your Father Was Emperor of China, and Your Mother an Indian Queen': Reverse Imperialism in *Wuthering Heights.*" In *Imperialism at Home: Race and Victorian Women's Ficition,* 96–125. Ithaca, NY: Cornell University Press, 1996.

Middleton, Joyce Irene. "From Orality to Literacy: Oral Memory in Toni Morrison's *Song of Solomon.*" In *New Essays on "Song of Solomon,"* edited by Valerie Smith, 19–39. New York: Cambridge University Press, 1995.

Mitchell, Timothy. *Colonising Egypt.* Berkeley: University of California Press, 1991.

Molloy, Sylvia. "Postcolonial Latin America and the Magical Realist Imperative: A Report to the Academy." In *Nation, Language, and the Ethics of Translation,* edited by Sandra Bermann and Michael Wood, 370–79. Princeton, NJ: Princeton University Press, 2005.

Moretti, Franco. *Atlas of the European Novel, 1800–1900.* London: Verso, 1998.

———. "Conjectures on World Literature." *New Left Review,* no. 1: 54–68.

———. "Dialectic of Fear." In *Signs Taken for Wonders: Essays in the Sociology of Literary Forms,* 83–108. London: Verso, 1988.

————. *Modern Epic: The World-System from Goethe to García Márquez*. Translated by Quentin Hoare. New York: Verso, 1996.

Morrison, Toni. *Paradise*. New York: Knopf, 1998.

————. "Rootedness: The Ancestor as Foundation." In *Black Women Writers: A Critical Evaluation*, edited by Mari Evans. New York: Anchor/Doubleday, 1984.

————. *Song of Solomon*. 1977. New York: Plume/Penguin, 1987.

————. "Unspeakable Things Unspoken: The Afro-American Presence in American Literature." In *Toni Morrison*, edited by Harold Bloom, 201–30. New York: Chelsea House, 1990.

Moses, Wilson Jeremiah. *Afrotopia: The Roots of African American Popular History*. Cambridge: Cambridge University Press, 1998.

————. *The Golden Age of Black Nationalism, 1850–1925*. New York: Oxford University Press, 1988.

Mottahedeh, Roy P. "'Aja'ib in *The Thousand and One Nights*." In *"The Thousand and One Nights" in Arabic Literature and Society*, edited by Richard Hovannisian and George Sabagh, 29–39. Cambridge: Cambridge University Press, 1996.

Mudimbe, Valentin. *The Invention of Africa: Gnosis, Philosophy, and the Order of Knowledge*. Bloomington: Indiana University Press, 1988.

Mufti, Aamir. "Orientalism and the Institution of World Literatures." *Critical Inquiry* 36.3 (2010): 458–93.

Mullen, Harryette. "African Signs and Spirit Writing." *Callaloo* 19.3 (1996): 670–89.

Musawi, Muhsin Jassim al-. *Anglo-Orient: Easterners in Textual Camps*. Tunis: Centre de Publication Universitaire, 2000.

North, Michael. *The Dialect of Modernism: Race, Language, and Twentieth-Century Literature*. New York: Oxford University Press, 1994.

Nwankwo, Ifeoma C. K. "Insider and Outsider, Black and American: Rethinking Zora Neale Hurston's Caribbean Ethnography." *Radical History Review*, no. 87 (2003): 49–77.

————. "The Promises and Perils of U.S. African-American Hemispherism: Latin America in Martin Delany's *Blake* and Gayl Jones *Mosquito*." *American Literary History* 18.3 (2006): 579–99.

Okpewho, Isidore. "Walcott, Homer, and the 'Black Atlantic.'" *Research in African Literatures* 33.1 (2002): 27–44.

Oliver, Lawrence J. "W. E. B. Du Bois' *The Quest of the Silver Fleece* and Contract Realism." *American Literary Realism* 38.1 (2005): 32–46.

Ouédraogo, Jean. *Maryse Condé et Ahmadou Kourouma: Griots de l'indicible*. New York: Peter Lang, 2004.

Padura Fuentes, Leonardo. "Lo real maravilloso: Praxis y percepción." *Iman* 1.1 (1983): 80–99.

Pollack, Sarah. "Latin America Translated (Again): Roberto Bolaño's *The*

Savage Detectives in the United States." *Comparative Literature* 61.3 (2009): 346–65.

Pollard, Charles W. "Traveling with Joyce: On Derek Walcott's Discrepant Cosmopolitan Modernism." *Twentieth-Century Literature* 47.2 (2001): 197–215.

Pope, Jeremy W. "Ägypten und Aufhebung: G. W. F. Hegel, W. E. B. Du Bois, and the African Orient." *CR: The New Centennial Review* 6.3 (2006): 149–92.

Prendergast, Christopher, ed. *Debating World Literature*. London: Verso, 2004.

Ramazani, Jahan. *The Hybrid Muse: Postcolonial Poetry in English*. Chicago: University of Chicago Press, 2001.

Rampersad, Arnold. *The Art and Imagination of W. E. B. Du Bois*. New York: Schocken Books, 1990.

Roach, Joseph. *Cities of the Dead: Circum-Atlantic Performance*. New York: Columbia University Press, 1996.

Rowe, John Carlos. "Opening the Gate to the Other America: The Afro-Caribbean Politics of Zora Neale Hurston's *Mules and Men* and *Tell My Horse*." In *Kontaktzone Amerika: Literarische Berkehrsformen kultereller Übersetzung*, edited by Utz Riese and Doris Dziwas, 109–56. Heidelberg: Universitätsverlag Winter, 2000.

Said, Edward. *The World, the Text, and the Critic*. Cambridge, MA: Harvard University Press, 1983.

Schmeisser, Iris. "'Ethiopia Shall Soon Stretch Forth Her Hands': Ethiopianism, Egyptomania, and the Arts of the Harlem Renaissance." In Fabre and Benesch, eds., *African Diasporas in the New and Old Worlds*, 263–86.

Schrager, Cynthia. "Both Sides of the Veil: Race, Science, and Mysticism in W. E. B. Du Bois." *American Quarterly* 48.4 (1996): 551–86.

Schulz, Hans-Joachim, and Phillip H. Rhein, eds. *Comparative Literature: The Early Years; An Anthology of Essays*. Chapel Hill: University of North Carolina Press, 1973.

Scott, David. "Introduction: On the Archaeologies of Black Memory." *Small Axe* 12.2 (2008): v–xvi.

———. "An Obscure Miracle of Connection." In *Refashioning Futures: Criticism after Postcoloniality*, 106–28. Princeton, NJ: Princeton University Press, 1999.

Seniff, Dennis P. "Orality and Textuality in Medieval Castilian Prose." *Oral Tradition* 2.1 (1987): 150–71.

Shaw, Ian. *The Oxford History of Ancient Egypt*. New York: Oxford University Press, 2002.

Strich, Fritz. *Goethe and World Literature*. Translated by C. A. M. Sym. New York: Hafner, 1949.

Sundquist, Eric. *To Wake the Nations: Race in the Making of American Literature*. Cambridge, MA: Belknap Press of Harvard University Press, 1993.

Tally, Justine. *Paradise Reconsidered: Toni Morrison's (Hi)stories and Truths.* Hamburg: LIT Verlag, 1999.

Tang, Chenxi. *The Geographic Imagination of Modernity: Geography, Literature, and Philosophy in German Romanticism.* Stanford, CA: Stanford University Press, 2008.

Tate, Claudia. Introduction to *Dark Princess: A Romance,* by W. E. B. Du Bois, ix–xxviii. 1928. Jackson, MS: Banner Books, 1995.

Terry, Jennifer. "A New World Religion? Creolisation and Candomblé in Toni Morrison's *Paradise.*" In *Complexions of Race: The African Atlantic,* edited by Fritz Gysin and Cynthia Hamilton, 61–82. Münster: LIT Verlag, 2005.

Todorov, Tzvetan. "Narrative-Men." In *The Poetics of Prose,* translated by Richard Howard, 73–82. Ithaca, NY: Cornell University Press, 1978.

Trumpener, Katie. *Bardic Nationalism: The Romantic Novel and the British Empire.* Princeton, NJ: Princeton University Press, 1997.

Van Seters, John. *Abraham in History and Tradition.* New Haven, CT: Yale University Press, 1975.

Van Wienen, Mark, and Julie Kraft. "How the Socialism of W. E. B. Du Bois Still Matters: Black Socialism in *The Quest of the Silver Fleece*—and Beyond." *African American Review* 41.1 (2007): 67–85.

Viswanathan, Gauri. "The Ordinary Business of Occultism." *Critical Inquiry* 27.1 (2000): 1–20.

Volney, C.-F. (Constantin-François). *The Ruins; or, Meditations on the Revolutions of Empires: and the Laws of Nature.* 1802. New York: Peter Eckler, 1926.

Von Sneidern, Maja-Lisa. "*Wuthering Heights* and the Liverpool Slave Trade." *English Literary History* 62.1 (1995): 171–96.

Walcott, Derek. "Afterword: Animals, Elemental Tales, and the Theater." In *Monsters, Tricksters, and Sacred Cows: Animal Tales and American Identities,* edited by A. James Arnold, 269–77. Charlottesville: University of Virginia Press, 1996.

———. *The Antilles: Fragments of Epic Memory; The Nobel Lecture.* New York: Farrar, Straus and Giroux, 1993.

———. "The Art of Poetry XXXVII: Derek Walcott." By Edward Hirsch. In Walcott, *Conversations with Derek Walcott,* 95–121.

———. *Collected Poems, 1948–1984.* New York: Farrar, Straus and Giroux, 1986.

———. "Conversation with Derek Walcott." By Robert D. Hamner. In Walcott, *Conversations with Derek Walcott,* 21–33.

———. *Conversations with Derek Walcott.* Edited by William Baer. Jackson: University of Mississippi Press, 1996.

———. *Dream on Monkey Mountain, and Other Plays.* New York: Farrar, Straus and Giroux, 1971.

———. "Interview with Derek Walcott." By Paula Burnett. *Agenda* 39.1–3 (2002–3): 295–318.

———. "An Interview with Derek Walcott." By David Montenegro. In Walcott, *Conversations with Derek Walcott*, 135–50.

———. "Meanings." In *Critical Perspectives on Derek Walcott*, edited by Robert D. Hamner, 45–50. Washington, DC: Three Continents, 1993.

———. "The Muse of History." In Walcott, *What the Twilight Says*, 36–64.

———. "On Robert Lowell." In Walcott, *What the Twilight Says*, 87–106.

———. "Reflections before and after Carnival: An Interview with Derek Walcott." By Sharon Ciccarelli. In Harper and Stepto, eds., *Chant of Saints*, 296–309.

———. "The Sea Is History." In *Frontiers of Caribbean Literatures in English*, edited by Frank Birbalsingh, 22–28. New York: St. Martin's, 1996.

———. "Thinking Poetry: An Interview with Derek Walcott." By Robert Brown and Cheryl Johnson. In Walcott, *Conversations with Derek Walcott*, 175–88.

———. "What the Twilight Says: An Overture." In Walcott, *Dream on Monkey Mountain, and Other Plays*, 3–40.

———. *What the Twilight Says: Essays*. Farrar, Straus and Giroux, 1998.

Walker, David. *Appeal*. 3rd ed. Boston: David Walker, 1830.

Walkowitz, Rebecca. *Cosmopolitan Style: Modernism beyond the Nation*. New York: Columbia University Press, 2006.

Wall, Cheryl A. "Zora Neale Hurston: Changing Her Own Words." In Gates and Appiah, eds., *Zora Neale Hurston: Critical Perspectives*, 76–97.

Washington, Mary Helen. "'I Love the Way Janie Crawford Left Her Husbands': Emergent Female Hero." In Gates and Appiah, eds., *Zora Neale Hurston: Critical Perspectives*, 98–109.

Weheliye, Alexander. "The Grooves of Temporality." *Public Culture* 17.2 (2005): 319–38.

Wheatley, Phillis. *Poems of Phillis Wheatley: A Native African and a Slave*. Bedford, MA: Applewood Books, 1838.

Whibley, Charles. Introduction to *An Aethiopian Historie*, by Heliodorus, vii–xxix.

Wilentz, Gay. "Civilizations Underneath: African Heritage as Cultural Discourse in Toni Morrison's *Song of Solomon*." In *Toni Morrison's Fiction: Contemporary Criticism*, edited by David L. Middleton, 109–33. New York: Garland, 1997.

Williams, George Washington. *The History of the Negro Race in America, from 1619 to 1880*. New York: G. P. Putnam's Sons, 1883.

Williams, Raymond. *The Country and the City*. New York: Oxford University Press, 1973.

Willis, Susan. "Eruptions of Funk: Historicizing Toni Morrison." In *Black*

Literature and Literary Theory, edited by Henry Louis Gates, Jr., 263–83. New York: Methuen, 1984.

Winnett, Susan. "Coming Unstrung: Women, Men, Narrative, and Principles of Pleasure." In *Narrative Dynamics: Essays on Plot, Time, Closure, and Frames*, edited by Brian Richardson, 138–58. Columbus: Ohio State University Press, 2002.

Winter, Alison. *Mesmerized: Powers of Mind in Victorian Britain*. Chicago: University of Chicago Press, 1998.

Wright, Melanie. *Moses in America: The Cultural Uses of Biblical Narrative*. New York: Oxford University Press, 2002.

Wright, Richard. "Between Laughter and Tears." In Gates and Appiah, eds., *Zora Neale Hurston: Critical Perspectives*, 16–18.

Yelin, Louise. "In Another Place: Postcolonial Perspectives on Reading." In *Reading Sites: Social Difference and Reader Response*, edited by Patrocinio Schweickart and Elizabeth A. Flynn, 83–107. New York: Modern Language Association of America, 2004.

Index